YOUR LIFETIME PERSONAL FINANCIAL PROGRAM

Robert and Thomas Brosterman, top experts in the estate planning field, explain exactly how to plan your personal estate, whether you are about to retire or just starting your career.

- They discuss such capital investments as real estate, insurance, corporate bonds, stocks, annuities.

- They define the benefits to be derived from divided ownership of property within the family and the maximum gift and estate tax savings possible.

- They explain how to calculate estate taxes and how they can be reduced.

- They thoroughly investigate estate management, offering pointers on what advisers to select, how to choose them, and what powers to give them.

- They include an Appendix containing Estate Planning Worksheets, a variety of Personal Schedules, and U.S. tax tables and summaries of the tax laws, including changes in estate and tax laws up to 1987.

ROBERT BROSTERMAN is a New York attorney specializing in estate planning, wills, trusts and probate law. He was formerly Lecturer on Taxation at New York University's Graduate School of Business Administration, and is the author of *Estate Planning for the President* (President's Association of the American Management Association, Inc.).

THOMAS BROSTERMAN is a financial advisor and independent portfolio manager with special interest in international finance and economics. He attended Massachusetts Institute of Technology and served as Assistant Professor at the University of Southern California and at the University of California, Los Angeles. Mr. Brosterman resides in West Los Angeles.

W9-CNE-949

THE COMPLETE ESTATE PLANNING GUIDE

Updated to Include Tax Changes to 1987

REVISED EDITION

by

Robert Brosterman
of the New York Bar

and

Thomas Brosterman
Investment Adviser

A MENTOR BOOK

NEW AMERICAN LIBRARY

NEW YORK AND SCARBOROUGH, ONTARIO

To our father and grandfather, Morris Brosterman,
who at age 93 was vigorously building his estate—
while breaking every rule in the book.

Copyright © 1964, 1970, 1975, 1977, 1979, 1980, 1981, 1982, 1984,
1987 by McGraw-Hill, Inc.

All rights reserved. This book, or parts thereof, may not be reproduced in
any form without permission of the publishers. For information address
McGraw-Hill Book Company, 1221 Avenue of the Americas, New York,
New York 10020.

Library of Congress Catalog Card Number: 87-61458

Published by arrangement with McGraw-Hill Book Company

MENTOR TRADEMARK REG. U.S. PAT. OFF. AND FOREIGN COUNTRIES
REGISTERED TRADEMARK—MARCA REGISTRADA
HECHO EN CHICAGO, U.S.A.

SIGNET, SIGNET CLASSIC, MENTOR, ONYX, PLUME, MERIDIAN and NAL
BOOKS are published *in the United States* by NAL PENGUIN INC.,
1633 Broadway, New York, New York 10019,
in Canada by The New American Library of Canada Limited,
81 Mack Avenue, Scarborough, Ontario M1L 1M8

First Mentor Printing, October, 1966
Seventeenth Mentor Printing (1977 Revised Edition)
Twenty-fourth Mentor Printing (1980 Revised Edition)
Twenty-seventh Mentor Printing (1982 Revised Edition)
Twenty-ninth Mentor Printing (1984 Revised Edition)
Thirty-second Mentor Printing (1987 Revised Edition)

32 33 34 35 36 37 38 39 40

PRINTED IN THE UNITED STATES OF AMERICA

Contents

Part One
CREATING YOUR ESTATE

Foreword

This book is about something that almost everyone has or wants to have: an estate.

The word is perhaps an unfortunate one, for it fails to indicate the universality of the subject. It summons up images of landed gentry, of vast fortunes or great property holdings. It is commonly associated with death; a man's estate is what he leaves behind him.

An estate is all of these things, certainly, but it is also much more and much less. The family savings account, a house, an insurance policy, the benefits from a job, even the monthly payments to a widow from Social Security—these are part of an estate as well. In fact, if you own any capital at all, you have an estate. Everyone wants a large estate because having one means financial security—security for himself and his family during his life and the family after his death.

How to accumulate capital, how to build an estate, how to increase it, how to keep it, and how to pass it on—this is estate planning, something we do all our lives. When you buy stocks, change jobs, start a business or sell one, pick a street to live on, give money away, you are planning your estate, whether you realize it or not.

Unfortunately, most people don't really *plan* their plan. Or at best, they do it spasmodically, when and if the spirit moves them—now writing a will, now making an investment, now buying an insurance policy. One action bears little relation to the other. The result is a crazy quilt; it lacks a visible and orderly pattern. Opportunities are lost, capital is dissipated and the goal of the plan—family security—is threatened.

Thus, the purpose of this book is to set forth the principles of estate planning, to point out how they can be applied, and, finally, to emphasize the very real and sizable gains to be had from the estate plan that is conscious and continuous as opposed to the one that is casual and makeshift.

We can think of no area where this approach is more meaningful than that of tax planning. Our government not only allows but, indeed, has consciously *created* opportunities for lessening the impact of taxation. It is up to the planner, however, to use these opportunities in every aspect and at every stage of his estate planning.

On this question one of the great jurists of our times, Judge Learned Hand, wrote: "Anyone may so arrange his affairs that his taxes shall be as low as possible; he is not bound to choose that pattern which will best pay the Treasury; there is not even a patriotic duty to increase one's taxes."

This does not mean that the government should be considered as an adversary to be defeated by manipulation, subterfuge, or clever tax tricks. The well-planned use of available tax shelters make this type of tax thinking both unwise and unnecessary.

This is what we hope the reader will gain from the extensive treatment of taxes which every chapter contains—not a series of gimmicks but an explanation of numerous clear-cut and acceptable examples of when, where, and how to save taxes at each point in the estate plan.

This book is not a treatise on estate planning—that would take volumes and would be for the use of experts. Look at it, rather, as a map—a contour map which reproduces the estate-planning landscape in broad perspective. All the main outlines are there, the avenues laid out, the guideposts indicated.

There is something in this book for nearly everybody: for the person of wealth, for the corporate executive or professional, for someone who is about to retire, and for the person who is just beginning his working life; for the independent businessperson and for the possessor of an inherited fortune. The problems of each are different. For all of them are suggestions and directions on how to evolve and develop their own individual estate plans.

No one should sit down with this book and plan to read it straight through. A young person at the start of a career will probably want to read the first part thoroughly, but the established professional who already has an estate can skip this entire section if he wants to, and concentrate on the latter part. A corporate executive isn't going to be interested in the parts which deal with the independent business-person or professional. They, in turn, will find large sections of the book which do not bear on their problems.

Then, too, the reader may find that some parts of the book have meaning for him today; others will take on greater importance 5, 10, or 15 years from now. It is our hope that readers will use the book not only for current information but as a reference which they can call on repeatedly during various stages of their lives and careers.

There is one element of the book which is meant for every reader. We refer to the "Estate Planning Worksheets," which are in the Appendix and are an important part of the book. They are designed to give you your estate picture at a glance. Used properly they can give you the information you will need to do your planning.

Don't just fill out the Worksheets, use them once, and then forget them. You must keep them up-to-date, just as you must keep your entire plan up-to-date. For estate planning is like life itself—continuous, changing, dynamic. The person who seriously sets about an estate planning program can never say the job is done.

The organization of the book is somewhat unorthodox, since it separates estate planning into two distinct parts—creation and transfer—and gives equal stress to both these aspects of estate planning. The more usual pattern is to give estate transfer the primary emphasis, relegating estate creation to a lesser, subsidiary role.

Our deviation from this pattern is due to the thesis of this book: family financial security. It is not enough just to have an estate to pass on; it must obviously be an estate of sufficient size so that, when transferred, it will truly provide security. Thus, the emphasis on estate building.

In addition, we have treated the two aspects separately because the problems they deal with, while interrelated, are separate. They affect different people in different ways and are made clearer by this somewhat arbitrary divorcement.

Out of it all, we hope that you will develop your own

philosophy of estate planning. It is up to you to do this, based on your personal evaluation of the long-range economic economic trends of our society. We have tried to suggest some of these directions in the book. It is obvious, for example, that we are now, and have been for some time, in a period of inflation. Therefore, any planning you do must, perforce, consider the effect of a continuing and possibly accelerating inflation. But times can change, we all know that. So can laws, especially tax laws. Hence the need for periodic re-evaluations to adapt your plan to changing times and opportunities.

And finally, we want to say that this book has been more than an individual effort, and is, we hope, the better for that. To Dorothea Garber Cracas, we are indebted for bringing her practiced legal abilities to the meticulous research and elaboration of its material. Without her dedication to the project, it is doubtful that the book would have been begun or could have been finished. We owe a special debt of gratitude to Madelon Bedell, public relations consultant and former member of the editorial staff of Fortune Magazine, who contributed her literary skills to the writing and organization of the book. Whatever felicity of style it contains is due to her.

Robert Brosterman
Thomas Brosterman

Authors' note: The material in this book applies equally to men and women. If the personal pronouns *he* and *his* are used most frequently it is because *he or she* and *his or hers* is often awkward.

Preface to Revised Edition

This paperback edition includes all the material from the original hardcover book, but has been revised to keep abreast of changes in laws and taxation in the more than 20 years since it was first published. The latest revision takes into account the many changes brought about by the Tax Reform Act of 1986. A summary of this far-reaching reform of our tax laws is included in the Appendix on page 353.

In setting down in print a book about estate planning, an author must contend with the fact that the law is ever-evolving. The basic principles of and reasons for estate planning, however, remain the same. The need for a will and trusts and the elements in their planning have not changed since this book first went to press; nor has there been a change in the need to build an estate toward retirement, for protection in case of disability, or for family security on the death of breadwinner.

We all know that building an estate and attaining estate objectives are often frustrated by tax erosion. In this respect, the 1986 tax law especially has imposed new and unusual pressures on the best laid estate plans. It is the most complex tax legislation enacted in recent years and its technical meanings and applications will not be precisely known for years. In the meanwhile new tax laws will come, possibly meant to simplify tax planning, but are likely to complicate it further. In these circumstances, a current review of your existing plan is required and continuing attention should be given to the way interpretations of the existing laws, and the enactment of new laws, will affect your estate and family planning.

As never before, you will need expert advice to lead you through the tax maze to the attainment of your objectives. This book can help you to understand your tax and estate planning problems and how and where to seek advice and solutions.

The 1986 Tax Reform Act establishes rates of income taxes on individuals based on two brackets for the year 1988 and thereafter, they are for single tax payers 15% on taxable income up to $17,850 and 28% on income over that amount; for tax payers filing joint returns, they are 15% on taxable income up to $29,750 and 28% on income over that amount. For 1987 only, there are five brackets that run up to 38.5 percent. *The examples included in this edition use the 1988 rates inasmuch as these will be the continuing rates for your estate planning purposes.* For more detailed information on the new tax structure, see page 294 of the Appendix and the summary outline of the 1986 Act starting on page 353. The reader should be aware that many cities and states have income taxes and that these examples will be affected by the local or state taxes that apply.

In the considerable task of bringing this edition up-to-date, we gratefully acknowledge the collaboration of Kathleen Adams and Elsa Brosterman and the special contribution of Barry S. Berg and Pamela A. Markley of the accounting firm of Ernst and Whinney in researching and developing much of this new material.

Robert Brosterman
Thomas Brosterman

PART ONE

Creating Your Estate

CHAPTER 1

The Modern Dilemma:
Creating an Estate in an
Affluent Society

Does security have a price tag?

And if so, what is the amount? How much money does it take in today's society to meet personal and family needs, now and in the event of a person's death, his retirement, or his disability?

Is the $40,000 a year person secure? Or should the figure be put at $60,000, perhaps $90,000? Somewhere in the income structure, the security threshold must exist, for surely, the $150,000 a year person is secure, rich even. Otherwise, what is the point of success?

We have had this question posed to us innumerable times over the years. Sometimes it is asked in casual conversation, but just as frequently it comes up in discussions with clients. It is a leitmotiv of our times, a problem that haunts the thinking of nearly every successful person. Recently, it was asked by four different people in various stages of successful careers.

Let's take a look at them. They are all real people incidentally, clients or friends whom we'll call by their generic rather than their individual names. In so doing, our purpose is more than disguise; it is also to underline the universality of their situation. One of them might be you, and if not you, surely someone you know.

Mr. Junior Executive:
A Person with Great Expectations

He is our $40,000 a year person. Just past 30 years old, a young executive in a small but growing advertising agency,

3

Mr. Junior Executive is talented, ambitious, and energetic. In the manner of his profession, he may shift from one agency to another, but he expects to double his income in 5 years.

Junior Executive's financial situation is a bit tangled. He and his wife just had a second child. To give his family more room and a better environment, he recently gave up his four-room apartment in the city and bought a modest house in the surburbs. Price $90,000, $20,000 down. The house and the inevitable purchases that accompany it—furniture, automobile, appliances, garden equipment—have taken all of Junior Executive's savings and more. He is in debt to the tune of $12,000. If he should die now, all that he would have to leave his family would be the house (with only a few hundred dollars of the mortgage paid off), plus $110,000 worth of personal and group life insurance—a net, after expenses, of about $95,000. But then, at his age, the chances of an untimely death are unlikely. Or so he reasons.

There is also his occupation. It has not escaped Junior Executive's attention that the only men in his office who are over 50 are the owners of the company. Advertising and the communications field in general are a young man's business. Junior Executive realizes that he has to make it within the next 20 years or face an uncertain future. But he is confident of his ability to succeed, on the whole, this confidence overrides any anxiety he might have about his security—present and future.

Mr. Corporate Executive:
Expectations Realized

Mr. Corporate Executive is a true successor to Mr. Junior Executive. He might well be the same man, 15 years later. At 45 years old he is making $75,000 a year. There are some differences between them, however. Corporate Executive is an organization man, plant manager, with a big corporation. He doesn't have to worry about getting fired or shifting jobs. Barring depressions and other unlikely eventualities, his position is safe. He also banks on the security of better corporate fringe benefits.

Corporate Executive is a suburban home owner too, but on a higher status level. His house is located in a more exclusive section of town. It is worth $150,000—mortgage

$40,000. He owns two cars—a new station wagon which his wife uses and a 3-year-old foreign car which he drives to and from work every day.

He has more expenses than Junior Executive. There is a son in college, a daughter who will be entering next year. The two younger children are in public school, but their music and dancing lessons, plus their summer camp, cost about $8,000 per year.

Assets? The house, of course, $8,000 in government securities mutual fund, about the same in his checking account, stocks worth $25,000 at the current market value, $120,000 in personal and group life insurance, pension and profit sharing in his company of about $60,000.

Less debts and other estate expenses, Corporate Executive's estate will amount to about $175,000.

Mr. Professional:
Non-organization Man

He is a physician, only a year or so older than Mr. Corporate Executive, but in a higher income echelon. His yearly net earnings amount to $120,000.

Mr. Professional's scale of living is correspondingly higher. He has a $175,000 house; he belongs to a country club; he entertains frequently; he owns two Cadillacs and a 24-foot sailing sloop. For his own part, he could do without some of these things, but he believes his status in his community— and by implication his future success in his profession— demand a display of this sort of affluence.

Unlike Corporate Executive, Professional has none of the benefits of corporate paternalism, no pension plan, no profit sharing. He belatedly started a self-employed retirement plan last year and has $12,000 to his credit. This plus $20,000 of group insurance through his medical society, $75,000 of personal insurance, $25,000 in securities, the $140,000 equity in his house, and $45,000 in the cars and the boat make up his estate.

His debts amount to $25,000 which he borrowed last year to meet some pressing bills. It all adds up to a net of $265,000 after expenses. This is the amount that would be left for his wife and his two teen-aged children if he died.

Mr. Professional, a heart specialist, knows all too well that he is reaching a dangerous age. One statistic on fatalities among doctors sticks in his mind: the death rate of physicians in the 55 to 70 age bracket is 15 percent higher than that of the general population. He also realizes that he cannot keep on working at his present pace. He doesn't dare think that if he were disabled, there would only be invested assets plus social security to support the family for the rest of his life.

These thoughts occupy Professional's mind at night when he should be getting his sleep, and that is why his blood pressure goes up and he gets irritable when he reads about "money-grubbing doctors."

Mr. Successful:
The American Dream Personified

At 55, Mr. Successful is the man who has everything—a job as vice-president in one of the country's largest corporations, which pays him $175,000 per year—two homes, a house in the country and an apartment in the city—a gardener and a full-time cook-housekeeper. He belongs to a country club and a men's club in the city.

Successful is constantly on the go, partly because he wants to be and partly because he has to be. He has practically no leisure time. All his pleasures are cast in the framework of his business. He plays golf with business contacts three times a week, not because he wants to, but because he finds it is good business. Several times a year he goes to conventions where he drinks too much, eats too much, and stays up too late. His wife goes with him on these junkets and she accompanies him out to dinner when he entertains his business prospects, or on weekends at the seashore spent with still other business contacts. In fact, he and his wife rarely spend an evening alone together.

It's not only that this life is wearing; it also costs him money. The company pays for some of these expenses, but not all. It doesn't pay a cent of the $8,500 a year his wife spends on the clothes she must have to fill her proper roles as his hostess and companion. Nor does it pay for marginal business entertainment, the two cars, or for many of his club expenses, not to mention the largesse he must display at Christmas or the many "little extras" that add up to $10,000 a year.

By any ordinary standards, Successful is secure. Let's see

how secure. There is his $25,000 of ordinary life insurance and $175,000 of group insurance, a total of $200,000. His stock options are now worth $60,000 and his estate could get $40,000 out of them if he died. His house is worth $250,000 but there is a mortgage of $80,000 (his apartment is a rented one).

There is the $23,000 he has paid into the pension fund. His securities are worth $15,000. Add it all up, count in $15,000, the value of his personal property, the $1,000 in his checking account, and it comes to a nice sounding sum of $464,000.

Now, subtract his debts of $30,000 (Successful has them too; like many people in his economic bracket, he has to borrow at income tax time), his funeral and estate administration expenses and taxes. Total net estate of Mr. Successful: $395,000.

THE STATISTICS OF SECURITY

So far I have spoken only of the total estate each man will leave if he dies now. This total sum represents the capital they have created. Some of these estates, especially Successful's, seem impressive. $395,000 is quite a large sum. Now let's analyze this capital (assuming all of it can be productively invested) in terms of the income it will produce for their families. This, after all, is the true measure of security.

Assuming an income after taxes of 5 per cent of investment, Junior Executive's family will collect about $5,000 per year; Corporate Executive's family, about $9,500; Professional's wife and children will have $9,500; Mr. Successful's survivors will receive about $20,000. In addition, all of the families qualify for social security in varying amounts, at varying times, depending on the ages of the widow and children. The most it will ever be for any of them, however, is $10,000 per year for differing periods and at different times, as we shall later see.

Will they be secure?

According to the Bureau of Labor Statistics, it takes an income of $19,000 per year to support a family of four on a moderate level in New York City and most urban areas. This is more than the estate of Junior Executive, Corporate Executive, and Professional will provide. Yet this sum isn't really enough to supply what most of us consider to be "necessities" for our families. There is no room in it for college educations, for advantages which will enrich the lives of our children, for emergencies, not even for the kind of food, shelter, and environment that we consider healthy. It represents survival only. Is that the fruit of success today?

If these men are in a paradoxical position, they are not alone. Most of the nation is with them, not only in its financial insecurity, but also in its financial affluence. That is what makes the whole picture so puzzling. Things are better now, better than they have ever been. Median family income is more than double that of fifteen years ago. Double jobs and working wives have been a major factor in this increase. Working wives contribute about 40 per cent to the total of their families' incomes. In addition there are approximately 10 million single and widowed women who work to support themselves and their families. They are faced with the same problems of their male counterparts in building an estate and creating security for themselves and their families.

Now look at the other side of the picture. Consumer debt had grown from $141 billion in 1970 to $612 billion in May 1985. Of this amount $489 billion was consumer installment loans and $123.5 billion was open or stated period credit. In the housing area, total mortgage debt rose from $37.7 billion in 1950 to one and a half trillion in 1984. In an era when pensions and retirement funds have become realities instead of theories, 60 percent of those families whose head is 65 or older show total income from all sources of less than $9,000.

In short; it was never easier to make or get money than now; at the same time, it was never more difficult to keep it.

THE MODERN DILEMMA

Most of these people—the Junior Executives, the Corporate Executives, the Professionals, and the Successfuls and all their counterparts—are not careless spendthrifts or hedonist by nature as some of the popular moralists would have it. Their trouble is simple to define, but not so simple to solve. Despite their relatively high earnings, they have been unable to accumulate capital which might be expected from such earnings. Capital, not earnings, is what produces security. Earning power diminishes or ceases with death, disability, or retirement. Only a large amount of capital has the ability to produce a sufficient income in these instances. This is the missing element in the lives of these men, and that is why none of them has been able to establish security for himself and his family.

This is the modern-day dilemma. It is a dilemma composed of three horns so strong and tenacious that most members of the affluent society have been unable to escape their clutches.

The First Horn:
The High Cost of Living

Everybody talks about it. We all know it. Money doesn't go as far these days as it used to. Your parents fed a family of four on $20 a week, and there was meat and potatoes, not to mention dessert, on the table every day. It costs at least seven times that amount to buy food for your family.

The word is inflation. Measured by its arithmetic, today's salaries are worth a good deal less than they appear to be. The cost of living has more than tripled since 1960, reducing the value of the dollar to less than 30 cents. Today an after tax income of $30,000 is worth $7,500 in the purchasing power of the 1960 dollar.

The Second Horn:
The High Cost of Living High

But although it is true that the high cost of living reduces the effect of affluence, it doesn't cancel it out. No equalizing process is involved here. Inflation notwithstanding, the nation is still far better off than it used to be. The rise in median family income since 1960 has surpassed the rise in the cost of living 50 per cent.

The trouble goes deeper. It's not so much the cost of living; it's the high cost of living high. The meals your spouse serves not only cost more; they are composed of richer, more varied fare. Your parents owned one car and thought themselves well off. You need two to supply the needs of your family. You went to college; your daughter feels she needs both a bachelor's and an advanced degree to succeed in her profession. TV sets and vacations for the family are considered necessities even in low income groups. Going up in the economic scale, the same applies to the country club, the second house, and private school for junior.

In higher echelons, the definition of necessities becomes even broader. It embraces the luxury travel, the pleasure yacht, the wardrobes, the large-scale entertainment, the sumptuous homes. Gross materialism? Perhaps, but if so, such materialism is the very fabric of society, particularly the society of success. In large measure, an open display of affluence is expected of the successful person today. Some of it, although not all, is unavoidable if he is to continue his climb upward in the economic strata. It takes determination and will power to separate the true demand, the true necessity of displaying affluence from its simulated counterpart, the social pressure to spend.

The Third Horn: High Taxation

If it costs an individual more to live today, exactly the same applies to the society. Or, in more precise terms, to the government which administers, sustains, and protects the economic life of the people. Thus the third horn, and one we all know and talk about too, the inevitable accompaniment of the successful life. In a word, taxes.

Spell out its implications in figures, and the present-day tax impact on capital and earning power is clear. In 1939, a married man with two children earning a salary of $25,000 paid out about $1,700 in income taxes. In 1988 a person on the same salary will pay some $2,550 in taxes. Do you want to earn a net of $75,000? Then you must gross $120,000. Back in pre-World War II days, it took only $100,000 of gross to produce the same net.

This is what economists call the "tax squeeze." The phrase is apt. A person's earnings, his profits or his inheritance are caught in the grip of a vise; the excess is squeezed out. What is left may be enough for support, but it often leaves precious little for security. Security, if you remember, is based on capital, and this is what taxes make it so difficult to accumulate. The problem is the same for nearly all the stages of success in society; for the salaried junior or top; for the businessperson; even in some degree, for the person of fortune.

THE GREAT EQUALIZER

Here, then, the three horns. There is no getting around them. Like the mythical ones of old, they are encountered by everyone who charts a course through the seas of the affluent society. Together, they form a great equalizer which is at the heart of the modern-day problem of estate creation.

To the woman who is earning $400 per week, hard put to make ends meet even on a day-to-day basis, an income of $50,000 or $100,000 seems like unbelievable wealth. She cannot believe there are any financial problems for the possessor of such an income. What she does not realize is that the dilemma for these incomes—widely separated though they are—is essentially the same. That is what makes the accumulation of wealth just as knotty a problem for the Joneses as for those who want to keep up with them.

TOWARD A SOLUTION:
FOR A MODERN DILEMMA,
MODERN TECHNIQUES OF PLANNING

Does all this mean that the situation is hopeless? Obviously not, or we would not be writing this book and you would not be reading it.

Certainly, some people have found the solution. If we all know cases like our "typical four," so also do we know their opposites, persons who have been able to create estates that provide security for themselves and their family despite the economic stresses of their time. They are many in number, and they are not limited to any one group. They are found in all strata, all situations, and all ages. The "secret" of their success is no secret but a matter of common sense; they have dealt with the dilemma on its own terms.

It is a modern dilemma, remember that, one that did not exist until recent decades. So, dealing with it on its own terms means the use of *modern* methods of estate building, methods that take into account the problems of both high living costs and tax erosion.

Classic estate planning was limited, based on two prime principles: thrift and sound investment. These still apply; they are still at the heart of estate creation, as you will see in the course of this book. But other elements, just as organic to the successful estate plan, have been grafted onto them.

One such element is surely at the core: tax relief. The old techniques paid only peripheral attention to taxes. They did not constitute a major block to capital accumulation in former days. But today, as we have seen, our economy is tax saturated, and no estate plan is worth its effort, unless it, in turn, is saturated with tax relief.

The guideposts which point the way to tax relief are contained in the tax laws themselves, in the numerous preferential openings these provide for tax-favored methods of capital accumulation. We call these openings tax shelters. And shelters they truly are, places of refuge from the heavy downpour of both estate and income taxes. In essence, the term "tax shelter" refers to various ways and means of making investments, transfers, and compensation arrangements which result in profits or accumulations from which some of the burden of tax erosion has been lifted. You will be reading about numbers of them in the following chapters. Tax shelters run like a thread through the maze of estate-creation techniques.

A second new element is equally important, equally integral to the contemporary estate plan. Properly speaking it is not a technique but an opportunity: the opportunity for capital accumulation that lies in a person's own occupation.

The catchall term for it is "fringe benefits," the variety of plans offered by many corporations to their employees as additional compensation above and beyond their salaries: the profit-sharing, pension, and savings plans, the deferred compensation arrangements, the group medical and life insurance contracts, all the extras that are tacked onto a persons's salary and which can—although he may not be aware of it—form the basis of a lifetime estate building plan.

Fringe benefits have been part of the corporate way of life for many years, but they came of age during World War II and have continued to expand during the ensuing three decades. By now the term "fringe" is really a misnomer. Depending on the individual and the corporation which employs him, they are no longer the frosting on the cake, but the cake itself—so far as estate creation goes.

For three reasons: first, they operate as a sort of semi-compulsory savings plan. Unlike regular salary compensation they are usually deferred and held in reserve for a number of years. This aspect has obvious importance to the planner, who is bedeviled by the pressures of our times to spend whatever monies he has on hand. Second, they are ordinarily invested for the benefit of the employee, thus providing him with a built-in investment program. And thirdly, most of them are tax-sheltered. All in all quite a package.

Moreover, fringe benefits are not necessarily limited to the employees of corporations. In recent years, professionals and independents of all types have sought and won the right to acquire them. An increasing number of the United States working force is being swept under the protection of their benevolent umbrella.

They are not there simply for the taking, however. They vary widely from corporation to corporation, and in many of the smaller ones they scarcely exist at all. In the case of high fringe benefits for high-echelon executives they must be bargained for. In all cases, they have to be sought after, pursued, and actively incorporated into an overall program. It takes individual planning and, above all, individual initiative to bring to life their great potentiality as estate builders.

NEEDED: A WHISPERING SLAVE

We have talked a good deal about the obstacles in the path of estate creation. But so far we have not mentioned the final and most important one. It has nothing or little to do with taxes or cost of living, or with the conditions of society. It goes deeper. It is a condition of human nature, called default.

It is easy to define default, harder to cure it. In terms of estate planning, it means a failure to take advantage of the opportunities that exist for estate building; failure to meet one's responsibilities as head of the household and guardian of the family; failure to provide security. It is a failure exemplified by the plight of Young Executive, Corporate Executive, Professional, and Successful and all their counterparts everywhere.

All manner of reasons can be put forth for default. The estate-planning picture is complicated. It requires energy and zeal for the average person to find out who to go to for help, or what to do. Successful people lead busy lives. It's hard enough for them to meet the demands of the day, let alone those of the distant future.

True enough, but we suspect that the real cause for default goes deeper. It is simply the all-too-human reluctance to accept the inevitability of age and retirement. Or, even beyond that, the inevitability of death. "No young man," said Hazlitt, "thinks that he will ever die." The fact is that few of us—young or middle-aged—face up to the prospect of either age or death.

The Romans had a way to handle this problem. Theirs was an age of heroes and the heroes tended sometimes to forget that they too were mortal. To remind themselves of this unpleasant fact they retained a "whispering slave." His function? To follow the hero through the streets as he rode in triumph and whisper in his ear the truth that all men, even he, must some day die.

The affluent hero of today could use a whispering slave. Sometimes, it is true, the slave does appear and issue his warning: to the person who has a serious but non-fatal heart attack, or to the person who sees his friend's unprepared widow forced to go to work.

But do we really need such drastic warnings to force us to attack the problem of default? We refuse to believe it.

The means to build and pass on a sound estate are within the reach of nearly every executive, professional, and businessperson today. They are not limited to the already successful but can be used by the would-be successful as well—by the young and old alike. The main thing is to get started, for if it is never too late to begin building an estate, it is also never too soon.

CHAPTER 2

Getting Started

Estate planning has sometimes been called social work among the rich. It is also described as a means of passing from this world into the next without passing through the Internal Revenue Service.

These wry statements are more notable for their nice grasp of the comic than for their accuracy of definition. In reality, estate planning is not limited to the rich but encompasses a broad group of society. Nor is its sole concern the reduction of the tax impact. Indeed one of its basic precepts is that family security must never be sacrificed for tax advantages.

What is estate planning then? We would define it in this manner: *the creation, conservation, and utilization of family resources to obtain the maximum support and security for the family during the lifetime and after the death of the planner.* In less formidable terms, it means making the most of what you have or can develop.

Estate planning has both long-term and short-term objectives. Its short-term goals are current support, providing for the needs of each of the family now, while the head of the household is actively employed. At the same time, the long-term goals have to be considered; providing for the same needs of the same people if and when the planner becomes *disabled, retires,* or *dies.*

Do you want to get started on your estate planning program? Then you must mesh both the short- and long-term goals together, and you must not neglect one for the other. You must actively plan for both present and future.

All this sounds rather elementary, and philosphically speaking, it is. But when the philosophy is put into action, deep-seated problems appear. The trouble is that the achievement of the current objectives is likely to interfere with and sometimes—in fact often—prevent the realization of the long-term goals.

THE DYNAMICS OF THE FOUR FIRSTS

Let's look at the problem of current support and security. When does a family have such security and when doesn't it? A time-honored definition says that it starts with the establishment of four elements: a *home*, that is, a place to live; an annual *income*, usually secured by a job; a *savings account*, a reserve fund which can be drawn on in case of emergency; and finally *life insurance*, a source of future income if the planner should die.

The manner in which you set about achieving these goals, however, involves far-reaching decisions which are going to affect your long-term objectives. Two of the four, your income and your home, have ramifications which go deeper than their surface definitions. Not only do they help establish an estate; they also establish a standard of living. This latter aspect usually operates to prevent or impede further estate building. The simple decision of selecting a home, for example, sets in motion complicated problems of estate creation. So too with the requirements of "living up to one's career or income position."

We can illustrate these dynamics with a concrete example. A young friend of ours just bought a home. He is 30 years old and, for his age, not just successful but extremely successful. He's a salesman; clever, ambitious, and energetic. His income is presently $60,000 and he has every reason to believe that it will go much higher in the future.

He bought the home to take care of the needs of his family—a wife and four children. It is large and expensive. He can afford the initial purchase price—that is not the question. The question is, can he afford to maintain the standard of living which residence in this house, in this section of the town, with these neighbors, will demand? He will need to hire domestic help; he will have to entertain and be entertained in a fairly luxurious style; he will acquire expensive tastes and so will his wife and children. The satisfaction of these tastes will soon appear to be necessities and he will work harder and earn more money to meet them. But will he build an estate?

TO RESOLVE THE DYNAMICS: DETERMINATION PLUS OBJECTIVES

So far, our young friend has not come to grips with his problem. For two reasons:

First—he has not yet acquired the *determination* to build an estate. By determination, we mean the conscious and active desire to make estate building an integral part of his financial planning—from now until the day he dies. Without this determination, it is almost impossible to build an estate; with it, the way is opened up. It is the foundation of the estate plan, the catalytic ingredient which sets the rest of the process in motion.

Secondly—and as a result of his lack of determination— our young friend has not yet made a conscious evaluation of his estate-planning objectives. Without such objectives, an estate plan lacks direction; it is like sending a ship to sea without a rudder.

THREE PEOPLE AND THEIR OBJECTIVES

Here are three people we know. Examine for a moment their attitude toward this problem of determining objectives.

The first is a doctor, just finishing her residency, married, no children yet. She has a clear idea of exactly how much money she can earn from her specialty, pediatric surgery. She has selected the locale where she will set up practice, made a rough estimate of her yearly earnings and expenses for the next 5 years. She has already started an insurance and investment program. All this done with some definite goals in mind. She wants to create an estate of about $500,000 before she is 45, and thinks she can do it.

The second is also a doctor, age 63, very successful. His income is substantial and has been for years. He has the usual accoutrements that go with success; he and his family live extremely well. He has saved very little, has no insurance or investment plan, has never really thought about where he is going, financially speaking, or why. In a vague way he knows he's going to have to work till the day he dies. But what about his family's security after that? He has for some years past resolved to do something about hedging against the possibility of his disability or death. But he has never really made a determination of what he wanted to do or how to do it—and certainly has never taken the first small steps in translating his wavering resolution into action.

The third is a businessman. married, three children. He is a real loner. He operates his export-import office without benefit of even a secretary. Some years he brings in a good deal, as much as $150,000 or $200,000. In others he earns only $50,000. He has no savings; he makes no investments; all he has in the way of an estate is a small insurance policy. When he has money he lives high. When he doesn't, he hauls in his belt and lives off his much reduced income. He is a nonconformist, who is not interested in security for either himself or his family. He believes that such considerations hamper his freedom and restrict his life. He is confident of his ability to produce enough income to support the family and educate the children. Beyond that, they must take their chances as he did.

Which of these three have determined their estate-planning objectives?

Obviously, our first person, the young doctor, is the very model of an estate planner. She knows exactly where she is going and what she wants and is taking measures to achieve these goals. But you will probably be surprised when we tell you that the last person has also determined *his* estate-planning objectives. They are far from orthodox and we do not recommend them. But nevertheless they are the product of a rational decision; they represent a life plan which is *consciously* arrived at.

It is our middle man who is in trouble. He is the only one who has not determined his objectives and therefore has no estate plan. He is a procrastinator. So much so that he hasn't even thought seriously about what he wants, let alone how to get it.

The Right and Wrong of It

There is no "right" or "wrong" set of objectives, you see; they must be personally determined by each individual, and one set is as good as another. The point is to have them. What income do you want your spouse to have available if you should die? How much will she and the children need? What will you need for the support of yourself, your spouse and your family, when you retire, or if you should become disabled?

The answers to these questions will determine your objectives. They require a good deal of thinking through. You will have to evaluate the needs of each member of the family, not forgetting any support obligations you may have for relatives outside your immediate family. You must make lifetime decisions about such things as the standard of living you expect yourself and your family to maintain. Do you want your children to go to college? To graduate school? And if so, do you plan to pay the full cost of this education or you will expect your children to help by working or getting scholarship aid?

Do you want to give them further security by leaving them an inheritance? By transferring part of your estate to them while you are still alive? Or do you think it better to send them out in the world to make their own way?

Each person's answer to these questions will be different. In addition, they will vary according to the individual's age and station in life. The determination of objectives is—as are all parts of estate planning—both flexible and continuous. It will change as you change.

But for the younger person, one thing is sure. Whether his objectives are modest or grandiose, he will need to scrutinize his current standard of living most carefully. In all probability it will have to be more modest than he might wish, for he must begin, now and not later, to set aside part of his income for capital accumulation, if he is to achieve those objectives. Therefore, he must ask himself at every juncture where a raise in the standard of living is indicated: is this necessary? Does my job really require more expensive living? Can I afford it and still continue my estate-creation program?

It is easier to make such decisions before rather than after the upward step has been taken on the status escalator.

Tastes once acquired are not easily abandoned. Few prospects in life are more agonizing to contemplate than the reversal of a standard of living, once it has become a habit.

STARTING POINT: INVENTORY YOUR ASSETS

So far we have only talked about the philosophy behind getting started—the frame of mind, the strength of character, and the objectives. Let us assume that you do possess the determination and you have established objectives. Where do you go from here?

You begin by taking stock. This is the first and absolutely essential step. Before you explore all the estate-creation opportunities open to you, you must know what you have to start with.

What is the value of your estate in terms of providing security for your family right now? This isn't determined by a mere listing of assets (although this must be done). The market value of assets alone is not a measure of their security value. This is capital, and to determine the security potential of your capital, you must determine how much annual income it will produce. When you know what this is, then you have a true idea of the ability of your estate to provide security for you and your family in the three situations: retirement, disability, and death.

A word here about the significance of capital. We say that capital should never be encroached on, for the moment it is, it loses a portion of its income-producing capacity. A rule of thumb says it should last the lifetime of the individual as well as that of his surviving spouse. For a person of 45 years with a spouse 5 years younger, that would mean about 35 years. Sometimes, of course, the principal of an estate will not be large enough to produce a sufficient annual income to meet a family's needs, and so principal will have to be used. How long, then, will the principal last? What if the estate owner and his spouse live long past their life expectancies? These days, 90 years or more is not an unusual life span. The need for support and financial independence must be projected on the basis of the possibility of such a long life. What happens, for instance, if capital is exhausted at some point and the widow lives on for an additional 10, maybe 20 years?

An estate owner should try to plan so that this situation never arises. The production of income and the inviolability of capital are, in other words, prime objectives of estate planning.

All estate planning begins with an estimate of income potential. You should make this estimate whether your estate is large or small, whether you are going to leave your family a fortune, or merely a sum to ensure their security. It is something you can do for yourself, without calling on any expert advice.

In the appendix of this book for your use are "Estate Planning Worksheets." Used properly, they will provide you with an immediate and continuing record of all your assets and the important facts about them from an income-producing point of view. The record, when completed, will show you at a glance whether your estate can meet your objectives.

You will have to do a number of calculations to use the Worksheets, not difficult, only time-consuming.

Begin by making a list of all your properties. Include everything you own or have a right in: securities; real estate holdings; business interests; corporate benefits, such as pension plans, stock options, and group insurance; personal insurance and annuities; personal property; even such things as veterans' benefits and social security.

Now determine the prospective income from each of these in three instances: death, retirement, disability. Use as a basis for figuring income a standard estimate of 5 per cent annual return after taxes on invested capital. (This standard will be used throughout this book. It may not be valid for particular types of investments, but it is useful as an overall guide.)

There will also be administration costs and estate taxes to be subtracted from the value of the after-death estate to determine how much property will be left to the surviving family.

ANALYZING THE INVENTORY: YOUR ESTATE PICTURE

With your inventory completed, how does the picture look? How much security have you assured for your family?

You may be shocked by what you see. The unplanned estate rarely presents a balanced picture. Usually, there are great holes left—especially in the retirement and disability columns. Estates that appear to be small can turn out to be quite productive in providing income and vice versa. We know of the estates of two persons, both of which had been described as worth $200,000. After the assessment was completed, it turned out that one of them—being largely invested in securities returning 7 per cent—had an income potential of $14,000. The other turned out to be comprised of a $100,000 home, a 30-foot cruiser, and a locked-in minority interest in a close corporation that paid no dividends. Annual income potential: zero.

The first part of this book will show you how to fill in the gaps. Numerous paths of estate creation will be analyzed. The many uses of insurance will be explored, the occupational opportunities clarified, the special problems of retirement and disability treated, principles of investment outlined.

The second part deals with the problem of estate transfer, progression of investment strategies explained, the methods of distributing your capital both during your life and after death, so that it can be conserved and best used for the benefit of your family.

Don't think you have to read the entire book through from beginning to end. Glance through it, read the sections that interest you most, or have the most bearing on your own problems, get an idea of what each chapter contains so that you will know when and how to refer to the specific information it covers. This will give you a broad picture of your own estate-planning problems and supply a frame of reference for utilizing the Worksheets. The Worksheets will help you analyze your estate. You should begin filling them in at this point, using the main book as a guide and aid. A careful reading of the book is the last step. It should help you in formulating your plans and finding the ways and means of improving your estate picture.

We begin with the "universal" estate builder: life insurance.

CHAPTER 3

Life Insurance:
The Universal Estate Builder

Jane Doe is a fortunate young woman. At age 28 she already has three of the necessary requisites for building an estate: *ability* (she is intelligent, hard-working, competent); *opportunity* (she has a good job with a corporation that will eventually provide her with a number of estate building sources); and *determination* (she has even established an estate-creation program and has the will and strength of character to carry it through). All she needs now is *time*, the time to use her ability, opportunities, and determination to create her estate.

In the usual course of things, Jane will get that time. She will probably live to a ripe old age. If she uses her ability and opportunities well and maintains her determination, she can accumulate the estate.

But what about her estate position right now? Suppose she were to die prematurely. Where's the estate going to come from, if the time is lacking?

Like many things in life, the time is for sale. It can be bought for an initial payment of as low as $200 to create an instant estate worth $100,000.

In a word, her answer is life insurance, for life insurance buys time; it is the only investment that does. This is its basic function; it is what makes it the "universal" estate creator and the first outside investment a family man should make.

The ordinary Jane goes ahead and makes that investment. Not being an insurance expert, she probably never does get around to reading the fine print in her policy. She has only a vague idea of such things as dividend options, investment versus risk, the taxability of insurance, modes of settlement, and the like. She is aware of the amount of yearly premiums she pays, the face value of the policy, and not much else. Yet the fact is that life insurance often represents the largest single continuing investment that the average person makes during the course of her life.

Beyond this, life insurance is, of all estate-building tools, the most flexible. Although its first and most important function is to create an instant estate, it has other uses and other ramifications, which make it of interest to the owner of the large estate as well as the small, to individuals and companies alike, to business owners as well as employees.

THE USES OF INSURANCE

It *indemnifies*, that is to say, it replaces a financial loss caused by the death of an individual. It is a *funding* device, used to supply monies for business purposes. And finally, it is an *investment*, providing an opportunity for capital accumulation, which is especially attractive to the high-bracket taxpayer.

Indemnification

• *Mr. A is a young man with a family*. Good job, good future—but no estate as yet. Since his children are young, he needs somehow to ensure their security if he should die and leave his family without a source of income. He figures that $200,000 would suffice to at least take care of his family till the youngest child reaches 21 years. He buys a life insurance policy in this amount and breathes easy. He has partially idemnified his family against his loss.

• *Ms. B is the president of Successful Enterprises, Inc*. She has been the prime organizer and motivating force behind the success of her company. Her death would represent a profound loss to the firm, if she were to die at this point in its development. Nothing could make up for the loss of her personal contribution, that is true. But life insurance could soften the blow considerably by indemnifying the company for the financial losses.

• *Mr. C and his wife have built their dream house*. The

mortgage payments are rather high, but he'll have it paid in full by the time he's 52—if he lives that long. He's afraid that his wife wouldn't be able to keep up the payments if he died prematurely. So he buys mortgage insurance. If he dies before the mortgage is paid off, the insurance takes care of it.

Remember, too, that in each of these cases, as well as in most others, the liquidity of life insurance is of great importance. The typical beneficiaries of insurance—widows, estates, and independent businesses—are usually in great need of ready cash. In most instances, insurance proceeds are transferred without delay or administration costs.

Funding

• *Ms. D and her closest friend are the sole stockholders in a small corporation.* Each of them wants to be sure that she would have complete control if the other one died; so they enter a stockholder's agreement providing for this. But neither of them, nor the corporation, has enough money to buy out the other's interest at his death.

They use insurance to provide it in the following way: each takes out insurance on the other's life, equal in value to a half interest in the corporation. If one of them dies, the necessary cash is immediately available to carry out the agreement. They could accomplish the same goal by having the corporation insure both of them. Then the corporation would redeem the dead partner's stock, using the insurance money to pay for it.

• *Mr. E is the sole owner of a million dollar corporation.* He wants to be sure that his company will continue after his death for the benefit of his family, but he knows there will be a heavy demand for cash in the period immediately following his death. It will be needed by the company to redeem stock so that his estate has liquidity to pay estate taxes. It may also be required to pay off creditors, to hire key people to replace him, and to maintain the business community's confidence in the firm.

Life insurance can supply his company with this money. The company can take out what is known as a "key man policy" with a face value of, say $200,000 on E's life and pay the premiums out of its surplus. When E dies, the proceeds will be available, tax-free, to help the business through the many difficulties that lie ahead.

• *People in her community say that Ms. F is rich.* They are right. When she dies, she will leave her family an estate worth $2 million. Having no surviving spouse, there is no marital deduction available to Ms. F's estate. Her whole estate, less the $600,000 equivalent exemption that everyone is entitled to, will be subject to the estate tax. The trouble is that none of her assets are liquid. Where, then, is the cash going to come from to pay the $525,000 in taxes and administration expenses?

Insurance is the answer. It will be immediately available on her death to use for this purpose. This means that the other assets in her estate can be passed on whole, undiluted by the losses that usually accompany a forced liquidation.

• *Mr. G is a man with a number of business interests.* In some years he has heavy debts. He is afraid that if he died in one of these bad years his creditors might wipe out his entire estate. To forestall such a disastrous event, he carries insurance sufficient to meet all these obligations.

Insurance as Investment

• *Ms. H earns $30,000 a year and can't save a dime.* She makes periodic resolutions to do something about savings, but as soon as she accumulates a little money, she finds something to spend it on. A strong-intentioned but weak-willed planner, she finally solves her problem by buying an insurance policy. She pays her premiums on a regular schedule, just like her mortgage payments, with not too much strain, as part of the family budget. The cash value of her insurance is her savings, and if she doesn't have time to complete her savings plan for her family, the death proceeds will complete it for her. It is a savings plan that is semi-compulsory, and therefore more likely to be continued.

• *Mr. I is a child of the depression years* who saw a family fortune disappear in a few days. This traumatic experience has turned him into an ultra-conservative investor. For years he has been sacrificing capital appreciation and high rates of return for safety. Now he wants to branch out into investment fields which offer more opportunity for capital appreciation, but he is still too conditioned by his "safety-first" code to give up his fixed-return investments.

He doesn't have to. If he substitutes insurance for some of his fixed investments, he can free a large part of his assets for equity investments, in the knowledge that his family will be taken care of, if he dies. Nothing is more risk-proof than insurance. It offers a fixed amount which the purchaser specifies in advance, and it is not subject to change because of business conditions, economic factors, or other circumstances beyond the control of the policy holder.

• *Ms. J. makes a good deal of money.* Her salary and other income put her in a 28 per cent tax bracket. When she makes her investment plan, she realizes that she has to either find an investment that earns 7.5 per cent (in order to realize an after-tax income of 5 per cent) or buy tax-free bonds yielding at least 5 per cent. The first is sometimes hard to come by. If she takes the second course, unless she purchases bonds through a tax-exempt fund, she may not attain the level of diversification she should have. Also, whether she invests through a fund or directly, she may realize capital losses if general interest rates subsequently shift upward or the underlying state or municipality suffers a drop in its credit rating.

She could get both yield and liquidity, however, if she substituted insurance for some of the low-yield investments she now owns. The cash value of her insurance, after figuring her insurance cost, will grow at an accumulating yearly rate of 8 per cent, or more if she uses her cash values as an investment medium for capital growth. She pays no income taxes on this growth while it is being earned, and the likelihood is that she never will.

Thus, the nature of insurance: a source of capital accumulation and a device to supply money whenever it is needed at someone's death. Moreover, its cash value is always available for borrowing, and it can be converted at retirement into a favorable annuity program.

TYPES OF INSURANCE

Today, there are insurance policies to meet any insurance need and many investment objectives. As only one element in the estate plan, the insurance program must be tailored to the needs of each individual estate. Basically, however, you will have a choice among several principal types.

Term Insurance

The chief thing to keep in mind about term insurance is that it is *temporary* insurance, which exists for a given period of time—such as 1, 5, 10 years. You pay a fixed amount in premiums for the period of its term. If you don't die in that period, the policy expires and protection ends. Most term policies, however, give the holder an option to renew. On each renewal, the premium rises, and usually the renewal option ceases at age 65 or 70. Term can usually be converted, however, at any time to permanent insurance with no physical examination required.

Term insurance requires the smallest outlay of cash. A man, aged 35, could carry $100,000 of 5-year term at a net premium of only $300 per year. He'd have to pay a net of $1,300 for the same amount of ordinary life insurance.

But in the long run, term is not inexpensive. It's costly. The premium keeps rising with every renewal. Over a period of years, your total net costs for term will exceed the total net cost (your net premium less cash value) of permanent insurance.

Remember, too, that since most term policies cut off at age 65 or 70, they cannot give either continuous or permanent coverage to a person with a normal life expectancy.

Should you buy term or not?

If you are a young person about to buy basic insurance, term insurance is not the answer. You need permanent coverage until you die, at the lowest net cost. But what do you do if you can't afford the premiums for permanent insurance? The best solution is to buy part term and part permanent, converting your term to permanent as your income rises. In other words, it's better to supplement permanent insurance with term than to carry no permanent insurance at all.

There are many situations, however, when term insurance is a useful solution. It's usually the best answer when there is a need for immediate protection for a limited period of time or for a particular purpose. This is the case with term mortgage insurance, which Mr. C bought to make sure his wife would never have to sacrifice their dream house.

So, too, with many business and investment situations. Take the case of an inventor seeking financial backing. He has a new product with great potential, but it will take several years to get it ready for the market. Investors, while interested, are cautious about advancing money. What will happen if the inventor dies before the product is ready? The solution: they take out term insurance on the inventor's life and thus protect themselves against loss, at the lowest cash outlay, in the event of his premature death.

Whole Life Insurance

Whole life is permanent insurance. It differs from term in that it will pay off at any time the insured dies, rather than within a specified period. It embraces two different types of insurance plans: ordinary life and limited payment life. These differ mainly in the length of time premium payments are to be made.

Ordinary Life

Under this type of contract, for a set premium payable for the whole of the insured's life, the policyholder gets permanent coverage. Ordinary life can function as part of an investment program and savings account. We saw some examples of how this works in the case of Ms. H, Mr. I, and Ms. J. Let's now take a look at the principles which underlie this aspect of ordinary life.

When you buy ordinary life, both your policy and your premium payments are divided into two parts: risk protection and investment. The risk part represents term insurance. The investment part represents your savings account in the policy; it forms the cash value of your policy.

At the beginning of your policy much of your premium goes toward risk and the "loading cost" of putting the policy in force. Gradually, however the cash value rises, the risk cost decreases, and a larger share of the premium is consequently added to the cash value. At the same time, the cash value has a built-in annual earning factor. This results in a continuous build-up of the cash value of your policy. How does all this affect an investment or savings plan?

If you have bought your insurance at age 35, for instance, within 3 years the yearly increase in the cash value (including dividends) of your policy will exceed your annual premium. In one company, for every dollar of premium paid in the ninth year, $1.63 is credited to the cash value and dividends. This is in addition to the fact that the term insurance part of the policy is being paid for.

The cash value gives you a liquid asset. It is always available for borrowing—sometimes in periods when no other source is available. We know of at least one person who was saved from financial ruin through the cash value of an insurance policy. He had overextended himself in the stock market, and was called for margin. He was able to meet the call by borrowing the cash value out of his insurance policies for a limited period of time and so saved his stock interests, and rode the slump through, on into the rise that providentially followed it.

Cash value should also be considered as a potential source of investment capital. When and if your insurance needs stop, you can terminate your policy, walk away with the cash value, and use it to make other investments—or conversely, you can use it to buy other forms of insurance or an annuity.

The build-up of the cash value is free of income taxes during the existence of the policy. This tax-sheltered treatment turns insurance into an attractive investment. If you are in a low income tax bracket, your return on your cash values is as good as your return after taxes on most other fixed dollar investments. You would have to earn 10 per cent or more before taxes on your other investments in order to equal your tax-free build-up of your cash values.

Let us look at the investment return on cash value life insurance. Assume you are 35 years old and need $50,000 of insurance coverage. At this age, you will pay out a total of $12,265 in premiums over a period of 20 years on an ordinary life policy.

At the end of the 20 years, the build-up of the cash value plus the dividends will amount to about $36,000 a gain of $23,600.

Obviously, however, you also have had term coverage during this period. The term cost of the risk portion of the policy is, in effect, also a return on the $12,265 you paid in.

If you add the amount it would have cost you to buy this term insurance, at the lowest available rates, to the after-tax gain on the $23,600, you will find that the return on your life insurance investment will exceed 7 per cent compound interest, tax free.

When you terminate a policy and take the cash value, you pay an income tax only on the amount you get back which exceeds the total amount of premiums you have paid less dividends you received, in this case $23,600.

Variable Life

Similar to whole or ordinary life, this policy is based on the payment of a fixed annual premium, the establishment of a cash value, and the guarantee of a minimum death benefit. It differs in that the insured may elect to have the cash value invested in stocks, bonds, money market, or other types of investments. In addition, he may change or transfer the investments from one type to another at stated periods, free of taxes or fees. The cash value of the policy at any given time will depend upon the success or failure of the investment program. The death benefit is guaranteed at its full amount. If the cash value has increased in value beyond the policy's assumed rate of growth, however, the amount of this increase will be added to the full amount of the policy and will be received tax-free by beneficiaries as life insurance death proceeds.

Universal Life

Universal life is basically an investment program tied to a term insurance contract. For income tax purposes it qualifies as life insurance and as such enjoys its tax advantages. It differs from most other forms of insurance in that once the initial premium is paid (in any amount necessary to pay the costs of establishing the policy, paying the term insurance rate, and setting up a cash value account), annual fixed premiums are no longer required. The policy-holder may invest as much as and whenever he wishes into the cash value account. The annual term cost will be taken out of this account as long as it has a sufficient balance. Like variable life, the cash value account may be invested in specified types of investment programs and may be transferred from one type to another at the election of the policy-holder. The accumulation of earnings in the cash value account is tax-deferred and may be withdrawn tax-free up to the amount of his investment in the policy. Any withdrawn amount in excess of his investment will be taxed. The death benefit will amount to the term insurance in force plus the value of the cash value account and will be received tax-free by the beneficiary.

Limited Payment Life

This is like ordinary life, except that the period of premium payments is limited to a certain number of years, such as 10 or 20 years, or until you reach a certain age. After that your policy is paid up and remains in force for the full face amount. You need make no further premium payments.

Premiums for limited payment life are, of course, higher than those of an equal face amount of ordinary life because the period of premium payment is shorter. At the same time the cash value increases at a much greater rate. The high cash value makes it an attractive investment for those who want to use their insurance to provide a retirement income. Limited payment is also a good type of insurance for a person who has a high income in early years which may go down as he gets older. Professional athletes, artists, and entertainers might consider it.

Paid-up Life

Another form of permanent insurance, it is similar to limited payment life except that here the entire premium is paid in one installment.

An ordinary or limited payment life policy can be converted to a paid-up policy for a reduced face amount. This amount will be determined by the cash values which are in the existing policy. The cash value is used as a single premium, based on the age of the insured at the time the conversion is made.

Endowment Insurance

Do you want to build a retirement fund, finance a child's college education, or have a certain sum of money at a particular time in the future?

Endowment insurance is one way of achieving these goals. It covers a fixed amount of time, pays out the face amount

either at the end of this time or on the death of the insured
if he dies before the period is up.

It is, thus, similar to limited payment life in that it
provides both insurance protection and a savings account.
The difference lies in the fact that endowment calls for
accumulating the face amount of the policy and is essentially
a plan of savings. Because a larger portion of the endowment premiums is allocated to savings (the cash value) the
premium is necessarily higher than other forms of insurance.

Endowment policies can also involve added taxes. If you
survive to the endowment time, the amount paid out as an
endowment is always larger than that paid in as premiums.
Therefore, there is an income tax to be paid on the excess
received over the amount paid into the policy.

Retirement Annuity

In a sense, this represents the opposite concept from life
insurance. With life insurance, the company that insures you
is risking its money against the possibility that you may die
before the age at which the actuarial tables say you will.

With annuity policies, the risk is still based on the actuarial
tables—but here the company takes the risk that you will
live beyond your life expectancy. It pays you a fixed sum for
the rest of your life, an annuity. The annuity payment
consists of the installment return on your investment as well
as an interest return on it. You might say that annuities are
really "life" insurance. What we call life insurance is actually "death" insurance.

This possibility—that you may live to retirement, and
perhaps many years beyond your life expectancy—is one
that every planner must take into consideration. Life spans
are increasing today. Life expectancies represent only an
average; it is not uncommon for a person to live to a great
age, 80, 90, 95 even. There may be 20 to 30 years of
retirement for which income has to be found. The value of
the annuity principle is that you can never outlive the payments of principal and interest which it provides; this is
something that no other form of investment can offer.

Chapter 9 takes up the problems of retirement more fully.
We deal with the annuity policy here, however, because it is
frequently combined with a life insurance element. The
retirement income policy is basically an annuity policy which

includes decreasing term insurance. Thus, if you die before your retirement, the policy pays off to your beneficiaries. If you live to retirement, it pays off to you. The term insurance part is less expensive than ordinary term because, like a rider, it is part of a combined policy.

Single Premium Life

This policy contains many of the features of term, variable, universal, and paid-up life insurance. For the payment of a lump sum, the policy-holder receives life insurance coverage in a greater amount than his premium. He has two investment options. He may elect to have the cash value invested at a fixed return that will vary with the change in general interest rates. In this case the insurance company will guarantee the principal. Alternatively, he may elect a variable investment plan similar to those of the variable and universal programs. The insured may borrow out accumulated earnings and a proportion of the cash value. This borrowing will be tax-free, if not in excess of his investment in the policy, and probably at little or no interest cost. The death benefit will vary according to the amount of the underlying insurance and the value of the cash value at the time of death and may be received by beneficiaries free of tax as a distribution of life insurance death proceeds.

INSURANCE RIDERS

For additional premiums most policies will include riders—provisions attached to the basic contract, which give the policy holder extra benefits or options. Some of these are so common that they are automatically inserted in the policy, and the premium is quoted as part of the whole policy.

Double Indemnity

A famous novel and movie turned this rider into a household word. If you have a double indemnity rider your beneficiaries will get double the face value of the policy should you die in an accident. Some policies triple the amount if the accident occurs while you are traveling in a common carrier.

Is it worth buying? We'd say it's a matter of personal choice. The chances are small that you will die as the result of an accident; on the other hand, the extra premium cost is modest and the returns are large.

Disability Waiver

For a small extra premium, your policy may include a waiver of premiums in the event of disability before 60 or 65 years of age (depending upon the company). This is an extremely important rider, and one that we advise you to consider most seriously. Here's what it provides:

If you become totally and permanently disabled, the company will pay your premiums for you. At the same time all the provisions of the insurance contract remain effective. Generally this covers only disability which lasts at least 6 months. But the waiver is retroactive to the beginning of the disability period.

The waiver is obviously a great protection against a loss of security in a time of emergency. But it is also a money-making machine. During the period it operates, the cash value keeps increasing, and so may be borrowed against if extra cash is needed, or withdrawn, if you want to terminate the policy later.

Family Income

If you die within a certain period the company will pay the family a monthly income for a fixed time and, at the end of this period, pay out the face amount of the basic ordinary life policy in a lump sum or on options. Family income riders are really reducing term insurance, but the premiums are cheaper than if you buy term separately.

Mortgage Redemption

This is another form of reducing term insurance attached to a basic policy. It is used for paying off a reducing mortgage, and so the face value of the rider diminishes. As a rider, the cost is less than a policy offering similar protection.

Insurability Protection

This is a new type of rider which is useful to the young family provider. It gives the insured the right to buy additional insurance of specified amounts at certain ages, usually up to age 40, without further physical examination. This is a valuable rider; the additional premiums are low; your insurability is guaranteed, even if you become ill or disabled.

MODES OF SETTLEMENT AND OPTIONS

This phrase refers to the ways and means available to you and your beneficiaries for payout of the policy proceeds. A number of alternatives are available.

1. *Lump Sum Payout.* Your beneficiaries get the whole face value at once. They may also have the right reserved to select other options, however.

2. *Interest Option.* The proceeds are left with the company, which pays a guaranteed rate of interest. The interest is taxable to the beneficiary as ordinary income. This option is used when the policy holder wants to prevent his beneficiary from dissipating the insurance fund. It can also include a "spendthrift clause" which protects the insurance from the beneficiary's creditors.

It's better, however, not to use this option too rigidly. Unless you specify that the beneficiary has the right to withdraw part or all of the principal, or elect other options, the insurance proceeds are not available for emergencies.

3. *Fixed Period Option.* Proceeds are paid out in equal installments over a specified number of years. The installments are made up of payments from principal (i.e., the insurance proceeds) and interest.

4. *Fixed Amount Option.* Installments are paid out in fixed amounts until the proceeds are exhausted.

5. *Life Income Option.* This is like an annuity in that the company agrees to make periodic payments during the life of the beneficiary. How much these payments amount to depends, of course, on the amount of the insurance proceeds and the life expectancy of the beneficiary. Its great advantage is that it provides larger annuity payments than a new annuity policy purchased with an equal sum of money.

* * *

What about settlement options?

Which one is best? There's no pat answer. They have to be carefully considered and fitted to the individual case. Very often they are simply too rigid. The payment should be made a flexible matter, depending on the particular situation at the particular time.

This can be provided by using the interest option with the right of the beneficiary to withdraw principal on an unlimited basis or in installments at stated intervals.

Flexibility can also be obtained by having the insurance proceeds paid into a trust. The trust proceeds can be invested by the trustees (people of investment experience) and then paid out to the beneficiaries on the basis of their changing needs. Thus, the insured does not have to make a rigid arrangement which may not meet his family's needs after he is gone. He has substituted personal representatives for himself who will make new dispositions as changed circumstances require. Insurance trusts are dealt with in greater detail in Chapter 13.

DIVIDENDS AND WHAT TO DO ABOUT THEM

If your policy is issued by a mutual company or as a special policy by a stock company, you will receive annual dividends. You have several choices in their use. Which one you select is of importance in your estate picture.

1. You can take your dividends in cash. Since a dividend is considered a return of a part of the premium, there is no income tax on the dividend receipt.

2. You can apply them to your premium payments, thus reducing your annual payments to the company.

3. You can leave them to accumulate with the company, and receive in return a guaranteed rate of interest on it. This interest rate is often increased because of increased company earnings. The accrued interest is taxable, and must be reported annually, whether or not you withdraw it. You may withdraw it at any time or leave it as a savings account.

4. You can buy additional paid-up insurance with your dividends. This is an attractive option; the insurance is at "pure cost" (meaning there is no overhead or "loading" charge); therefore, it is cheaper than insurance purchased in

the ordinary way. The additional insurance will have a cash value like any other type of permanent insurance.

5. You can use a portion of your dividends to buy automatically each year 1-year term insurance equal to the cash value of the policy. No physical examination is required for this purchase.

This option is called the "fifth dividend option." If you use it, you are purchasing additional protection at "pure" insurance rates.

The fifth dividend option is important. It cancels out one of the major objections to life insurance as an investment: the fact that the owner becomes a "co-insurer" with the insurance company on the policy.

How does this happen? Ordinarily as the policy continues in force the cash value grows; the death value, however, remains the same. When the death claim is finally paid, the company is in effect returning the cash value (which belonged to the insured anyway) plus the balance of the face value. This balance is the only amount which really represents the insurance risk. But when the fifth dividend option is used, the company must pay at risk, over and above the cash value, the full face value of the policy at most ages.

In addition, the fifth dividend option has a number of uses in helping to *finance* a policy—which is a subject in itself.

PREMIUMS AND HOW TO FINANCE THEM

Up to now, we have been speaking about the purchase of insurance by the regular payment of premiums out of pocket.

Prior to the enactment of the 1986 Tax Reform Act, it was possible to pay the insurance policy by borrowing all or part of the premium payments by using the cash values of the policy as collateral. Some of the borrowing plans offered considerable tax savings and, in effect, allowed the policy owner to buy insurance at an extremely low cost. The interest paid on the loan was wholly deductible under prescribed conditions.

Unfortunately, the 1986 Tax Act disallows the deduction of interest paid on life insurance loans but on a phased-out basis. During 1987, 65 percent of interest paid is deductible; in 1988, 40 percent; in 1989, 20 percent; in 1990, 10 percent. Thereafter, no interest paid is deductible.

An alternative to borrowing against the cash value of the insurance policy is to obtain a loan or line of credit secured by your residence. Interest on loans secured by your residence will continue to be fully deductible up to the cost of the home plus improvements.

The cost of obtaining such a loan, commonly referred to as a "home equity loan," varies with the lending institution. Closing costs include an appraisal fee, title fees, and recording fees, and may range from $500 to $900, although some banks have waived these closing costs.

Although the loss of the deduction of interest in connection with the financing of premiums reduces the flexibility and the alternatives that were previously available to individuals in high tax brackets, we were always believers in keeping cash values intact. They are a valuable savings medium. There may be a time when the fund is the only money available to you to meet an emergency or other need. Systematic borrowings against cash values often had the effect of reducing the coverage amount of a policy and in most cases increased the net cost of the insurance.

Split-dollar financing is commonly used between relatives. A father-in-law, for instance, wants to ensure his daughter's support if her husband dies prematurely. At the same time, he recognizes that his son-in-law may not be able to afford costly life insurance premium payments. The solution is to enter into a split-dollar arrangement with him and still get a fair return on any money he invests.

Thus Mr. Jones, aged 45, enters into a split-dollar arrangement with his father-in-law, Mr. Smith, in which Smith takes out $500,000 of insurance on Jones's life. Smith owns the policy and Jones has the right to name his wife or children as beneficiaries of the death proceeds in excess of the policy's cash values. Jones pays the first year's premium of $8,910, and $6,910 of the second year's premium. Smith pays the rest of the premiums. By the third year, the cash values will always exceed the annual premiums paid by Smith and his investment in the policy will be protected.

If Jones should die in the tenth year, the cash values of the policy would be $116,826, which Smith will receive (he will have paid in $75,690). His daughter, Jones's wife, will receive the balance of the death proceeds. Assuming the dividends have been used to buy paid-up additions, the daughter will receive $481,673.

This is a very effective way of financing a family insurance program in cases where an individual has limited capital or income but at the same time has need for a large amount of insurance. Split-dollar insurance is often and advantageously used by corporations and their stockholders or key people. More about this in Chapter 5.

INSURANCE AND THE INCOME TAX

Insurance death proceeds are specifically exempted by law from income tax liability whether they are paid to an individual, an estate, or a corporation.

There is one major exception to the rule, however, and that is where a policy is sold or transferred for "valuable consideration." In such a case income taxes are payable on the part of the death proceeds which exceed the new owner's cost.

Thus, if a $25,000 policy is sold for its cash value of $5,000 and the new owner later pays a total of $5,000 in premiums, she will have to pay a tax on $15,000 when she receives the death benefits of the policy. This is considered to be ordinary income and will be added to her other income for tax purposes.

This tax treatment holds even though a policy is sold to the insured's spouse. When transferring a policy to a member of the family, you must be certain that it is done as a gift and that nothing of value is paid for it.

Exceptions are made to the so-called "transfer for value" rule in the case of transfers to a corporation where the insured is a stockholder or officer, to the insured's partner or partnership, or to the insured himself. In these cases, even though consideration is paid for the policies, the death benefits are not subject to the income tax.

INSURANCE AND THE ESTATE TAX

There is a prevalent notion that insurance isn't subject to the estate tax. This isn't necessarily true. If it is payable to your estate or if you retain ownership of the policy, the death proceeds are going to be included in your taxable estate. Included in the definition of ownership are what the law calls "incidents of ownership" such as the right to sur- render or pledge the policy, the right to borrow on it or assign it, and the right to change the beneficiary.

One way to remove insurance from your taxable estate is to relinquish all rights in it by assigning the policy to someone else. However, there might be a gift tax imposed upon such an assignment. The gift tax rate is the same as the estate tax. However, only the cash value of the policy and the unearned and subsequent premiums paid by you are subject to this tax, not the face value of the policy. The gift tax can be avoided or reduced. By virtue of the unlimited marital deduction, there is no gift tax payable on an insurance policy assigned to your husband or wife nor any estate tax on the proceeds of insurance which are paid to your spouse.

The increase in the gift tax annual exclusion to $10,000 ($20,000 if your spouse consents to the gift) means that a tax-free transfer can be made of a policy with a cash value of up to that amount and of subsequent premium payments of no more than the amount of the annual exclusions. However, if death occurs within three years of the transfer, the proceeds of the policy will be subject to estate taxes.

But are you sure you want to make such an irrevocable assignment? Are you certain you will never need to borrow on the cash value? Never want to change your beneficiary? Better look before you leap, because here as elsewhere in estate planning, family security and needs should not be sacrificed to save taxes.

Additional point: If a man transfers his policy to his wife and she dies before he does, the cash value of the policy is taxable in her estate. Unless his wife's estate is substantial this won't create a tax problem. But if it is large, there is not only this problem to consider, but also the fact that, if she survives him, the entire proceeds will go to her. Then, when she dies they will be part of her taxable estate.

In such cases, you should consider other forms of ownership. It may be worthwhile to have other members of the family own and be beneficiaries of the policies; or it may make more sense to assign the policy to an irrevocable living trust, with income and part of principal payable to your spouse or children according to their needs, and the remainder of the principal to your children after your spouse dies. Some taxable gift may be involved depending upon the cash value of the policies, the amount of the subsequent premiums paid by you, and whether or not the trust qualifies for the use of the $10,000 annual exclusion. The proceeds, however, will be exempt from taxation in both your estate and that of your spouse.

HOW MUCH INSURANCE?

This is, after all, the most perplexing question for most people, and one that is not answered by all this talk about options, modes of settlement, types of insurance and financing, regardless of their importance.

But no one, except yourself, can really answer that question for you. Let us show you why.

Ideally, you might consider life insurance as being like other types of insurance. It should be used to replace an asset—something that has been lost, destroyed, or stolen. In the case of life insurance, the asset is your economic value to your family in the event that you die.

How do you assess the economic value of a human being? Suppose that you are 30 years old and are now earning $30,000. Realistically, assessing your future you decide that your future earnings will look like this:

$30,000 per year for 10 years	$300,000
$35,000 per year for 10 years	$350,000
$40,000 per year for 15 years (to age 65)	$600,000
$20,000 per year for life—as retirement income— life expectancy of 15 years	$300,000
Total economic value	$1,550,000

Theoretically, you should then take out insurance coverage for a million dollars. But, of course, you can neither afford nor would you want to do that. Unfortunately, the economic value of a human being just doesn't operate as a practical measuring rod.

Let's try another "ideal" way of determining how much insurance you should have. A time-honored principle says that the face value of your insurance policy should equal four or five times your current earnings.

Here's Mary Smith then, on the first rung of the success ladder and earning $35,000 per year. The rule says she would need only $150,000 of insurance. But this amount wouldn't begin to provide even minimum support for her two small children.

Take another case, Bob Brown, upper-echelon executive earning $75,000 a year. The "rule" tells him he needs $300,000 worth of insurance. But Bob has a wife with a large estate and a number of family trusts which have amply provided for the future welfare of his descendants. For support purposes, Bob doesn't need any insurance at all (although he may need it for other purposes), regardless of the rule.

The Realistic Approach: Assessing Your Family's Needs

The only realistic way we know of to arrive at a proper figure for life insurance coverage is to assess it in terms of your family's needs—now and in the future. How much income will they need for adequate support if you die? Your "Estate Planning Worksheets" will give you an approximation of how much they can expect. The difference beween the income expected and the income needed is your deficiency. The amount and type of insurance you select should be adequate to make up that deficiency.

In determining that "income needed" figure, bear in mind that your estate will be depleted by taxes, funeral and administration expenses, and the payment of debts. Remember, too, that income needs will vary. Your spouse will need more income while the children are young. Their educational costs will rise sharply when they reach college age. Your spouse may have large medical expenses in later years. All these factors have to be considered.

We realize that women like Mary Smith just beginning their careers with small salaries, large responsibilities, and no estate can't afford to buy the amount of insurance they need. But they can make a start by providing at least enough to tide their family over for a period of years and then add to it later, just as they are adding to the rest of their estate.

Moreover, if they begin their insurance program at a young age, the cost will be less. Letting time go by also means risking the possibility of becoming uninsurable.

And when you come to select the type of insurance and

decide on its amount, don't be misled by the idea that the "best kind of insurance is the cheapest." With insurance, as with every kind of purchase, you get no more and no less than what you pay for. The best kind of insurance is the kind which is tailored to your own specific needs.

CHAPTER 4

Your Occupation and Its Opportunities: The Corporate Compensation Package

The time is the present, a fine evening in the spring. Mr. Young Executive, 35 years old, $30,000 a year man, and employee of Corporation Americana, bounds up the walk to his house, throws open the doors, and announces the glad tidings.

He has just been given a $4,000 raise. If things continue the way they are going, it won't be too many years before he clinches that $50,000 a year spot he has his eye on. Already he has big plans for using the $4,000. Here is the extra cash he needs to do some investing in the market. At last, he has the opportunity to build up some capital. Mentally, he savors the prospect of $4,000 growing to $10,000 to $20,000, and more. The taste is sweet.

Push the clock ahead to April of the following year and look in on Young Executive again. The season is the same but not the weather. It is raining, an appropriate setting for his mood, which is considerably gloomier than it was 12 months ago. Young Executive is hard at work, filling out his income tax return. As he works, some unpleasant facts begin to dawn on him. The $4,000 raise wasn't really worth $4,000. It upped his income taxes from $4,500 to $5,620, leaving only $2,880 of additional spendable income.

"Spendable" is a fitting description, too, because he hasn't invested a cent of it. What's more, he doesn't exactly know where the $2,880 has gone. It has apparently been dropped, along with the rest of his salary, into that bottomless pit labeled, "family needs." On the whole, his position hasn't changed a bit. He has more possessions perhaps, but that priceless one, security, seems as far away as ever.

It takes only a little figuring for Young Executive to calculate that when he reaches the $50,000 a year salary he is aiming at, he may well find himself in exactly the same straits. The increase won't really represent $16,000 but only $11,520 after taxes. He wonders if it will be just as easy to fritter away that amount, and knows in his heart that indeed it will.

But our hero need not despair. The picture he is painting for himself is only half completed. He has faithfully depicted the darker aspect of estate creation—the fact that salary increases alone very often do not result in capital accumulation—but he has neglected the sunnier side. The opportunities he seeks for building capital lie within his reach—within his occupation, his own company.

At Corporation Americana, Mr. Young Executive receives not only a salary, but a set of "fringe benefits" as well: the various plans, arrangements, and contracts which his company provides to give him and his family greater security against old age, illness, disability, and finally death. This is the "corporate compensation package" available in one form or another to nearly every corporate employee in the country.

The package had its origins in the incentive theory of labor compensation. The idea was to offer the employees something extra in return for extra effort. Much of that character has been lost today; employees and companies alike now look on the package as part of the standard and expected compensation. It has become private enterprises's own form of "cradle to the grave security."

If Young Executive examines the package carefully, he will discover that it will help him overcome the two major obstacles to capital accumulation he faces: the erosive effect of taxation and his inability to save out of salary alone. As such, it offers him the most valuable oportunity for estate creation he is likely to meet during his life.

How so? Because of two unique features which the compensation package has, but the individual salary does not: favored tax treatment and favored investment prospects.

Thus, with the tax treatment:

1. Some benefits are entirely tax-free when received; with others, taxation is deferred.

2. Some benefits may be taxed when received at a 20 percent rate or other preferential rates rather than at regular income tax rates.

3. Others can be made to pass at death free of estate taxes.

And with investment:

1. Investment is made for the employee with untaxed dollars. This means there is a larger fund available for investment for him than if he were to use his own after-tax dollars.

2. Since income and capital gains on these package investments accumulate tax-free, the fund builds up faster.

3. The individual invests as part of a group, not by himself. Hence, wider and more diversified investments are made.

4. The funds are handled by professional management.

5. The individual is provided with an enforced savings plan.

6. And finally, under certain plans, windfall benefits can result for the remaining employees, when departing employees forfeit part or all of their shares in the fund.

THE CONTENTS OF THE PACKAGE

The compensation package varies from company to company. Some corporations offer a very full package indeed; with others, the pickings are slimmer. Some corporations give the benefits across the board to all employees. Others limit some or all of them to particular groups, categories, or departments. Some of the plans contain much greater estate creation opportunities than others. It pays the executive to scrutinize the package provided by his company (or prospective employer) and then to compare it with others.

At this point, however, let us explore the contents in a more general way, looking for the types of benefits provided by the various plans.

Profit Sharing: Qualified and Unqualified

Profit sharing is a popular word in today's corporate lexicon. It appeals to the union member and clerical worker as well as to the executive. Basically it is an arrangement whereby a percentage of corporate profits goes into a profit-sharing kitty, either according to a formula or on the basis of merit. Some plans cover only executives above a certain salary. Other companies have different plans for different levels of employees. Still others cover all employees.

Profit-sharing plans hark back to the incentive philosophy because they tie the employee's financial gains to those of the company. In a good year the return to an employee may be great. The profit-sharing benefits received by executives have equaled, even exceeded their salaries in high sales years.

The important consideration for estate-creation purposes is whether a plan is "qualified" or not. The adjective "qualified" refers to tax treatment. Qualified plans meet certain requirements of the tax laws and therefore get favored tax treatment. Unqualified ones do not.

1. *Unqualified plans* usually provide for the profit-sharing fund to be paid out at the end of a period, monthly or yearly. The share, when the employee becomes entitled to it, represents additional compensation to him and is taxable as ordinary income in the same way as his salary. The company can take its tax deducation for its contribution into the fund in the years in which they are taxed to the employees.

2. *Qualified plans* have tax advantages for both employer and employee. They allow the corporation to get an immediate tax deduction. They defer or postpone taxation for the employee. And finally, they give him further tax benefits.

Such plans are formalized in writing. They must contain a definite formula for allocating contributions and for distributing funds after a fixed number of years, at a certain age, or upon a certain event, such as retirement or termination of employment. The qualified plan is not allowed to discriminate in favor of any employees within the group. The same does not hold for the unqualified plans, many of which discriminate in favor of the higher-paid executive.

The profit-sharing fund in a qualified plan is set up in the form of a trust. The company pays into this trust a share of its profits according to a predetermined formula (limited to no more than 15 per cent of each participating employee's compensation).

EMPLOYEE CONTRIBUTIONS: Some plans allow the employee to put in as much as 10 percent of his salary. The investment opportunities here are attractive. Although the contribution is made with after-tax dollars, the build-up of the fund is tax-free; the part of the income and capital gains which otherwise is taxed away remains in the fund for further investment. In addition, the employee gets the advantage of an enforced savings account and professional management of his own funds as part of a group investment.

TAXES: The corporation gets a deduction for the share of its profits which are contributed to the profit-sharing trust. The employee pays no tax on the amount contributed to his account at this time, regardless of whether his interest is forfeitable or non-forfeitable. The full untaxed amount is invested by the trustee.

Taxes for the employee enter the picture when withdrawals are made. Some plans allow you to withdraw part of your share while you are still employed. This is taxed as ordinary income, unless you have contributed to the funds. In that case, if the withdrawals do not exceed your contribution, there is no tax.

If your employment ends and the profit sharing fund is paid out to you within one taxable year, here is the way the lump sum distribution you receive will be treated:

1. Your own contributions come back to you tax free.

2. If you reached age 50 before 1986, the taxable portion attributable to your participation in the plan before 1973 can be taxed, at your option, at a flat 20 percent rate or with the benefit of a 10-year income averaging rule under 1986 rates, or a 5-year income averaging rule under current tax rates.

3. The taxable portion attributable to post-1975 participation is subject to the above averaging rules if you were a participant at least 5 years.

4. If you received stock of your corporation as part of the distribution, the unrealized appreciation on that stock is not included in the taxable amount. It is not taxed until you sell the stock.

5. If you have not attained age 50 prior to 1986, favorable lump sum treatment is limited to a one-time election of 5-year averaging after you have reached age 59½. The 20 per cent flat tax on pre-1974 participation is repealed.

It is possible to defer taxes on a lump sum distribution if the retiring or departing employee places the distribution (less his own contribution) into an Individual Retirement Account (or an IRA annuity or an IRA retirement bond) within 60 days of receipt. Until he draws down from the IRA, earnings within his fund will accumulate tax-free. He can begin drawing from his IRA, at age 59½ and up until age 70½, at which point some form of annuitized payments could be elected. Funds drawn from IRA's are taxed to the recipient. Premature withdrawals (prior to age 59½, except for death or disability) result in a nondeductible 10 per cent penalty tax. See pages 56–58 in this chapter for more information and other uses of the IRA.

Some people prefer to take out their benefits in installments over a period of years. In this case, the payments are taxed when received. Even though capital gains treatment has been eliminated and the top tax bracket is now 28%, there is some likelihood that you will pay lower taxes. These payments are generally received in retirement years when you may be in a lower tax bracket.

Suppose you die before you retire? If your beneficiary takes the proceeds in installments, he would have the same income tax treatment you would have had, plus a $5,000 income tax exemption. If the proceeds are taken in a lump sum, in addition to the $5,000 exemption, your beneficiary may make use of the 20% rate and/or 5-year income averaging rule.

FORFEITURES: Ordinarily your interest in a qualified fund is forfeitable at the start. Plans must provide for gradual "vesting"—i.e. a certain per cent becomes non-forfeitable from time to time.

One plan might allow for vesting to begin 3 years after you are hired, and to continue at the rate of 20 per cent per year. By the end of 7 years, the vesting would reach 100 per cent and your interest would become entirely non-forfeitable. Another might start vesting immediately and continue at the rate of 20 per cent for 5 years. That way, vesting would reach the 100 per cent mark within only 5 years. Most plans provide that if you leave or die before your share is fully vested you forfeit the non-vested portion of your account.

FRINGE BENEFITS: Profit-sharing plans can encompass other fringe benefits within themselves. Some plans include health insurance, make provision for layoff payments, and permit the employee to borrow from the fund. Some even provide for disability income. In addition, funds from a profit-sharing or pension trust may be used to buy life insurance for the employee. This is a way to supplement your personal insurance at little cost to you. It is true that the term part of the premium is considered part of your taxable income. This usually amounts to only a fraction of the total premium, however, and the actual tax is, ordinarily, nominal.

If you resign, you can take the policy with you (buying it from the trustee, if it hasn't vested), and continue to pay the premiums without having to pass a further physical examination. If you retire, you can take the cash value or elect to have a lifetime annuity—at the rates which were in effect when the policy was first issued.

It is often advantageous to fund life insurance through a profit-sharing plan. Take the case of a 40-year-old executive who is in the 28 per cent tax bracket. If he were to take out an ordinary life insurance policy for $50,000, he would have to pay about $1,500 in premiums every year. To pay those premiums, he has to earn $2,100 before taxes. But if the profit-sharing trust takes out the insurance instead, then this $1,500 (less a small income tax on the term rate) is available to him for other investments.

THE END RESULT: How does qualified profit sharing work out in dollars and cents?

Here is Ms. Young Executive. If she had received a salary increase of $3,500 she would have about $2,800 left after taxes. Assuming that she invested this amount each year at 6 per cent compound interest after income taxes, she would have $210,000 available to her at age 65. On the other hand, if instead of taking the increased salary, she had the $3,500 credited to her in qualified profit-sharing and pension plans and invested at 6 per cent she would receive a distribution of $335,000 at retirement—an increase of $125,000. However, the $335,000 is subject to taxation when received.

A drawback, but sometimes, also an advantage to profit sharing as an estate builder is that the ultimate distribution is subject to two variables. Obviously, if the company does not earn sufficient profits it will not make its annual contribution to the profit-sharing fund. Also, if the investments in the fund lose some of their original invested values the overall value of the fund will be decreased. This will, of course, depend upon the type and success of the fund's investments.

If they are fixed return or insured, there is little problem of capital loss. On the other hand, if the fund invests in equities, the amount to be distributed to the participants will be in direct proportion to the increase or decrease of their values. Some profit-sharing funds have had phenomenal success. We can think of several which have doubled and trebled as the result of the increase in the market value of the securities they hold.

As we know, a participant will receive at his retirement his share of the value of the fund on that date. What happens then if at this time there is a temporary drop in the value of the fund?

Consider the case of two persons who worked for the same company at the same salary. I'll call them Mr. X and Ms. Y. Both were due for retirement at the same time. Mr. X retired on the due date and took out $200,000 from the profit-sharing fund, Ms. Y was asked if she wouldn't stay on for another year, and did. This action proved to be disastrous for her. In that period, the market drop of 1973–1974 occurred. The value of the fund's securities shrank and the value of her share on her retirement date was correspondingly reduced from $200,000 to less than $135,000. Or in other words, profit sharing can seem to promise, but it cannot guarantee you a fixed sum on retirement.

Pension Plans

A pension plan, on the other hand, can make such a guarantee. The amount you get when you retire doesn't depend on profits or vary with business conditions, but can be actuarially determined. An employee might prefer a company which offers the security of a pension plan to one which has a profit-sharing plan, but some companies provide both.

Most pension plans are qualified. As such they get the same type of tax-favored treatment as the qualified profit-sharing plan. There are tax-free accumulations and tax advantages on payout, which in this case is retirement. If the employee contributes to the plan himself, he gets favored tax treatment on the income earned on his own contributions. But, unlike the qualified profit-sharing plan, pension funds cannot be used for layoff, sickness, accident, or hospitalization benefits.

Benefits. Usually, the income you get from a pension plan

is determined by your salary, your age, your length of service, your social security, or a combination of these factors. There is usually a regular increase in benefits over the course of employment so that the longer you work, the greater your benefits. In one company, these ranged from $8,000 a year for a person at the $20,000 salary level who has worked for 25 years to $44,000 for the person in the $100,000 level who has worked the same amount of time.

You can sometimes elect to have the pension paid out to you on your retirement in a lump sum rather than in installments. The plan must also provide for an optional selection of a joint and survivor annuity to ensure income for you during your life and for your spouse if she survives you.

What About Inflation? Inflation can greatly reduce the value of a pension. The person who 25 years ago looked forward to getting $300 per month on retirement finds, when the great day arrives, that $750 per month is hardly enough to support him and his wife.

Some companies recognize the effect of inflation and make provisions for it. In others, the fund is divided into two parts. One part is in fixed investments or is insured to provide a guaranteed pension, the other is in equity investments. The latter is intended to act as a hedge against inflation. Still other companies increase and decrease the amount of pension payments with the rise and fall of the cost of living, somewhat like the escalator provisions of union contracts.

What If You Leave or Die Before Retirement? Ordinarily if you leave before you retire you will get back from the pension fund only what you have contributed to it, plus a small interest return. The purpose of the pension fund, after all, is retirement security.

If you die before retirement, your beneficiaries may get little else than your contribution. Some plans, however, like profit-sharing plans, allow the pension trust to purchase a limited amount of insurance on the employee's life, so that your family will receive some benefit if you die prematurely.

401(K) Plans and Saving Plans

Under a cash or deferred plan (commonly referred to as a "401(K) plan") you may elect to have your employer make contributions to the plan that will not be included in your gross income for the year. The advantage of such a plan is the deferral of income tax to the year in which the distribution from the plan is made.

The deferred arrangement often takes the form of a salary reduction agreement. In addition, your employer may make matching contributions that are based upon a percentage of your total elective contributions.

Your annual elective contributions to a 401(K) plan are limited to $7,000. Inflation adjustments on this amount will begin in 1988.

One year's employment may also be required before you are eligible to participate in the plan.

Corporate savings plans offer more than their name implies. They are a valuable means of capital accumulation and growth because they can qualify for favored tax treatment and because the employer contributes as well as the employee.

Qualified savings plans operate in this manner: You put into the plan a certain amount—up to 10 per cent of your salary. The corporation then matches your contribution in a fixed proportion and, in some cases, as much as dollar for dollar. These plans have the same tax-free accumulation benefits as qualified pension and profit-sharing plans.

Plans vary as to time of vesting. If you withdraw from the fund before time of vesting, then you forfeit the non-vested portion (but not your own contributions and the fixed interest return on them).

As with profit-sharing and pension plans, savings plans often include other features within the plan, such as stock purchase or profit sharing. You may also be able to select the type of investment you want, including life insurance.

Group Life Insurance

This can be a valuable supplement to personal insurance. It is purchased on a group basis by the employer from an insurance company. The employer pays a part of the premium; sometimes he pays the whole thing. His contributions are tax-deductible. The employee's contribution, if any, comes out of after-tax earnings.

The cost of group premiums is averaged out, based on the

overall costs for a number of people, whose ages can vary from 25 to 65.

If the employee is required to pay part of the premium, he should always compare the cost of his contribution with the premium price he would be paying for the same amount of individual insurance. If the group price is less, then obviously he has a good buy. But if it is more—and it can be for a younger person—then it may not pay for him to enter the group plan.

Term Insurance. This is the usual form of group insurance. It is issued annually and remains in force as long as the employer chooses. In most states, when you retire, or if you leave your job, you must have the right to convert the term policy to an individual ordinary life policy, without a physical examination. Don't overlook this right. It is a valuable one.

The employer's cost is tax-deductible. The employee, in turn, pays no tax on the part of the premium which the employer pays up to $50,000 of coverage. If the employer pays for more than $50,000 then the premium for the excess is taxable to the employee according to a Treasury table which is based on the employee's attained age.

This means that the employee is really receiving income, to the extent of the employer's contribution, in that he gets insurance, at no cost or at a cost below what he would have to pay for it himself.

Like individual term insurance, group term offers only temporary protection, but at ages over 40 years, even though the employee contributes, it is so inexpensive it usually makes a worthwhile benefit.

Paid-up Insurance. Here a single premium is paid each year to buy a fixed amount of insurance for the employee, which will remain in force throughout his life. Since this is an expensive form of insurance, the employee pays part of the premium, generally the cash value portion. The employer pays the term part.

During his employment the employee may not take the cash value, but on his retirement or termination he is allowed to take over the policy and retain it as paid-up insurance. Or he can claim his cash value, which because of dividends will usually be larger than the total amount of premiums he paid in.

Group paid-up insurance is more than insurance protection for the employee; it is also a valuable means of savings. While he works, it creates an ever-growing fund for his use during retirement. If he dies prematurely, the proceeds will then be available for the support of his family.

Family Life Insurance. This is a type of group insurance which covers not only the individual employee, but his immediate family as well. So far, it is issued by only a few companies and approved in only a few states, but it may one day become as widespread as group health insurance.

Group Medical, Health, and Accident Insurance

These types of insurance are common. They can include disability income, hospitalization, medical and dental care, surgical benefits, maternity care, and beyond this, major medical insurance, for the individual and his family.

Corporate plans which require part payment by the employee should be examined carefully to see if they provide worthwhile benefits for the estate planner at comparatively low cost.

In general, however, this type of insurance carries the same advantage as many other employee insurance plans; being group rather than individual, it is usually cheaper than the individual policy and does not require a physical examination.

Moreover, it can either be fully paid for by the employer (to whom it is a tax deductible expense) or partly paid for by him and contributed to by the employee.

The inclusion of these insurance coverages in the compensation package can be of substantial value to the employee. If the benefits were not available through his company, he would have to arrange for it on his own. To the extent the cost is borne by his employer, it does not have to be paid for by him. The savings he thus enjoys are therefore equivalent to a tax-free raise in pay.

Individual Retirement Plans

The maximum allowable IRA contribution if you are not an active participant in a retirement plan is $2,000 or 100 percent of compensation, whichever is less. When there is an additional contribution to an IRA for your unemployed spouse, the maximum is $2,250.

The $2,000 IRA deduction limit is phased out for single taxpayers with income over $25,000 and married taxpayers with income over $40,000. An individual who is partially or totally prevented from making a deductible IRA contribution may make a nondeductible IRA contribution for the difference up to $2,000.

If you are single and not an active participant in an employer pension or profit sharing plan, you may make a deductible contribution to your own IRA, regardless of your compensation level. If your company's retirement plan permits, you can make your contribution to that plan instead of setting up your own IRA. If you are an active participant in an employer's plan, however, the IRA deduction limit is phased out based on your own level of income and marital filing status. If you are married and file a joint income tax return, the phaseout applies to both you and your spouse even if only one of you is an active participant in a plan. You will generally be considered an active participant under a plan if you are eligible to participate in the plan, even if you choose not to do so.

While the funds are in the IRA, they build up tax-free. Payments from the account except for amounts attributable to non-deductible contributions become subject to income tax when paid out. If you take your payment in a lump sum, you will not be eligible for the special tax-reducing rates afforded to qualified plans, including 5-year averaging and possible capital gains treatment. However, you cannot start taking payments from the account earlier than age 59½ or later than age 70½ without penalty.

There are a wide variety of IRA investment vehicles. They include trust and custody accounts which can be invested in securities, mutual funds and savings accounts. You may also purchase endowment contracts, retirement annuities, and Federal retirement bonds.

Rollovers. Individual Retirement Accounts afford other benefits. They can provide tax-free portability for an employee receiving a lump sum distribution from a qualified benefit plan or termination of the plan or when you leave or retire from your job. As long as you "roll over" the lump sum distribution into a proper IRA vehicle within 60 days, you can defer its taxability. The fund can be switched between different types of IRA investments, and even back to a new qualified retirement plan in which you may later participate. One valuable IRA provision permits a lump sum distribution payable to a surviving spouse to be rolled over into a "spousal" IRA. No income tax liability accrues until, and to the extent that, the IRA pays out to the surviving spouse. The fund in this account, however, cannot be later rolled over into a qualified retirement plan in which the surviving spouse participates.

SIMPLIFIED PENSION PLANS

Your employer can set up a simplified pension plan, which must be non-discriminatory, and contribute up to $30,000 or 15 per cent of your compensation, whichever is less, to your IRA. If your employer contributes less than the IRA limit ($2,000), you may contribute and deduct the difference, subject to the IRA phaseout rule for active participants in an employer retirement plan. You can participate in other qualified retirement plans and also be included in a simplified pension plan.

SUMMING UP

The young executives of this world, those in the lower middle income brackets, usually have no opportunity to bargain with their corporations, for special benefits. They are either available to them or not, as part of the overall corporate employee benefit program.

This does not mean that the middle-echelon employee has no control over his compensation benefits. They vary from company to company, and what one company doesn't offer another will. From the estate planning point of view, they should be evaluated as carefully as the salary offered, the opportunities for advancement, and all the other things that make a job offer an attractive one.

When negotiating for employment the executive should seek out the company whose benefit plans will provide his family with the most comprehensive security. What is involved is often more than a difference in immediate income; it may be the difference between an eventual estate and no estate at all.

Moreover the compensation package is only the base, not

the sum total of the occupational opportunities offered by corporate employment for estate creation. If a young executive stays with Americana and becomes one of its key players, avenues will open for him to negotiate *individual* corporate benefits, tailored to his needs and producing capital accumulation far beyond that offered by the basic package.

Let's turn the clock ahead and move on to the second act in the career of a young executive.

CHAPTER 5

Your Occupation and Its Opportunities: Selective Bargaining for the Executive

The season and setting are the same, a fine spring evening outside the door of Mr. Young Executive's house. The time is different, however, and so is Young Executive. He is 15 years older and 15 years wiser. His salary is now $80,000 a year.

The main change in Young Executive, however, is that his name is different. In corporate circles he is known as Mr. Key Executive, a person whose business acumen and devotion to his company make him a valued asset. As Mr. Key, he is no longer merely a hired man. He has become a valued partner in the corporation, in spirit if not in fact. He is a decision maker, a planner, and a member of the corporate management team, performing many of the functions that the old-time individual business owner used to perform.

Corporation Americana wants to hang on to its Mr. Key. He is one of the important people on the team that makes the profits. They would like to build a fence around him, if that were possible, to keep him from straying down the street to a competitor.

By a not-so-odd coincidence, this is exactly what Mr. Key is thinking of doing on this very spring evening. He is returning from a most interesting meeting with a person known in the higher-echelon circles he frequents as a head hunter, a person who specializes in finding top executives for her corporate clients. The most likely place to find such top executives is in *other* corporations.

This particular "head hunter" has just "found" Mr. Key. The client in question is Corporation Columbiana: powerful, big, and successful, just like Mr. Key's own Corporation Americana. Mr. Key got the idea, although no precise terms were discussed, that there would most certainly be a substantial salary hike for him, plus certain other unnamed benefits that they could "work out" if Mr. Key were interested.

He doesn't realize it, but the advent of the head hunter, her offer, and all that it implies, has just opened the door to a fruitful estate-building opportunity for him.

Mr. Key is now in a bargaining position. Both companies want him, and are willing to negotiate with him for additional benefits which will secure his services and his loyalties. Most corporations regard these additional benefits as inducements and incentives for key employees. They realize that people like Mr. Key are hard to come by, that they devote all their time and energy to their work often to the neglect of their own financial problems. They know that they must help Mr. Key make up for that neglect by offering special opportunities to ensure the financial security of Mr. Key and his family. They know an unworried executive can concentrate on the company's needs instead of diverting his time and attention to his own financial problems.

These additional benefits, if Mr. Key bargains well and wisely for them, will provide him with a custom-made program of capital accumulation which can be keyed to the rest of his estate plan and to his regular compensation package. Its long-range benefits may be worth far more than a mere salary raise.

The companies will make offers, undoubtedly. But if Mr. Key is to drive a good bargain, he must not only listen to offers; he should also make proposals of his own. To do that, he needs to analyze two important factors, his own needs and the range of possible benefits open to him.

THE EXECUTIVE'S GOALS

We know them in a general fashion: some form of tax-sheltered compensation; an opportunity to invest in the company and so accumulate money via the capital gains route; help in purchasing family benefits with before-tax dollars at no or little cost to him. All of those are available in some form or another, as we shall shortly see.

Before he puts together his package of proposals, however, the executive must make an important decision. How much is he willing to sacrifice (if need be) in the form of salary to attain them?

The high-salaried married executive will be taxed at a 28 per cent rate with an additional 5 per cent on taxable income between $71,900 to $149,250. If Mr. Key were given a raise from $80,000 to $95,000, only $10,050 of that raise would be left to him after taxes.

This isn't the whole story, however. In reality, there are also intangible benefits to a salary raise. Since many package benefits are based on salary levels, these usually go up in value, along with the increase of the salary.

The intangibles are more difficult to assess, but just as meaningful. How important to Mr. Key is the status which $95,000 would give him within his company and industry? This is not a flippant question; future opportunities, advancements and offers may be contingent on this status-salary position. And what about his own immediate needs and desires? Will they be satisfied with the substitution of fringe benefits for a salary increase?

And finally, as Mr. Key weighs Columbiana against Americana, he must take into account the effect on his estate of the loss of the non-vested parts of the Americana compensation package, if he makes the change. What will Columbiana do to replace this loss?

He must analyze all these factors and come up with a balanced proposal—a package of his own that he has fashioned out of his own and his family's needs, a package built out of benefits and salary that will work continuously to build his estate and secure the independence of his family when he dies, or ensure his support if he retires or becomes disabled.

What is the range of corporate benefits possibly available? There are a number. They vary from simple bonuses to highly complicated plans for deferring compensation. He needs to know them all so as to select, for his proposal bag, those which would best develop and supplement his estate plan. At the same time he should keep his negotiating partner in mind—the corporation. How will these arrangements affect it? Are there mutual advantages to be obtained, and if so, what are they?

Our particular Mr. Key, incidentally, isn't the only executive in his corporation who should consider these proposals. They apply equally to other key players who are not considering a change, but who do want a custom-made set of benefits from their company.

BONUSES: CASH, STOCK, OR DEFERRED

Individual bonus arrangements are commonplace today. They suit the company which doesn't want to commit itself to a high salary or whose bylaws do not permit it to pay salaries above a certain level. The president of a company who gets $200,000 a year in salary and $100,000 in bonuses is no longer an unusual figure on the corporate scene. Neither is the lower-echelon executive whose $70,000 per year compensation is made up of $50,000 salary plus $20,000 bonus.

There are many ways in which bonuses can be dispensed. If you are thinking of negotiating a bonus arrangement, you should be sure that you know which kind you want.

Cash and Carry Bonuses

This is the simplest type. Generally, it is given annually, and is based on the company's profit or the executive's productivity. There may or may not be a written agreement between the executive and the company. Cash bonuses are taxable in the year they are received. They are thus not true estate builders but more like a salary raise; they provide additional spendable income, theoretically available for investment.

Stock Bonuses

A stock bonus gives an executive a personal stake in the future appreciation of the market value of his company's stock and thus is often a greater incentive to him. It also has an advantage over other stock plans in that the executive doesn't have to pay out any money for his investment.

A word of caution about stock bonuses. They are taxable

income, so it's wise to arrange for a part payment in cash to pay the tax.

Deferred Bonuses

One way to overcome the tax impact on a lump sum bonus is to arrange to have your bonus paid out on the installment plan. This is a particularly good idea if the bonuses are tied to profits and so are liable to be high in some years, low in others.

Will the corporation agree to defer bonus payments? The only reason for objection is that it cannot take its tax deduction until the bonus is paid out. But this objection is offset by the fact that the corporation gets the use of the bonus monies until the payout time arrives.

The government will not consider a bonus deferred, however, if the recipient can be said to have "constructively received" the whole bonus; that is, if he had the right to take it all immediately. In that case it demands an immediate tax payment on the full amount of the bonus.

The constructive receipt problem is a ticklish one. To make sure that your deferred bonus does not fall under it, you should make an agreement with the company specifying that the payment of bonuses as earned will be deferred. This agreement can state that your right to the bonus is a conditional one, i.e., contingent on your remaining with the company until the bonus is paid out.

STOCK OPTIONS

One of the most prevalent and popular fringe benefits, the stock option, can be of great value to the executive. It is another way of giving him a personal stake in the corporation, geared to the market value of its securities. It allows him to make investments using a minimum amount of capital, or in some cases none at all, and to take advantage of a rising market with small risk to himself.

A stock option is a right, in this case the right to buy corporate stock within a certain period of time. The option entitles you to purchase the stock at a fixed price—regardless of what the market price may be at the time you exercise the option. A few companies offer these options to all employees, or to all employees above a certain level, but generally speaking, they are offered to key personnel only or else as an inducement to lure key people away from one corporation to another.

Options usually aren't granted outright but on the installment plan. If the executive leaves before his option period has expired, he forfeits his right to the unexpired part of the option. In addition, companies usually add other restrictions. In some plans the executive must agree to hold his stock for investment only; he is prevented from selling in the open market. Sometimes the company requires that if the executive dies, the stock be sold back to the corporation (this incidentally can be a valuable right to an executive if the stock has no ready market and would thus be a nonproductive asset in his estate).

Executives like Mr. Key who are negotiating stock option agreements should look at these company restrictions carefully; they can result in a limitation, or conversely, an increase in their future profits.

What happens if the market price falls below the option price? If the executive has already exercised his option rights, he is now the owner of the stock and he loses just as any other investor does. If he hasn't bought the stock yet, he is under no obligation to do so and thus incurs no loss. In other words, the value of stock options is tied to the value of the corporate stock. They do not represent guaranteed benefits the way pension plans and some other items in the compensation package do.

A few companies, however, try to make up for this by setting up a variable option price within a certain range. Other ways to assure the benefits of stock options are to make provisions for reducing the option price under specified conditions, or to issue new options at a lower price when the market drops.

Stock options fall into two classes for tax purposes: those that are tax-sheltered and those that are not.

Tax-Sheltered Stock Options

These options get special tax treatment provided they meet specified requirements of the tax laws. Until January 1, 1964, the only tax-sheltered stock option was the "restricted stock option." The Revenue Act of 1964 revoked the restricted stock option and substituted in its place two new classes: "the qualified stock option" and the "employee stock purchase plan." However, restricted stock options issued before 1964 continued to enjoy the advantages in effect at that time.

While these tax-sheltered options varied in the requirements necessary to qualify them for special tax treatment and also in the manner in which profits or losses are taxed, they all had certain elements in common. Thus, the employee pays no tax either when he gets the option or when he exercises it, except possibly as a tax preference item. He pays a tax on his profits only when he sells his stock. The corporation, on the other hand, gets no deduction for the value it gives the employee—the difference between the option price and the market value of the stock at the time the option is exercised.

The Tax Reform Act of 1976 called a halt to future tax benefits of qualified and resricted options. To get the tax break, these options must have been exercised before May 21, 1981.

The Incentive Stock Option

This is a tax-favored option which incorporates provisions of the former restricted and qualified stock option plans. To qualify as an incentive stock option, there must be a shareholder-approved plan which requires that options must be granted within 10 years and an option must be exercised within 10 years of grant, the option price must equal the fair market value of the stock on the date it is granted. Options to purchase no more than $100,000 worth of stock may be granted to an employee in any calendar year.

The tax advantage of an incentive stock option is that there is no tax at the time the option is either granted or exercised (however, the spread between the option price and market value at the time of exercise is a tax preference item for purposes of the alternate minimum tax. There's an added tax break when an employee already owns stock of the corporation and the market value is higher than the option price. He can use the stock he owns to pay for the new stock on the exercise of the option without being taxed on the gain, if any, on the old stock.

In order to qualify, the employee must have been continuously employed by the corporation from the date of the option grant to within three months of the date of exercise. A disabled employee or the estate of the deceased employee, however, may, within 12 months of termination of employment, exercise an option.

Non-tax Sheltered Stock Options

In this type, the option price can be set at any amount and the option can be exercised at any time, limited only by what the stockholders of the company will approve. In a rising market, an executive can make a substantial profit.

It is true, of course, that the executive must pay ordinary income tax on the difference between the option price and the stock's fair market value at the time the option is granted. If the option is subject to a condition which affects its value, there's no taxation until the condition is met or removed.

Again, let's look at some actual figures. Suppose Corporation Americana agrees to give Mr. Key an option to buy 1,000 shares of Americana stock at $50 per share. The agreement states that Key can exercise the option in four installments of 250 shares per year, starting 1 year from the date of the agreement. There is a further condition that Mr. Key must still be employed by Americana at the time he exercises each of the installments.

At the time Key is given the option the market value of the stock is $75 per share. At the end of the first year, it goes up to $100 and Mr. Key exercises the first installment, paying the company $12,500 for 250 shares. On paper, he now has a profit of $12,500. This is the value of the first installment of the option, and therefore he must pay ordinary income tax on this sum.

If he sells the stock sometime in the future for $100 per share, he owes no taxes. But if he sells it for more (or for less) then the usual income tax rates apply.

To the corporation, the taxation aspects of unrestricted options are more advantageous. It gets a tax deduction for the value of what it gives the executive: the difference between the option price and the market price at the time the option becomes taxable to the employee.

Financing Stock Options

An executive is often faced with the problem of finding the money to exercise his stock options. There are a number of alternatives available to him.

1. He can arrange for a loan from the company or from existing pension or profit-sharing funds. However, the interest expense deduction will be subject to phaseout.

2. He can take a bank loan. In most cases collateral will be required, however. He will have to put up other securities in addition to the optioned stock. This is because the loan is made to buy stock and the usual margin requirements for this type of transaction must be met. Once again, the interest expense will not be fully deductible and will be phased out in 1990 except in cases when the loan is secured by a residence.

3. If the option is exercisable over an extended period of time, he can exercise part of the option and then use this stock to pay for the new stock as each installment is exercised, without gain on the stock used in payment.

Regardless of how he arranges his loan, of course, he will have to pay the money back. If he's bought in a rising market, however, that can be fairly painless. He can sell some of the stock, repay the loan, and still have his profit.

Stock Options and Estate Taxes

If an executive dies before he's exercised his stock options, what happens then?

Sometimes the options are not exercisable and therefore lapse. Or the estate may be allowed to exercise them. If so, they are considered as part of his *taxable* estate. His estate will have to pay an estate tax on the value of the options, i.e., on the difference between the option price and the market price at the time of his death.

This estate tax liability, incidentally, occurs whether or not the estate actually exercises the option. Thus an estate tax can be assessed even though the estate doesn't receive any profit. This usually means that the estate will want to exercise the remaining options. But the cash to do this may be hard to get because of the margin limitations on stock purchase borrowing. Key executives therefore would be well advised to provide for sufficient insurance proceeds to make ready cash available for this purpose.

OTHER STOCK PLANS

Stock options are not the only way in which an executive can tie his fortunes to those of the corporate stock. Many other arrangements are possible, some well known, others not.

1. *The stock warrant* resembles a stock option. The difference is that the warrant is negotiable. It is a right to purchase a specified number of shares of a corporation's stock at a fixed price, usually within a stated period. The warrant is immediately salable at its market value. This is a way to make a quick profit in a rising market without paying out any money at all except in taxes.

Stock warrants are often used as an inducement to obtain the services of an outside person, or as a bonus to a present key person. The value of the warrant (the difference between the market price of the stock and the warrant exercise price at the time the warrant is issued) is subject to income tax. Any profit above the market price at the time the warrant is issued is also subject to tax.

2. *Restricted sale stock plans* provide that the executive may purchase company stock at book value or even nominal value. In some cases the purchase is financed on an installment basis out of his dividend proceeds. He must sell the stock back to the company, however, when he leaves. The price he gets depends on the particular plan in force in his corporation. It may be based on the book value at the time of the resale or on a valuation based on earnings. Or there may be a set figure which is agreed to in advance, but adjusted periodically.

Restricted stock plans are particularly useful to small corporations. They give an executive all of the benefits of stock ownership except the right to sell on the open market. They keep the control of the stock within the company. They are frequently used in the communications industry, where turnover of top personnel is high.

3. *Shadow Stock.* Not too many executives in Mr. Key's position know about this unusual fringe benefit. It offers a

unique way of participating in the increase in value of corporate stocks without investing any capital.

Shadow stock is a bookkeeping device. The executive doesn't actually receive stock at all, but he participates in stock appreciation and dividends just as if he did.

Here's how it works. A key executive is credited on the company books with a certain number of units equivalent to stock, but no stock is actually issued. Any dividends declared on the stock are credited to his account, paid out to him, or retained, depending on the provisions of the plan. He is also credited with any increase in the value of his mythical shares, and he gets the benefit of stock dividends and splits. When he leaves or retires, he receives an amount of money equal to the increase in value of his shares, plus whatever retained dividends have been credited to his account.

When he takes out his profits, the executive pays income tax on the gain. The tax impact can also be spread out if he takes his payments in installments. The corporation gets similar tax treatment. No deduction is allowed until the time of payout.

DEFERRED COMPENSATION

The trouble with success is that its rewards are reaped during high-earning years and often don't carry over into later, less productive years. This is a key problem for all of today's key executives. They get their major salary increases at the time when they have to pay the largest taxes on them. How much more advantageous it would be if the increases could be paid out in retirement years, when the tax burden is lower. Or if the executive died, how much more secure his family would be if they could have the benefit of that salary increase then.

Actually both these alternatives are available to the present-day executive, through corporate deferred compensation plans. These are payment devices which, in effect, level out the executive's earnings curve and spread out his compensation during his entire life instead of concentrating it during his working years. The resultant tax savings increase the amount of spendable cash available to him during his life. If he dies, his family gets the benefit of both the earnings spread and the tax savings.

Many items in the compensation packages, such as pension and profit-sharing funds, are really a form of deferred compensation. But because they are qualified, and hence nondiscriminatory (i.e., paid out according to a standard formula to *all* employees in the group), they are of limited value to the key executive. The kind of deferred compensation we are discussing now is discriminatory and limited to selected personnel. It is the result of an individual contract between the corporation and the executive, tailored to the needs of that particular executive.

Supposing our friend Mr. Key received an offer of a big salary increase from his company, Corporation Americana. Assume he decided that he wanted this increase deferred. What precisely does he ask for?

The Deferment Contract

Deferred compensation agreements generally provide that a salary increase—let us say $10,000—is not to be paid out at the present time but postponed until retirement or termination of employment, when the accumulated sum is paid in installments to the executive either for the rest of his life or for a certain number of years. If the executive dies, his family gets the payments he would have received.

Usually these contracts also provide for the post-retirement consultation services of the executive. This assures the company that it will continue to have his valuable services, and that he will not go over to a competitor. This part of the contract should be carefully worked out, however, in order to ensure that the executive will not lose the capital gains treatment, if any, of his package compensation deals (pension, profit sharing, etc.) because his employment hasn't "terminated." The dangers of his being taxed for constructive receipt must also be guarded against.

In actual monies received, how does the executive benefit? If Mr. Key takes a $10,000 increase immediately he will have only $7,200 left from it after the 28 per cent maximum tax. Under the deferment contract, he may have as much as $8,500 per year left after taxes, if he receives it during the low-income-tax bracket years of retirement.

There is one possible thorn in this rosebush called deferred compensation, which a key executive should keep in mind. Deferred compensation is a general liability of the corporation. The fund cannot be set up as a trust or set aside for the employee in any way which would remove it from the reach of the corporation's creditors. That means that there is always a possibility that a corporation may not be able to meet the obligations of the deferred compensation contract when the payout is due. The risk may be small, but it is there.

The Use of Deferred Compensation Funds

During the years when part of Mr. Key's salary is being deferred, the corporation has use of these funds. By all rights they should be used by it for the benefit of Mr. Key and not the corporation. If he hadn't chosen to have it deferred, after all, the money would have been paid out and therefore wouldn't be available to the corporation. A common method of using these funds for the employee is to use the funds to buy insurance on the executive's life.

1. *Key Person Insurance.* When a company takes out insurance on a key person, it is, in effect, indemnifying itself in the event he dies and his services are lost. When key person insurance is used in conjunction with a deferred compensation agreement, however, it is also a way for the company to finance the deferred compensation. Should Mr. Key die, the proceeds from the insurance policy can be used by the company to meet the obligations of his family. If he retires, the cash surrender value can be used to meet its responsibility to him.

This insurance will often completely finance the company's obligation to Mr. Key and his family at no, or little, cost to the company. This is so because: (*a*) the premiums are paid for out of the after-tax amount that the salary increase would have cost the company; (*b*) the insurance proceeds are received tax-free; and (*c*) the benefits paid to Mr. Key or family are tax-deductible.

Thus the cost to Corporation Americana of a $20,000 raise to Mr. Key would have been $13,200 after taxes. This amount pays the annual premium on a $200,000 paid up at 65 policy on him. If Mr. Key should die before retirement, let us say, at age 60, the company would get $260,000 (including dividend additions) of tax-free proceeds, or $182,000 more than it paid in premiums.

On that basis it would be possible for the corporation to

pay out as much as $450,000 to Mr. Key's family over an extended period without dipping into any reserves, and still have a profit of $37,000. The $450,000 that is paid out is tax deductible at a 34 per cent rate, so the actual cost to the corporation is only $297,000—just $37,000 less than the company got in insurance proceeds.

On the other hand, if Mr. Key does not die but retires at age 65, the cash surrender value of the policy, including the dividend additions, is about $224,000. This is enough for the company to fund a deferred payout of $30,000 a year for 15 years after its tax deductions, at a cost of $18,000 more than it received when it cashed in the policy. Thus Mr. Key has guaranteed a total of $450,000 to himself or his family whether he lives to retirement or dies anytime prior to it.

These are figures that Mr. Key should certainly have well in mind when he sits down at the bargaining table.

2. *Split-dollar Insurance.* Another ingenious way of using deferred funds to buy insurance is for Mr. Key to enter into a split-dollar insurance agreement with his company.

Here's an example. Part of the after-tax surplus of $13,200 is now used to finance the company's advance (the increase in cash value) on the premium of a $300,000 ordinary policy. Mr. Key's costs will be less than comparable costs for the term policy carried by him alone. Suppose Mr. Key dies within 5 years. Assuming he has used the fifth dividend option to maintain the face value of the policy, his family would get the entire face amount, that is, $300,000 *plus* the deferred compensation. The company gets back the full amount of its advances, and thereby has the money to make the deferred compensation payments to the family.

If Mr. Key retires, the company is still able to make the deferred compensation payments out of its cash value return. Of course the policy will have to be terminated in order for the company to get this cash value. But if Mr. Key wants to continue the policy, he can borrow the cash value from the insurance company and pay off the advances which the company has made. If he does this, he will have a policy issued at an early age—at low premium rates and without further medical examination.

Tax Implications of
Deferred Compensation in the Estate

Deferred compensation is subject to the estate tax in an executive's estate. It is also taxable to the beneficiary as income, although the estate tax paid can be a deduction from the income received. Even so, the income tax impact can be serious. When deferred compensation is paid to a widow, in addition to other income she may be receiving, her income tax bracket goes up, sometimes so much that the benefits from the deferred payments can be reduced. This heavy tax erosion of the deferred payments can be lessened by dividing up the payments among a number of beneficiaries, or making them payable to a trust which is taxed as a separate entity.

Split-dollar insurance proceeds are also usually taxable in the estate. One possible way to avoid this is to tranfer ownership of both the policy and the split-dollar agreement over to the beneficiary, and thus take them out of the executive's taxable estate.

THE ESTATE BUILT FROM BARGAINING

Can it be done? That is to say, could a key executive build an estate out of no more and no less than the best compensation agreements he can make with his corporation?

The answer is yes.

Here's one estate we know of personally. It's composed of the following items: $200,000 from the pension plan; $65,000 from the profit-sharing fund: $150,000 from group insurance; $110,000 in stock purchased by the use of stock options; $150,000 in split-dollar insurance. It will amount to $675,000 if he dies before retirement, or provide him with $30,000 per year on his retirement.

Or in other words, a good bargain, even though he is not a top echelon executive.

CHAPTER 6

Your Occupation and Its Opportunities: Self-help for the Self-employed

So much for Mr. Key Executive and his forerunner, Mr. Young Executive. As employees of Corporation Americana, their occupations offer them a unique and contemporary source of estate building.

Now we want to introduce another character into the drama, a professional woman who is nobody's employee. Her name is Ms. Doctor, the young physician who earns $50,000 a year from her new practice. She has no compensation package and no negotiated benefits, no company to give her any of these niceties. Where are the estate-building opportunities in *her* occupation? Who is going to help her?

Thus, in a nutshell, the situation of some 10 million citizens of this country—all the doctors, lawyers, dentists, accountants, architects, engineers, writers, artists, and actors; other independent professionals, and along with them the independent businesspersons: the sole owners or partners of businesses, large or small.

These are the self-employed. They range from the actress who commands $100,000 for a single performance and the individual business owner who grosses a million per year, to the corner grocery store operator who nets only $15,000, or the writer who makes $50,000 in a good year, half of that in a bad one..

There are no ready-made pension plans, deferred compensation arrangements, or profit-sharing funds for them. If they are not active participants in a retirement plan, they can put up to $2,000 a year into an IRA (or $2,250 where there's a nonworking souse). Unlike the rest of their fellow citizens, their occupations do not automatically provide them with substantial built-in tax shelters. They are compensated as well or sometimes better than the corporate employee. But since all of this compensation is in the form of income, it is subject to tax.

The heart of their dilemma is in the very word that describes their economic situation: *self-employed*. Our tax laws were set up originally to benefit the employee, the person who works for someone else. Large though their numbers, the self-employed used to be an economic anachronism in our society.

But the fence that once separated the tax-sheltered employee from the non-sheltered self-employed person is no longer impenetrable. Over the years it has been opened more and more, until the Tax Equity and Fiscal Responsibility Act of 1982 gave the self-employed the opportunity to provide himself with most of the same employee benefits that his corporate counterparts enjoy.

"Self-help" is still the concept, however. More than the corporation employee, the self-employed has to take the initiative and put together his own compensation package, utilizing the various opportunities available to him.

THE PROFESSIONAL:
FIVE AVENUES TO SECURITY

First, just who is the professional? A person with advanced technical training—a lawyer, a doctor, or an engineer—who performs a personal service.

"Personal" is the key word here. The very meaning of the corporate identity is impersonal. In law, if not in fact, it cancels the personal nature of the professional's relationship to his client or patient. Thus, until recently, society had been reluctant to grant most professionals the right to incorporate. At the same time, the professional had not been allowed to build up any tax-protected pension or retirement funds for himself. These the government has reserved for employees.

This is no longer true. Today, there are no fewer than five avenues open to the professional which will allow him to accumulate tax-sheltered capital, and thereby help him find economic security for himself and his family.

Two of these avenues involve some form of corporate tax treatment for the professional. Two are concerned with compensation devices that afford advantageous tax treatment for professional income. The final one is a special law, which permits professionals to build their own tax-sheltered retirement funds. Together, the five make up a package of advantageous professional compensation ideas.

The Unincorporated Association: Avenue Number One

The first blow in the battle for fringe benefits for the professional was struck in 1948, in, of all places, Missoula, Montana.

A partnership of eight doctors decided to form an unincorporated association. As members of the association, they set up a group pension plan for themselves. The U.S. Treasury demanded payment of ordinary income taxes on the amount in the pension reserve fund which had been allocated to Dr. Arthur R. Kintner.

Dr. Kintner became the man who carried the ball for his association, and as it turned out, for professionals all over the country. He paid the tax, but sued for a refund in the U.S. District Court. His contention: his association, although unincorporated, was enough like a corporation to warrant the tax treatment of a corporation.

In 1952, the courts sustained Dr. Kintner, and after he won on appeal, the Treasury acquiesced. Now members of unincorporated associations which meet certain qualifications can take advantage of various corporate plans and benefits. The qualifications are:

1. *Continuity.* The association will not end if one of the members dies, retires, goes bankrupt, or becomes insane.

2. *Limited Liability.* No member can be personally liable for any of the debts of the association.

3. *Centralized Management.* A committee or a group must be given exclusive management of the business.

4. *Transferability of Interest.* Any member can transfer his interest to a non-member without the approval of the other members, although he may be required to offer it first to them.

The Professional Corporation:
Avenue Number Two

Wouldn't it be better to avoid the ambiguities of the unincorporated association and form a professional corporation instead?

By all means, and fortunately, that is now possible. The success of Dr. Kintner and others who followed in his footsteps led to the enactment of state laws giving professionals the right to incorporate. The majority of states grant the privilege to all professions. The others limit it to specified ones such as medicine, dentistry, and law. Needless to say, the professional who forms a corporation or association has really found the way out of the self-employed wilderness. Now he can avail himself of the fringe benefits which corporate employees enjoy: qualified pension and profit-sharing plans; group life insurance, group medical, accident, and health insurance; and deferred compensation arrangements.

Self-employed Retirement Plan:
Avenue Number Three

For the professional who cannot have or doesn't want either the unincorporated association or the corporation, there is a third avenue open. It provides retirement benefits which are now similar to corporate plans.

The third avenue was created by Congress in 1962, in the form of the Self-Employed Individuals Tax Retirement Act, popularly known as the Keogh Act. This allows self-employed people of all types to set up retirement funds for themselves. Here's how it works.

Dr. Jones is a successful surgeon, in the 28 per cent income tax bracket. He has an earned income of over $150,000 per year. He can set up a retirement fund for himself under the provisions of the Keogh Act in the form of a defined benefit plan or defined contribution plan. If he chooses a defined benefit plan, he can decide how much retirement income he wants, up to a maximum of $90,000 a year, adjusted for inflation. His annual contributions into the plan, actuarially determined, will be the amount needed to accumulate a fund sufficient to provide the fixed benefit he wants to receive after retirement. With a defined contribution plan, it is the amount of contribution that is fixed. The legal maximum is 25% of earned income or $30,000, whichever is less.

Dr. Jones decides on a defined contribution plan and puts in the maximum $30,000. All of this contribution is tax deductible. This means that he has a tax savings of $8,400.

Dr. Jones's fund accumulates both income and gain, tax-free, just as it does in a qualified corporate fund. In effect his $30,000 contribution can earn approximately one-third more income for him as it would if the income were subject to his 28 per cent tax bracket.

Jones can take out his money any time after he reaches 59½ years old. Or he can take it out at any age, if he is disabled. He must begin making withdrawals, however, no later than the year in which he reaches the age of 70½. If withdrawals are made before age 59½, except because of death or disability, a 10 per cent tax penalty must be paid.

When payout time arrives, Jones is taxed at preferential rates under the same rules that apply to retirees under corporate plans. Exempted, of course, is the portion of the payout which represents his contributions for which he did not have a tax deduction when he made them.

Dr. Jones can also take out his fund in the form of an annuity. If he does this, the portion that is non-taxable (the amount he contributed for which he received no deduction) is spread over the selected period of years or his life expectancy. The amount he receives annually over and above that is taxable income.

Suppose that Jones has employees—a secretary, an assistant, or a technician. Then his plan must also cover them. If it is a "top heavy" plan—that is, the key employees' accrued benefits or account balances are more than 60 percent of those of all participants in the plan—there are special rules for non-key employees. Dr. Jones's will be a "top heavy" plan, so he'll have to make an annual minimum contribution of not less than 3 percent of each participant's compensation. Moreover, the employee must have a non-forfeitable right to 100 percent of the benefit either after 3 years of service or after 6 years with 20 percent becoming non-forfeitable after 2 years and increasing 20 percent each year thereafter.

For some professionals, particularly when office staff may change every 5 to 10 years, this non-forfeitability provision can be irksome. On the other hand, it works out quite nicely for those who have relatives as employees.

Jane Jones works for her husband, Dr. Jones, as a receptionist and bookkeeper, at a salary of $15,000 per year. He sets up an owner-employee plan and contributes $3,000 per year for her. Since this is tax deductible, this contribution costs him only $2,160. It is not reportable on their joint return as income to Jane.

Thus, Dr. Jones will be able to build a tax-sheltered retirement fund for himself and his wife totalling $33,000 a year. He gets a tax deduction on all of this.

All other things being equal, will Dr. Jones be better off with a Keogh plan or a corporate one?

Though the amount of the retirement fund he can build would be the same under each, a corporate plan still has certain advantages over a self-employed one. The self-employed can't deduct the portion of his Keogh contribution that goes to purchase life, health or accident insurance, while premium costs are deductible for a corporate plan. Nor can he borrow from a Keogh plan, while he could, subject to certain limitations, from a corporate plan.

Moreover, the professional corporate employee can have wider benefits made available to him on a tax-free basis. The corporation can provide him with group term insurance. The premium cost on the first $50,000 of coverage will be tax-free to him. The cost of coverage over $50,000 paid by the corporation will be taxable income, but usually he will be paying much less than if he were to purchase this added coverage with before-tax dollars.

Another tax-free fringe benefit available to the incorporated professional, but not to the self-employed, is a medical reimbursement plan. With an individual's medical-expense deduction limited to amounts in excess of 7.5 per cent of adjusted gross income, this fringe benefit is more attractive than ever.

Building a Retirement Fund Through Tax-exempt Institutions: Avenue Number Four

Ms. Successful Commercial Artist, like many independent professionals, is a woman of varied interests and varied activities. Partly because she likes it and partly because it adds to her prestige, she has for many years been teaching courses at an art school. Her salary for this work—$7,000 per year—adds little to her spendable income since it merely piles additional taxable income on top of her yearly income of $80,000.

Someone tells her that she should use part of that salary to build a retirement fund for herself, and so she investigates the possibilities. She learns about the tax-sheltered annuities available to her as an employee of a tax-exempt institution. She asks the school to take $1,000 of her salary, and instead of paying it out to her, to use it to pay a premium on an annuity for her. Now she is getting only $6,000 of taxable income in salary. There is no taxation on the $1,000 which is invested in the annuity contract. This contract will be paid out in installments at age 65 years. She then will have to pay income tax on the annuity payments as she receives them.

If she dies before she retires, the annuity is paid out to her beneficiary. The beneficiary has to pay income taxes on it.

Can every professional who has a part-time job with a tax-exempt organization avail himself of this kind of arrangement?

Unfortunately not. All tax-exempt institutions cannot offer this tax advantage to their employees. However, the class which can is very broad and generally embraces charitable and educational organizations.

There is another way, however, of providing retirement benefits through tax-exempt institutions. Any organization may set up a non-qualified retirement plan. Most corporations don't avail themselves of this opportunity because the contributions to such non-qualified plans are not tax-deductible when made. But this aspect is obviously not important to the tax-exempt organization. It can create a retirement fund for an employee in the following way. Instead of paying out a salary to the employee on which he must pay income taxes, it makes the payments into a separate account to be paid to him when he retires.

Let's look at the case of Ms. Accountant, aged 55 years. She agrees to handle the finances for her college alumnae organization on a part-time salary basis. Ordinarily the salary would be $6,000 per year. Because of her high tax bracket, however, she decides to ask instead that $3,000 of the money be put into a trust for her, to be paid out in installments when she reaches certain ages or on her death. Her right to the fund, however, is conditioned on her continued service—until the payout. Because it is a forfeitable right, this money isn't taxed to her at the present time. The income earned by the trust is taxable to the trust (as a separate taxpayer) at its lower tax bracket. When the installments are paid out to her as she reaches the specified ages, she pays income tax on them. Assuming that she is in a lower tax bracket then, she will have more spendable cash available to her.

Taking a Piece of the Deal: Avenue Number Five

This is the final—and sometimes the most lucrative—way in which a professional can accumulate capital as a result of his occupation. It is a method, incidentally, that is not available to the corporate executive.

We once knew an architect who built an entire estate in this way. He started his unique estate plan unintentionally back in 1928. In that year he agreed to design a commercial building for a fee of $15,000. When the time came for payment, his clients were unable to pay any part of it. They had become insolvent. They offered him instead a 25 per cent interest in the property.

The architect had a choice between becoming one of their creditors or taking a share of what appeared to be worthless realty. He took the latter and mentally wrote off his fee as a bad debt. But the property interest somehow survived the financial difficulties without being foreclosed, and by 1940 it had become a profit-making investment. In 1955 the property was sold. His share of the proceeds: $240,000.

That experience encouraged him to take shares in other property. During the years from 1940 to 1960 he had frequently taken part, and sometimes all of his fees for services in income-producing real estate. He ended up with an estate of $950,000—although his net income rarely exceeded $35,000 in any one year, and he was by no means a great or popular architect.

This is what we mean by "taking a piece of the deal." It is a method which many other professionals besides architects could well utilize. Often they are in an excellent position to judge the potential success of an enterprise with which they are associated.

Take the case of the attorney who accepts stock in a new company in lieu of a $10,000 fee. Assuming she is in a 28 per cent tax bracket, she pays a tax of $2,800 on this stock. Three years later, she sells the stock for $15,000. She pays tax of $1,400 on her $5,000 profit. Her net gain on the whole deal was then $10,800 versus the $7,200 she would have netted from her $10,000 fee, after taxes.

Of course, every deal doesn't work out this well. Like most investments, the professional "deal" involves a risk. Bird-in-hand professionals will want to use more orthodox methods of estate building. The investment-minded lawyer, accountant, architect, and engineer, however, should examine the opportunities available here for a unique means of capital growth.

THE INDEPENDENT BUSINESSMEN

Until recently the independent enterpreneur, the owner or partner of a business was in an ironic position, compared to his executive counterpart. the manager-employee of a corporation. On the one hand, the independent's situation had greater growth potentialities. If the business went well and the times were propitious, it was possible for him to accumulate a fortune. The corporate executive's occupation generally affords him no such possibility.

On the other hand, the independent businessperson could not have the built-in tax shelters which were available to the corporate executive. His income might be greater but a large part of it was taxed away.

New developments have given the independent new opportunities. In fact, there is no reason why the independent now cannot avail himself of the same type of favored tax treatment. He is in business. Nearly every business can incorporate. And once incorporated, as we know, the business comes under the sheltering spread of the tax-favored umbrella.

It used to be that independents shied away from the idea of incorporation because of that famous bogey, double taxation. Today this can be avoided. There are a few ways to overcome this problem.

But first, what is it?

THE MEANING OF DOUBLE TAXATION

Corporations are taxed on their profits. The first $50,000 of profits are taxed at 15 per cent; the next $25,000 at 25 per cent. Profits over $75,000 are taxed at 34 per cent. An additional 5 per cent tax up to $11,750 is imposed on income over $100,000 up to $335,000. Therefore, corporations with income of at least $335,000 will pay a flat 34 per cent. Double taxation occurs when the profits are paid out as dividends to the stockholder. They were first taxed to the corporation at its brackets but are again subject to income tax to the stockholder at his bracket when he receives them. Thus if the corporate net profit is $50,000 to begin with, the corporation pays an income tax of $7,500. Then, when the remaining $42,500 is paid as dividends to the stockholder (who we'll assume is in a top bracket of 28 per cent), the tax is $11,900. A total of $19,400 in taxes is paid, leaving only $30,600 available for use to the stockholder out of the $50,000 original profit.

Naturally no one likes the idea of paying taxes twice on the same income. To see how it can be overcome, let's take the case of Mr. White, Mr. Brown, Mr. Green, and Mr. Black. Each of them is independent; each of them incorporates his business but overcomes the double-taxation factors in a different way.

Mr. White Draws Out the Entire Corporate Income in Salary

He is the owner of a small manufacturing firm. Its net earnings are $25,000. White incorporates the business, but since its income is small, he can reasonably withdraw it all as salary. Now there is only a single tax on the income, the tax on his personal salary. His corporation gets a full tax deduction on the payments to him. The situation is essentially the same as before except that White is now free to set up a program of corporate benefits for himself if he wants to use some part of the profit for that purpose.

Mr. Brown Splits the Income Between Himself and the Corporation

Mr. Brown is the sole proprietor of a textile distribution

business which has net earnings of $70,000. All this is taxable as ordinary income to him, and with a tax bracket of 28 percent, he pays a heavy tax bill—about $15,000. This leaves him with $55,000 per year of after-tax income.

Brown thinks he can get along on less than that. He incorporates his business and pays himself a salary of $50,000. His income tax on that is $10,000. The balance of the profits—$20,000—is left in the corporation. It is taxed now at only 15 percent or $3,000. The total tax bill of Brown Inc., *and* Mr. Brown is $13,000, as compared with Brown's former tax bill of $15,000. He has reduced the total tax paid by $2,000.

Now, too, Brown can avail himself of all those corporate fringe benefits, using the income he leaves in the corporation which, if used to fund a pension or group insurance program for Brown, would reduce the corporate tax still further.

Not everyone will want to follow in Brown's path, of course. Splitting income will depend upon the relative tax brackets of the corporation and the owner. There is also a limit on the amount which the corporation can reasonably accumulate without incurring certain tax penalties. In such cases, why not emulate Mr. Green?

Mr. Green Elects to Have His Company Taxed as a Subchapter S Corporation

Subchapter S refers to a section of the Internal Revenue Code which came into being in 1958 and was substantially revised by the Subchapter S Revision Act of 1982. Under it, stockholders of a corporation may elect to have their corporation considered as a partnership for tax purposes. The income, credits, deductions and losses are passed through pro rata to the shareholders. For all other purposes, the corporation has the attributes and advantages of a corporation.

Mr. Green, the president of Close Corporation, Inc., Mr. Gray, the vice-president, and Mr. Outsider, an investor, own the corporation equally. Green gets a salary of $30,000. Gray gets $20,000. The corporation has profits of $50,000.

Gray, Green, and Outsider decide to file an election under Subchapter S. Green and Gray are taxed on their $30,000 and $20,000 salaries. In addition, the three stockholders are taxed on their shares of the $50,000 profit, even

though the profit is retained in the surplus of the corporation. If the corporation later distributes that $50,000, it is
not taxed again to the stockholders.

Green (and Gray) are able to enjoy the tax-favored employee benefits of the corporate setup with one exception:
an employee owning more than 2 per cent of the stock of a
Subchapter S corporation is not eligible for certain fringe
benefits such as tax-free accident and health plan and $50,000
of group term insurance.

For those who are interested in Sub-Chapter S treatment,
here are the qualifications which a company must meet to
elect to be taxed under its provisions.

1. There must be no more than 35 stockholders, none of
whom are non-resident aliens or a corporation or partnership.

2. The corporation must be created under the laws of the
United States, or one of the 50 states, or one of the territories.

3. There must be no more than one class of stock outstanding, but there may be different voting rights among the
shares.

4. The corporation may not own 80 per cent or more of
another corporation.

If the corporation receives more than 25 per cent of its
gross receipts from rents, royalties, interest, dividends annuities, and gain from the sale or exchange of securities and
also has accumulated earnings and profits, it will be taxed
on that passive income. After 3 consecutive years of such income it will lose its Subchapter S status.

The maximum corporate tax rate now exceeds the maximum individual tax rate (34 per cent vs. 28 per cent).
Because of the rate differential, shareholders of a closely
held business should consider electing S corporation status
in order to shift the burden on corporate earnings solely to
the shareholder level.

Mr. Black Uses the Excess Earnings
of the Corporation to Expand His Business

Mr. Black is one of three brothers who owned a small
New England manufacturing corporation. After World War
II, the profits of the firm increased considerably. Black and
his brothers took stock of their situation. What should they
do with their profits?

Their salaries were already high, so much so that they

couldn't raise them substantially. They didn't want to pay out dividends; this meant double taxation. Besides, their personal tax brackets were already high. They couldn't accumulate any more earnings in the corporation without being subject to the imposition of the accumulated earnings tax (an additional tax imposed on accumulated earnings in excess of $250,000, not justified by the reasonable needs of the business).

Their decision: to plough the profits back into the business, using them for an extensive advertising campaign. The result: because of the advertising campaign, sales tripled, the business grew . . . and grew . . . and grew . . . until it had become a national distributor, its chief product a household byword. In effect, the pressure of high taxation forced Black and his brothers into a highly successful expansion they might otherwise never have undertaken.

THE PAYOFF

When all is said and done, what is the payoff? Are the independents, businesspersons and professionals alike, as well off as their corporate brethren so far as their tax-sheltered estate building opportunities are concerned?

Though there are still some restrictions for the self-employed and Subchapter S stockholders, the independent has the opportunity to create his own tax-sheltered package almost equal to that available to the executive of Corporation Americana. The independent doesn't have the security of a large corporation and is dependent on his own ingenuity and success—meaning his business or professional fortunes—for his estate plan.

Yet he has a great advantage. He can, if he is successful, accumulate a real fortune from his business or profession, an estate which is truly worthy of the name. In the long run, this may be an occupational opportunity which cannot be equaled.

CHAPTER 7

Investments: Making Your Capital Work for You

Today nearly everyone is an investor. The idea of accumulating money and putting it to work in the hope that it will produce income and perhaps appreciate in value appeals to all classes and all ages. The investment programs of individuals, of course, differ widely. Thus, a fourth-grader may put one-half of his allowance in a savings bank each week with his grandest goal a strictly limited one: the purchase of a new 22-inch English bicycle.

His father, on the other hand, buys stocks when and if he has the money to invest, and his eyes are fixed on broader, if somewhat vaguer horizons—who knows what the future in the securities market may bring?

Looking at the two investment programs from a strictly technical point of view, we'd say the boy has a definite edge on his father. His program meets the classical requirements for a sound investment philosophy. He has a fixed objective and a systematic savings and investment plan. What's more, the amount of his investment is realistic in relation to his resources, and its form is well suited both to his circumstances and to the attainment of his fixed objective.

But what about the father? In fact, his objectives are undefined. He vaguely knows he wants to ensure his family's security, or perhaps he hopes for riches. But his savings program is not systematic at all. Haphazard is the word for it. As a result, he never accumulates enough capital really to initiate and carry through a sound investment program. He lacks the two basic ingredients which form the basis of any estate planning investment program—objectives and resources.

It is not the purpose of this chapter to discuss how to make a million (and certainly not how to lose it). It is, rather, to set forth the essentials of an investment program and discuss the nature and meaning of investments from the estate planning point of view.

This point of view is long-range. It is not concerned with haphazard buying of securities, when and if funds are available, and then selling when cash is needed. An estate planner's program must be predetermined and conscientiously carried out over the period of his investing life, which may be 40 to 45 years or more. It is part of a larger plan, and its goals are the same as that larger plan: to provide funds for retirement, disability, and family security, both before and after the planner's death.

Surplus Capital: The Basis of Investment

To invest you must have surplus capital, funds which are not needed for current family requirements or for other aspects of estate building, such as insurance or the emergency savings account.

Thus, the estate planner-investor must, at some point in life (and that point is far better reached earlier than later), examine his resources, assess his needs, and put into motion a systematic savings plan. The funds devoted to it are for investment; not for a vacation, not for Christmas, or not even for that second automobile or home.

There are all kinds of methods open to a person today to help him set up such a savings system: payroll deductions, corporate savings plans, banking programs, and mutual funds with automatic re-investment plans, to name only a few. And, of course, the time-honored method of budgeting family expenses to leave some surplus out of earnings, although painful, is always possible. Just about anything will do so long as there is regular saving.

The story of the eccentric who puts his money in a mattress is an old one, but we sometimes wonder if those who scoff at it aren't really missing its message. The fact is that he has succeeded in saving surplus capital. What's more, if this "savings program" of his is regular, i.e., if he takes a part of his weekly salary and stows it away over a period of years, he will end up with more money at retirement age than the great majority of his more sophisticated fellow citizens.

The real mistake of our hoarding friend is not *using* his excess capital; that is, in failing to put it to work so that it produces income or provides principal growth, or both. This is what we mean by investment and these are its prime attributes: income production and capital appreciation.

ESTATE-PLANNING PRINCIPLES OF INVESTMENT

For the estate planner, investment acumen lies not so much in the ability to select a certain "right" security as it does in the ability to create a long-term, well-balanced investment program which will produce the capital needed to carry out your estate planning objectives.

How you as an investor-planner accomplish this and how well you accomplish it is a highly individual matter. There are your aims and objectives; the amount of capital you have available; your age (how much time you have to carry out your program); your other resources; your experience and competence; the tax bracket you are in; the amount of risk you are willing to take or can afford to take; even your personality and temperament. All these factors enter into the success or failure of your investment program.

There is a wide, and often confusing, variety of investment opportunities available. When you come to the problem of selecting investments, each one should be assessed from different points of view.

1. *Diversification*. Does your portfolio show variety? You must seek to achieve diversification, not only in the relation of each investment to the other, but also in the relation to the rest of your assets and your sources of income.

2. *Safety*. How safe will the principal be? The amount of risk varies with each type of investment. Here the planner must balance the classic contradictions. One the one hand, since you are looking for safety, you should seek investments which carry a minimum of risk. On the other hand, low-risk investments usually offer low returns and little ap-

preciation. And just to make things more complicated, this tradition doesn't always apply. In recent years, for instance, blue chip (i.e., "safe") stocks have shown greater capital appreciations than many successful risk investments; and savings accounts have produced larger income returns than most equity investments.

3. *Inflation Hedge.* How well will this particular investment preserve your capital against inflation? It is just as important to protect the purchasing power of your capital as it is to protect yourself against the possible loss of capital. In any inflationary period, it won't do to just maintain the number of your dollars. If that is all you do, you will still suffer an economic loss. Here again, the whole question of diversification enters the picture. A portfolio that is invested entirely in a savings account, returning 5 or 6 per cent, is often no protection against inflation. Only a portfolio based on a variety of investments—some with fixed returns and some with potential for capital appreciation—will do that.

4. *Growth.* What is the growth potential? Here we are speaking of the inherent ability of the investment, not just to protect against inflation but in addition to appreciate the capital beyond a normal inflationary increase. Generally speaking, these investments are found in the industries which have great growth potential. In the early part of the century, it was the railroads and the steel industry. In recent years it has been first automobiles and chemicals, then electronics, now space and new products.

5. *Income.* What is its expected income return? Here we refer to expected *future* income production as well as to current. Is the income guaranteed? Will the income return be available in the bad times as well as in good times? Is it fixed? Will the rate of return move up and down with general money rates so as to reflect the state of the economy and the probable changing costs of living?

6. *Marketability.* What is its marketability? Is this a security that you can readily sell? Or will buyers perhaps be hard to find? There are many securities which are not readily marketable, but still make worthwhile investments. Obviously, however, your investment portfolio should not be weighted with these. Liquidity is extremely important to many aspects of estate planning.

7. *Taxation.* How will taxation affect your program? As in many features of estate planning, taxation plays a funda-

mental role in the investment program. At this point it may be worthwhile to deal with some basic tax concepts which will be involved in our later investment discussion.

INVESTMENTS AND TAXATION

Your build-up of capital will be much greater if you utilize available tax shelters and thereby reduce the amount of taxation. This applies to the two aspects of income taxation—the taxation on income received from dividends, interest, rent, etc., and the taxation on profits that may occur from a sale of property.

In both cases the regular income tax rates of 15 and 28 per cent will apply. The income you receive from your investments is added to the rest of your ordinary income and taxed accordingly. There are a few exceptions and exclusions. Interest is generally taxable; there is one major exception—interest on bonds which are issued by a state or one of its sub-divisions. Net income from real estate is taxable also, but the deduction for depreciation can greatly reduce the tax burden. The same applies to the deductions and depletion allowances for investments in natural resources and cattle. Capital gain or loss tax treatment occurs when a capital asset is sold. Most investments which you will make outside your business will come within the capital asset category, and so will qualify for such treatment. The types of properties which do not qualify are: copyrights and other artistic properties; assets held for sale to customers in the ordinary course of business; notes and accounts receivable acquired in the course of doing business; certain government obligations issued at discount.

The Basis of Capital Gains Taxation

When you sell a capital asset, the tax you pay is imposed on the difference between the sale price and what is called the "adjusted basis" of the asset. If the sale price is less than the adjusted basis, you have a tax loss; if it is more, you have a gain.

Generally, the "adjusted basis" is the price you originally paid for the asset, plus any additional capital expenditures you may have made on it. Thus, if you paid $20,000 for property and put capital improvements of $5,000 into it over the years, your adjusted basis would be $25,000.

However, the adjusted basis may be less than cost. The adjusted basis of a piece of real estate, for instance, is the purchase price plus added capital costs minus the depreciation allowance. (Gain attributable to accelerated depreciation may be subject to ordinary income tax.)

Other special rules apply. For gifts made before 1977, there are two rules for determining the basis, one for gain and one for loss. For gain, the basis is the same as the donor's basis plus the gift tax. For loss, however, the basis can be either the donor's basis or the fair market value of the property at the time of the gift (plus the gift tax), whichever is lower. If the asset is a gift received after 1976, the same two rules apply for determining basis, one for gain and one for loss. However, only that portion of the gift tax attributed to the appreciation over the donor's cost can be added to basis.

Sometimes these two rules make a tax no-man's land out of the sale of gift property. Here's a father who gives some securities to his son. The father paid $10,000 for them, but at the time he gives them away, their market price is only $6,000. Sometime later the son sells the securities for $9,000. Has he incurred a gain or loss?

Under the rule for determining gain, he takes his father's cost of $10,000 as his basis. Since his sale price was only $9,000, he has no gain. Using the rule for determining loss, he takes as his basis the lower value, the fair market value of the securities at the time his father gave them to him— only $6,000. Again, since he sold the asset for $9,000, there is no loss. For tax purposes, he realized neither a gain nor a loss.

For inherited property, the estate tax valuation establishes its basis. The general rule is that property in a decedent's estate is valued at its fair market value on the date of death. The property gets a new basis which may be more or less than the decedent's. If less, the decendent's paper loss is never realized. If the fair market value of the property is greater than the decedent's basis, the step-up in basis means that the unrealized appreciation escapes the tax on capital gains. Suppose a woman invested in a new enterprise in the

1950s when its stock was selling at $100 a share. When she dies, it's being traded at $200 a share. Her daughter, who inherits her estate, gets a new basis of $200. If she sells it for $210, she has a taxable gain of only $10.

Congress decided to eliminate this tax break by replacing the stepped-up basis with a carryover basis in the Tax Reform Act of 1976 so that inherited property would have the same basis the decedent had with certain adjustments. The new law was so complicated and difficult to apply that Congress first postponed and then repealed it, reinstating the former law.

An exception to the rule that the basis of inherited property is its fair market value on the date of death is a special provision that permits real property used in family farming or by a closed corporation to be valued at its "actual use" value rather than its "best use" value. For example, a piece of property while used as a farm might be worth $100,000, but as part of a shopping center, its best use, it would have a value of $300,000. If certain conditions are met, the estate can elect the actual use value for estate tax purposes.

There is another exception to the rule that property inherited from a decedent takes as its basis the estate tax valuation. To prevent an heir from giving appreciated property to a person on his deathbed in order to get a step-up in basis to market value at the time of death, there is no stepped-up basis for any property the decedent received as a gift within a year of his or her death if that property is left to the original donor or donor's spouse. Note: If the property passes to another person the step-up basis rule does apply.

The tax law permits the executor to value the estate's assets at their value 6 months after the date of death or, if sold or distributed within 6 months, at the value of the property when transferred. If the total value of the assets in the estate declines, the executor will usually elect the alternate value to save estate taxes. When the estate has increased in value during the six months and the assets are to be sold soon, it would be better to elect the alternate estate tax value to get a higher basis if the estate tax on the post-death appreciation would be less than the income tax on the taxable gain. For estates of decedents dying after July 18, 1984, however, the alternative valuation date can only be elected if both the value of the gross estate and the estate tax are reduced as the result of the election. The alternative value can no longer be used solely to increase the basis of the assets in the estate.

Taxes on Sales

As we have previously pointed out, taxation of capital gains is the same now as that of other taxable income—at 15 or 28 per cent to the individual. The holding period of the asset is irrelevant to taxation. There is no longer a 60 per cent deduction on net long term capital gains as the result of the Tax Reform Act of 1986.

The distinction between capital gains and losses and other types of income, however, does still have significance. Capital losses are first deductible in full against capital gains. Thereafter, any additional capital losses may offset other income only up to $3,000 on a dollar-for-dollar basis in any taxable year. Losses in excess of the $3,000 limitation may be carried forward to the following tax years.

In certain instances, the law will not permit tax losses. Loss deductions, for example, are not allowed on "wash sales" (i.e., a sale of securities at a loss made 30 days before or after the purchase of substantially identical securities by the same person). Nor are they allowed for losses which result from sales between closely related people, such as husband and wife.

TYPES OF INVESTMENTS

With these tax principles firmly in mind, the potential estate planner-investor is ready to look at the considerable variety of investments from which he can pick and choose.

Savings Accounts

The most common and one of the most conservative types of investment. It has its drawbacks—the principal is static so there is no opportunity for appreciation of capital, and no protection against inflation. But there is a guaranteed return. Rates, though usually regulated by the supervising government authority, tend to rise somewhat during periods of inflation. Recently, in fact, short-term savings accounts have been returning 5 per cent (savings and loan accounts 5¼ per cent). Longer-term accounts offer returns between 6 per cent and 7 per cent; certificates of deposit, 7 per cent or more.

Short-term savings accounts also offer liquidity. Ordinarily when you deposit money in a savings account, you can take it out any time you choose. Some institutions retain the right, however, in fine print, to condition withdrawals on 60- or 90-day notice— and in times of extreme economic depressions, such as that of 1929, this has been exercised.

Most savings accounts are insured, either by the Federal Deposit Insurance Corporation or the Federal Savings and Loan Insurance Corporation. Except for federal savings and loan associations, however, which are required to carry FSLIC insurance, the insurance need not be that of a federal agency. It can also be private. Depositors should always check on this.

1. *Mutual Savings Banks.* These are state-chartered institutions which exist in approximately one-third of our states, chiefly in the East. They follow a conservative investment policy, since state laws limit their investments to prescribed securities. Currently, about 65 per cent of their assets are invested in mortgages, the rest in government securities, gilt-edged corporate bonds, and a few common stocks.

2. *Savings and Loan Associations.* The return paid on this type of savings may be higher than that paid by other major savings institutions because savings and loan associations specialize in home financing. They therefore have large earnings to distribute because home mortgages earn a greater return than government securities. Savings and loan associations operate under either state or federal charters with close government regulation. Most associations are thus able to provide a high level of safety and return for their depositors.

3. *Commercial Banks.* Many offer savings accounts but the interest rates are usually lower than either the mutual savings banks or the savings and loan institutions because the Federal Reserve Bank limits maximum interest rates they may pay with respect to certain time deposits. The difference is generally about one-quarter of 1 per cent.

4. *Credit Unions.* A credit union is an association formed by any group of people who have a common interest— employees of a particular company, professionals, church

members, etc. The group pools its savings and makes them available for loans to members. They are federally or state-chartered. Credit unions are tax-exempt and their administrative costs are low; this makes it possible for them to pay higher interest rates than most other savings institutions. Credit unions, however, do not have the professional management which most banks and savings and loan institutions do; therefore, some of them do not have the same degree of safety although many of them do have federally backed insurance against depositor loss similar to banks.

Payroll Savings Plans

If you have made the decision to save regularly, but don't want to bother with the mechanics of deposits and purchases or if you want to supplement your savings program, many employers offer savings plans in which deposits can be automatically deducted from your paycheck before you receive it. In some cases employers will contribute a percentage of your savings to your account.

Many companies offer 401 (k) programs that provide options for saving as well as investing. It is important to remember, however, that since 401 (k) programs are actually retirement-type or tax-deferred funds, they are not really liquid. They come under the umbrella of a program that carries delays and penalties for withdrawal before retirement age. Among the options available in 401 (k) programs are investments in money market funds or annuities, usually provided by an insurance company.

U.S. Saving Bond plans provide for regular deductions from wages to purchase bonds for you.

Government obligations are debts which the government owes. They are two types: marketable and non-marketable securities.

Most people are personally familiar with the non-marketable type, namely, U.S. Savings Bonds. They may not be sold or used as collateral, but their redemption by the government upon demand is guaranteed.

Series E and EE bonds offer a special tax advantage. The owner may report the income on his tax return as it accrues or in a lump sum when the bonds are redeemed. This tax feature is of value in a retirement plan, since, having a number of years within which to redeem his bonds, he can wait until the lower income tax years of retirement to report this income. Holders of E bonds should make certain as to their maturities, even though they may be extended, because when the maturities are reached, they may stop accruing interest.

Series H and HH bonds have no special tax advantage. They are sold at par. The interest is paid semi-annually and must be reported each year. They mature 10 years after issue. They can be redeemed any time after 6 months from the date of issue.

Both E's and H's have the advantage of *safety*: the credit of the United States government stands behind them. But since their return is fixed, and there is no potential appreciation in market value, they offer no protection against inflation. They have been yielding between 6½ and 9 per cent if they were held to maturity, less if they were cashed in earlier. The new issues are paying 6% per cent if held to maturity.

Marketable securities are issued in the forms of bills, notes, certificates, and bonds. Unless the Treasury calls them in sooner, they are not redeemable until their maturity date. They are traded like corporate securities, and so their value is subject to the changes of the marketplace. Except for recent issues their interest rates have been lower than many other fixed return investments.

But from the estate planning point of view, this low interest factor, which has caused them to sell at a discount, has resulted in making some of them attractive estate investments. On the owner's death, certain issues of U.S. Treasury Bonds can be redeemed to pay estate taxes at their par values. The person who purchases these Treasury issues, which have been selling as low as $80, for example, can add to his estate an asset which will be valued at $100 at his death.

Municipal Bonds

The investment importance of municipal bonds is that their interest is tax-free both federally and in the state where they are issued. Industrial revenue bonds are no longer federally tax free.

Municipal bonds are issued by a state or its subdivisions (towns, cities, counties, and the like) or its agencies (highway, bridge, or other authorities). They are of three kinds:

general obligations, which are backed by the credit and taxing power of the government entity; *revenue bonds*, issued for a specific purpose (such as financing a bridge or sewage system), the income and principal of which are payable out of the special project or enterprise; and *moral obligation* or *agency bonds* issued for purposes of financing state housing, hospital, and university construction. Although the latter type are basically revenue type bonds, the state legislature is supposed to have a moral obligation to vote for allocating funds toward payment of interest and principal if the underlying projects do not generate sufficient income to do so. The general obligation issues are safer investments, but, being less risky, they usually yield a lower return.

Being tax-free, municipals are offered at a lower rate of interest than most corporate bonds. If you buy municipals and save taxes, then, will you end up with more spendable income than if you had invested in higher yielding corporate bonds?

For the person in a high tax bracket, the answer would definitely be yes. Take a taxpayer in the 28 per cent bracket. A tax-free bond yielding 7 per cent gives him a return equivalent to a taxable interest of 9.5 per cent.

But there are disadvantages to investing in some municipals which should be weighted against their tax advantages. Many of them are not as readily marketable as United States government or corporate bonds. If the owner is forced to liquidate them in a hurry, he may have to sell them in a narrow market and sell them below their face value. The estate planner who invests in them should consider them as long-term investments, not as a source of ready cash.

Furthermore the safety of municipals depends on the credit of the local government or the municipal project—often a difficult matter to determine. Recently even some of the largest municipalities have had difficulty in redeeming bonds issued by them. Also how dependable, for example, is the issue of a small town's sewage disposal bonds? This is obviously a question that can only be answered by experts. Anyone contemplating such investments should consult investment advisors who are specialists in the field.

All this means that the return from municipals should be substantially greater than the after-tax income received on other types of investments. Otherwise, the return doesn't compensate for their less desirable features.

Suppose an issue of municipals pays 7 per cent. A taxpayer whose top bracket is 28 per cent buys them and gets a return equal to 9.5 per cent in taxable interest. A taxpayer with a 15 per cent top bracket, however, would get a return equal to only 8 per cent taxable interest.

I'd call this a worthwhile investment for the 28 per cent person; he would likely receive a lesser yield from other investments. But the 15 per center is getting no more than the return he would receive from a safe, liquid investment such as a certificate of deposit in a savings bank or savings and loan association.

Corporate Bonds

When you purchase a bond of Company X, you are lending money to it, and it guarantees to pay a certain rate of interest, and to repay your loan in full by a specified date. Your bond may be *secured*, that is to say, it is backed, by a lien or pledge on all the company's property or on specific assets to ensure repayment. Or it may be unsecured, a *debenture* bond. The former is a safer investment. In either case, however, your claim takes precedence over stockholders.

What are the investment features of a corporate bond? First of all it is marketable; second, it yields more than government obligations; third, it provides the security of a fixed rate of interest; fourth, it guarantees repayment of the face amount if you hold it to maturity, and usually has an active market to ensure liquidity.

The chief disadvantage of the bond, however, is that since its interest is fixed, its market value will decline in a time of rising interest rates. One way to offset this effect is to buy *convertible* bonds. This type gives the bondholder the right to convert the bond into a certain number of shares of the common stock of the company.

Suppose you buy a convertible bond. Sometime later the stock of the corporation has a substantial market rise. You can either convert the bond to the stock, or sell it in the open market at a gain which will reflect the increased value of the stock to which it can be converted. Thus, a convertible bond offers the security of a fixed return investment as well as the growth opportunities of an equity investment. It is a hedge against both deflation and inflation, and therefore represents a most useful type of investment in an estate planner's long-term portfolio.

Taxation of Bonds. Bond interest, except for municipals, is taxable income. If interest is in default at the time you buy the bond or if you buy "income bonds" (i.e., bonds where the interest is contingent on earnings) on which back interest is due, when and if you eventually get the back interest, it is not considered taxable income but a return of capital. This reduces your basis. When the bond is sold or redeemed, your taxable income is increased by this amount of paid back interest. Therefore, this is merely a deferral of income.

Similarly, if you buy a bond at a discount and then you sell it at a profit or it is retired, the amount of the discount (other than an original issue discount) is taxable income. Suppose you buy a bond, for example, at discount, purchasing it at 85 when it had it had been issued at 100. When the bond matures, the company retires it, and you have a taxable income of 15.

A final word on bonds: except for convertibles, they have growth potential only if general interest rates decline. Their safety is dependent on the soundness of the company that issues them and its continuing ability to pay interest and repay principal.

Stocks

Until now we have been concerned with fixed return investments. They are usually safe, they are conservative, and they should be included in a sound investment portfolio. But in most cases they must be balanced by investments with growth potential. The need for growth investments is two-fold. They tie your capital to the prevailing economy. Thus, in an inflationary period they may protect your capital from a loss of buying power. Also, growth investments provide opportunity for capital appreciation apart from an inflationary rise.

Investments in corporate stocks serve this function. The holder of such an investment is not a creditor of the company like the bondholder; he is an owner. As such, he shares in both profits and losses. The expectation of increased profits provides the growth potential, but it should not be forgotten that loss potential is there also. That is why stocks are more of a risk; they traditionally offer higher yields than bonds of the same company. (This tradition, however is sometimes more honored in the breach than in the observance; currently, for example, few stocks yield more than 7 per cent, about the same as bonds.

Preferred Stock. This stands midway between a bond and a stock. There is a fixed return, but there is no specified maturity date. Usually preferred stock may be called, but the callability is an option which the corporation need not exercise. A preferred stockholder's claim is subordinate to those of the holders of bonds and other corporate indebtedness, but prior to those of common stockholders. In addition, his right to dividends is usually cumulative: that is, if dividends are in arrears, they must all be paid before any dividends are paid on the common.

Preferred, then, is like a bond in that its market value increases and decreases with prevailing interest rates. It is like a stock in that the payment of dividends is dependent on earnings. The preferred stockholder, however, is entitled only to the fixed dividend; everything over that belongs to the common stockholders. On the other hand, if the corporation cannot pay dividends, the preferred shareholder, in effect, participates in its losses.

There are two special types of preferred, however, which offer greater potential for appreciation by giving the preferred the opportunity to share in the company's growth.

CONVERTIBLE PREFERRED: Gives the shareholder the right, after or during a certain period, to convert his stock into a fixed number of shares of common. Thus, if the market price of the common rises, he can sell his preferred (which will have increased in value), or he can convert to common at no additional cost.

PARTICIPATING PREFERRED: Gives the shareholder the usual fixed dividend, but includes the right to share excess dividends with the common stock.

Convertible preferred is offered by many companies; participating preferred is rarely offered by public corporations.

Common stock. The common stock of a company is junior to bonds and other indebtedness and preferred stock. A company may have only common stock outstanding, or more than one class of stock. When a company has more than one class, as a general rule it will have one class of common and one or more classes of preferred. However, it may have more than one class of common. Although common stock is the junior security, it usually has the voting power. Occasionally preferred stock has voting rights, but generally it is the common stockholders who control the corporation.

The common stock bears the greatest amount of risk along with the greatest potential for growth. In the average portfolio, common stocks are necessary because of their capital appreciation potential. The proportion of investment which should be made in common stocks will vary with each individual's particular circumstances.

For example, the stockholder of a closely held corporation will not have a great need for investing in common stock because part of his assets is already in a growth investment, his business. A corporate executive or professional person with a steadily rising income may not need as large a percentage of investment in common stock as perhaps a person with a fixed salary or retirement income requires. His increasing earning power is a hedge against inflation and an estate-builder.

Stocks vary greatly in quality from the "blue chips" to the "cats and dogs." The choice depends on how much risk one is willing to take. For a person who depends solely on investments for income, the amount and regularity of dividends are important. Dividends fluctuate, and there is no guarantee that dividends will be paid out at all. However, an investor can look to a corporation's past dividend record and its current earnings as a guide to its future dividend paying policy.

Since the investment program of an estate plan is a long-range program, upwards of 40 years, the element of long-term growth is an important factor. But how do you determine where to find it?

Potential for growth is not limited to new enterprises. Older companies may offer great possibilities of growth, as for example, public utilities located in areas of the country with expanding populations.

However, the greatest potential or opportunity for growth often lies in the common stocks of the riskier new enterprises. The estate planner with substantially all of his reserves invested in fixed return or "blue-chip" securities can validly commit a small part to venture enterprises. He may risk the loss of a small part of his capital but might garner a windfall in the long run. Our products and services are constantly changing. A new product or invention may create a multimillion dollar corporation or an entire industry in years to come.

Unfortunately, there is no scientific way of selecting the right industry or corporation. If a person like Bernard Baruch claimed to have difficulty in making investments, how good a job can the average person do? Not only determining what to buy, but when to buy, is difficult. For the long haul put your money in the large organizations which have shown an ability to prosper and meet the changes of our changing economy. Let the management of these companies do the economic forecasting and planning for you.

Special Investment for High Tax Brackets

The person in the high tax bracket looks for investments which provide large tax deductions and allowances for depreciation and depletion. The actual cost of these investments is often reduced by the amount of income tax savings. Such a person should investigate a number of special types of investments which we will merely indicate here. In the proper case they offer opportunities which should not be overlooked. There are specialists and brokers who handle only these type of "deals." Often they are individuals working on their own, or even "wild catters." We would strongly suggest you carefully look into the background and experience of anyone you deal with. Your local bank or stockbroker can get you the names of the more reliable organizations which operate in these fields.

Oil and Gas Wells. There is a deduction for drilling expenses as well as depreciation on physical equipment purchases. However, the Tax Reform Act of 1976 provides for recapture (ordinary tax treatment) of past intangible drilling cost deductions when such interests are disposed of by the investor. If the well is successful, there is a deduction for depletion of 15 per cent on income received for most investors. When the investor's cost is recouped by depletion allowances, future allowances become tax preference items.

Cattle. There are substantial tax benefits. Expenses of care and feeding are deductible from ordinary income. The cost of purchase of the cattle can be depreciated over the scheduled lives of the animals, subject to taxation on the depreciation as ordinary income when sold. Breeding, dairy, or draft cattle get special treatment on sale, if they have been held for two years or more. If there is a loss, it is considered an ordinary loss, deductible against ordinary income if the taxpayer participates in the management or operations of the activity. If the taxpayer does not participate in the activity such losses can only be used to offset gains from similar investments. And as the herd increases in number and weight, there is a capital appreciation.

Timber. If you own an interest in timber, you will get a cost depletion allowance. This applies whether you own standing timber, a right to cut the timber, or merely hold timber royalties.

Investment Companies and Variable Annuities

Investing on one's own is a difficult task. It calls for skill, experience, and above all, time. A person with large resources can afford to pay for individual professional assistance, but the small investor is usually dependent upon whatever information he can gather from disparate sources in the limited time he can devote to this effort.

Few so-called small investors attain success in the investment field. The lists to choose from are so long and the comparative values as among stock issues are so difficult to assess. The amateur or part-time investor may be wise to turn his selection of investments over to a professional group. Here he gains not only experienced management, but also wider investment diversification than he would otherwise be able to afford.

Investment Companies and Trusts. When you buy stock in an investment company, you are investing in a company whose sole business is the investment of its capital in securities.

There are two types of investment companies: *closed end* and *open end*.

The *closed end* investment company operates like the ordinary corporation. It sells a fixed number of shares to investors which are regularly traded on the market. The company uses its funds for investments and pays the profits from dividends, interest, and capital gains to its stockholders.

The shares of these companies are subject to market fluctuations, just as are any other corporate shares. The price usually reflects the value of their underlying net assets, i.e., the securities held by the company. But they may sell above or below this value depending upon their success and market conditions.

The *open end* company, popularly known as the mutual fund, has no limit on the number of shares it can issue. The more money it receives for investment, the more shares it will issue.

When you buy a share in the mutual fund the price you pay is based on the net value of the fund plus a loading or sales charge. Make sure that you find out what proportion of the price is accounted for by this loading charge; sometimes it can go as high as 6 or 7 per cent. A few funds have no loading charges.

Shares of mutual funds are not traded on the market. They are purchased and redeemed either directly by the company or through a broker. The redemption price is determined by the net asset value of the fund at the time of redemption plus (occasionally) a redemption fee.

Since the market value of the securities held by the fund fluctuates, the value of the fund's shares fluctuates as well. Thus, the price at which you buy or have your shares redeemed is determined by the market value of the underlying securities at the time of the transaction.

Many mutual funds offer a "packaged investment." This is a systematic savings or investment plan, sometimes accompanied by term insurance to complete the plan in the event the investor dies.

Some funds even include accident and health insurance; if you become disabled, the insurance pays your investment installments during the disability period.

Both closed and open end companies offer different types of investment portfolios. Some are balanced funds, investing is preferred and common stocks and bonds. Some are limited to a particular type of security, offering only common or only bonds. Others limit their holdings to particular industries, such as chemical or electronics.

In any case these companies offer the investor a wide

diversification of securities or diversification within a particular industry—much more than he could develop on his own. His costs will be the loading charge (unless it is a no-load fund), a possible redemption fee, and the investment fee charged by managers.

Variable Annuities. The variable annuity is a new development in the attempt to combine the security of the fixed dollar investment and the growth opportunity of the equity investment. Some part of the funds you pay to the company for your annuity is invested in fixed dollar investments. Thus, there is a guarantee that a certain amount will be available when the annuity is due for payout.

Another portion is invested in equity securities. This hopefully ensures that if inflation continues, and the buying power of the fixed return portion is thereby reduced, there will nevertheless be an increase in value in the equity portion. Theoretically, the increase will roughly equal the increase in the cost of living.

A variation of this plan is based on the investment of a portion of the annuity payment in cash value insurance and a portion in equity stocks. Thus, if you die, your family gets a substantial death benefit. If you retire, the company terminates the policy and invests the cash value together with the equity value to produce the annuity return. There is no guarantee of what the return will be. If inflation causes the cost of living to rise, then the annuity payments should rise accordingly, but if it goes down, so too should the annuity.

The holder of the variable annuity, however, is placing his investments in professional hands. He is getting the advantage of experienced management which ideally should do a better job of selecting investments than he as an individual can.

Selecting a Mutual Fund

It is good to know that mutual funds are valuable investment media. But how do you, as a small investor in the limited time you can devote to the investment of your resources, make an informed judgment of which funds best fit your individual investment objectives? You should try to choose a fund that meets your standard of safety, diversity, and return. Each mutual fund or group of funds has its own philosophy and approach to managing its investments. These are set forth in the company's prospectus, which can be a basic tool to help you assess whether you will achieve safety, diversity, and return. What you will need to know, then, is the performance of the fund over time and the types of investments that make up the fund. To obtain information on the funds that are available, simply look for their ads in major newspapers—usually in the business section. It will contain information about their performance and investment focus and give you an 800 phone number to call for a prospectus. You should send for prospectuses from several companies to make comparisons. Once you receive a prospectus there are several factors to look for which will help you make comparisons among funds, and to decide which one is right for you.

1. The best criteria for making a selection amongst fund companies is past earnings. Look at their earnings/performance over many years. Look at their long-term growth, how they performed in good and bad markets during those years. This information is partially available in the prospectus. It can also be found with comparable data on other funds in *Investor's Daily* under the section labeled "Mutual Funds," with percentages of performance in the year to date as well as for the preceding years. Yields will always fluctuate with the market (unlike, say, a CD). Major newspapers provide information on the current prices of each of the mutual funds in their business sections on a daily basis.

As a starter, it is probably best to consider the established mutual funds with conservative, diversified stock or bond portfolios. As you become more experienced, more used to the fluctuations of the fund price in the market, and perhaps have more discretionary income, you might consider funds with portfolios that are less diversified, more invested in speculative businesses with potential for substantial growth, and thus involve greater risk.

2. Each fund details the assumptions upon which its projected growth is based, along with its philosophy of investing. This is subjective information, but will give you an idea of how it plans and makes investment decisions, and how aggressive or conservative it may be.

3. Most funds offer several types of portfolios with varying investment objectives and types of investments. Types of investments that make up each portfolio are given in listings.

4. Usually the prospectus will give you a guide for select-

ing amongst the various portfolios—investment objectives, types of investments emphasized in the portfolio, degrees of risk, and rates of expected return (i.e., low, medium, high) are provided. Some are balanced funds, investing in preferred and common stocks and bonds. Some are limited to a particular type of security, offering only common stocks or only bonds. Others limit their holdings to particular industries, such as chemicals or electronics. Many groups will allow you to transfer your funds from one mutual fund to another at little or no cost. These are called sector funds.

5. Costs of getting into and out of the fund (load costs): Some funds charge a load fee to enter; others offer no-load entry. These vary in cost. Check the prospectus for each fund to find out what and when load and/or management fees are charged. They vary from fund to fund. If the fund is well managed and performing well, the fees are worth the cost.

6. If you are about to invest in a mutual fund, we suggest that you buy into it directly through the parent company. In this way you save yourself the expense of brokerage fees. Professional advice can help you pick the fund which is right for you.

INVESTMENT ADVICE AND ASSISTANCE

If you feel that an investment company such as a mutual fund does not render the tailor-made service that fits your individual investment needs and believe you could put together a better package on your own, you will need advice and assistance from professionally qualified sources. Foretunately, there are a great variety of individuals and organizations that offer investment, informational and counseling services to the serious-minded investor.

Market Letters and Security Reports

Today there is a huge quantity of published material available to the prospective investor. It varies from the dope sheet put out by an individual operating from a hole in the wall to the comprehensive statistical reports issued by firms like Moody's or Standard & Poor's.

What do these services offer or purport to offer? Their information is theoretically based on independent investigations of the investment value of major corporations. To do a good job of this investigation, the service has to have competent research people who interview the heads of companies, study the records of the firms, and analyze the industries they represent. On the basis of this information, they make independent judgments as to the company's financial condition and its prospects for success. Moreover, they put all this information and analysis into a readable and understandable form. All of this is something that the individual can't possibly do for himself; it is a full-time job and requires a large organization. Hence the great attraction of the services for the individual investor.

But you must realize that the information presented is general and does not necessarily reflect your individual needs. You must still make your own critical evaluations as to what such information means in terms of your own investment program.

Brokerage Houses

These offer advisory and investment services and many are also equipped to take over the complete management of a portfolio. They are subject to the rules and regulations of the stock exchanges in which they operate and hence must measure up to standards of reliability.

When you deal with a firm which is a member of the New York Stock Exchange, the person who acts as its representative must have passed an examination given by that exchange. He will be registered with it, the National Association of Securities Dealers, and, usually, with the state in which he functions.

Does all this automatically guarantee that you will get good service from any representative? Not necessarily, for the job he performs is a highly individualized one. He uses the research provided by his company and then adapts this research to your own individual needs. This takes acumen, judgment, and interest, things that can never be guaranteed by formal registrations or even examinations. Remember, too, the representative is paid to buy or sell. This gives him a personal stake in his dealings with you that could impair his objectivity.

The Individual Broker

Many investments cannot be traded without a broker. In an arena with so many possibilities and variables it is important to have a specialist whose focus and expertise can guide you through the investment maze. Service, proficiency, and general approach of these individuals will vary. You may need to interview a few to find one you feel comfortable with. The effort can be worthwhile, since individual brokers are of varying experience, competency, and conscientiousness. Their training and experience should enable them to succinctly explain how particular investment opportunities may meet your specific goals. Many brokers are trade-oriented. Although they offer advice on estate-oriented investments, their main emphasis is on day-to-day trading. Because of this you need to keep in mind that their earnings are based on fees charged to you for trading into or out of investments. Thus, you should carefully make your own decision based on information and your own judgment as to if and when to make such moves. Before placing any investment orders it is a good idea to meet your broker in person for a strategy session. In this way you can discuss and clarify your objectives, based upon the advice of a knowledgeable specialist with whom you have established a relationship of trust and confidence.

The Investment Counselor

The advantage of this type of counseling lies in the fact that you will get individualized attention. Moreover, you can be sure that attention will be completely objective. The counselor has nothing to sell but his services, represents no other interests either directly or indirectly, except that of the client, earns only his fee.

If you select competent and experienced investment counsel you will get both the information and the professional advice you need to do a good investment job. Investment counselors don't guarantee success, of course, but your chances of winning it are much higher than if you tried to do it yourself.

One of the drawbacks is that most firms in this business cannot afford to take small accounts. You will need to have at least $50,000 to $100,000 as a minimum to invest before you can utilize such a firm. On this, you usually pay a fee of a percentage of the managed amount.

Ordinarily this percentage gradually declines with the increase in the size of the account. Also there is frequently special consideration made for government bonds and municipal bonds which are in the account and require little professional supervision.

Your Local Bank and Trust Company

All the major banks, as well as many local banks, maintain trust departments. As a matter of fact, this tendency to create trust and custodial departments in the banking fraternity has increased substantially in recent years.

Essentially, these trust departments have as their objective the preservation of an estate, whether that estate comes as the result of an inheritance or is still in the hands of the estate creator.

In actuality, however, many of these trust departments do manage estates that have a growth objective. You should not therefore be deterred from inquiring at your bank as to the suitability of their trust department in taking over the management of your estate building plan.

Make certain that the bank that you have chosen is set up for the aggressive type of investment action you may require.

There is also a question as to the minimum size of the account that can be accepted. In many of the larger banks and trust companies, the minimum account is $500,000, but there are many, especially in regional centers, that will take them from $100,000 or less. This, of course, precludes the use of this investment aid for the majority of the people who are starting to build an estate, and limits it to those who already have a substantial portfolio.

Fees tend to run along roughly the same lines as the fees outlined above for investment counselors. There again, there is a variation. One bank rarely has exactly the same fee structure as another.

To sum up, the selection of investments for the estate planner follows no magical formula. Your own portfolio's composition will depend upon your financial status, the state of the economy, your needs and taste for risk versus rewards, and most important, your objectives. Estate planning objectives are not meant to be tied to sudden success but to the accumulation of a sufficient capital base to supply income for major expenses such as college education for your children, and for disability, retirement, and death.

With all this as basic information you can now take a look at the resources provided in the Appendix on page 323, which are designed to help you construct your portfolio and have an overview of the types of investments available.

CHAPTER 8

Investments: Putting Your Capital in Real Estate

Of all investment opportunities, real estate may offer the big chance. Here is one area where property value is inherent in the property itself. Indeed, now, as in the past, the demands of an advancing civilization tend to increase land value. As even such an early economic thinker as Henry George pointed out, land represents a basic need of society; as this need grows, so also does the value of real estate. Population pressures, in terms of both higher standards of living and a rising birth rate, create new and larger demands for both land and buildings. Land for development becomes scarcer and more valuable.

The past two decades dramatically illustrate this essential character of real estate. Its values—both rental and property—have risen sharply. Given a continuing increase in the population, a well-situated piece of real estate is almost automatically sure to rise. At the same time, its income yield is unusually high. A 10 to 15 per cent return is not uncommon. In addition, real estate has other advantages. It has special tax-sheltered opportunities. It protects its owner against the erosion of inflation; rentals and values move with the economy.

Why, then, do we so often hear that real estate should represent the later, not the first use of investment money for the part-time investor? If we can predict with more certainty that a piece of land will increase in value than a share of stock, why buy stock before buying real estate?

For two reasons. First, there is the problem of liquidity. Despite its great potentiality as an estate builder, real estate lacks ready liquidity. It is subject to cycles within the long-term growth pattern, is greatly affected by real estate market swings—local, temporary, and specific though they may be—which occur even when the overall trend is inflationary. The person who is forced to sell real estate to get liquidity during one of these cyclical periods runs the risk of incurring losses because he cannot find a ready buyer.

Second, there is the question of knowledge and experience. Real estate investment in improved property is really a matter for professionals or those who have available time and are willing to devote it to their investment program. It involves the management and, often, the improvement of property. Expert help is not easily obtained, and even if it is, it still must be paid for—sometimes to the extent of leaving small profits to the owner.

Thus, the place of real estate in the estate creation structure for the part-time investor is as one element in an overall program. It is an opportunity which may bring long-term capital returns. But it is also an asset that must be supported by more liquidable properties such as insurance or securities and, if it is improved property, managed by someone with skill and experience.

THE FIRST REAL ESTATE INVESTMENT: THE HOME

A person's first venture into real estate, however, contradicts what we have just said. Since he must live somewhere, no matter what his stage in life is, he is going to be concerned very early in the game with at least a peripheral aspect of real estate investment—the purchase or the rental of a residence. Thus, at the beginning of the estate planner's program, when the "four firsts" are being established, your occupation, savings, life insurance, and residence—real estate investment questions enter into the picture.

Most people don't look at it this way. They place personal considerations above investment ones when they look for a place to live. We do not quarrel with this. Obviously, the personal factor is, and should be, paramount. But since buying a house usually represents one of the largest single purchases an individual makes during his life, he must also consider the investment aspects of the purchase. In fact, before buying a home he should, as an estate planner, weigh the advantages of ownership versus rental. Whichever road he chooses can have a long-term effect on his estate planning future.

To Rent or Buy?

Personal consideration aside, the question comes down to one of relative costs. Real estate agents will tell you that the person who pays monthly carrying charges of $400 for his home is better off than the one who pays the same $400 in rent because the home owner gets a tax deduction for the part that is taxes and interest, while the renter can't. Also, some part of that $400 is an amortization of the mortgage principal.

All well and good—if the $400 really represents the home owner's full cost. Too frequently, however, these blithe estimates overlook certain costs of home owning. There is commuting, the need to buy one or more automobiles, the purchase of larger amounts of furniture, and even with a new house, at least a certain amount of repairs, decoration, and land development. These are all real costs of home owning. And finally there is another hidden cost: the net income which the home owner could otherwise realize on the amount of capital invested in his home.

Or, in other words, the person who cannot decide which path to take—to rent or own—should calculate the true, not the supposed costs of his ownership. To do this he takes first his estimated annual home owning expenses; secondly, his capital investment in the house itself and its remodeling and improvements, prorated over a number of years, and the net income he loses by not investing this capital. He adds these together and then subtracts from this total sum the income tax savings from allowable deductions for taxes and interest. The figure he arrives at is his actual cost for home ownership.

Is it less than the rent he would have to pay for a comparable apartment? Then home ownership is cheaper for him. If it is higher, then renting may represent a better choice.

Home Ownership: Individual

If your decision is to buy, then you are making an investment. What should you look for from the investment point of view? What are the disadvantages and advantages of such ownership?

The limitations are clearly demarked. A house is not a liquidable asset. Depending on market considerations it may take a short or long period to find a buyer for a house. Generally speaking, it is not a short-term investment either. The costs of buying and selling, and the capital expenditures involved, need to be amortized over a long period of time before the investment becomes a worthwhile one. Look at your house as a good short-term investment only if you are able to buy it below the market value. If you buy at the market, then your costs of buying and selling will almost always end in a loss on the deal.

On the plus side, count in your mortgage as a definite advantage. It represents a systematic savings plan. The amortization is a repayment of a loan, but at the same time it is a method of capital accumulation. Part of each monthly payment to the mortgage holder increases the home owner's net worth. In addition, the interest paid on the mortgage is tax deductible, if the mortgage is on your principal residence or on one second residence and does not exceed the original cost of each of these residences plus the improvements on them.

The potential for increase in market value is another advantage. Depreciation notwithstanding, homes have in the recent past sold for more than the amount they were purchased at. The key factor in growth potential is location. Is the prospective house in an area that is growing—not static or on the decline? Is it situated near public transportation, schools, playgrounds, shopping areas? Is it in an area in which the houses are well built and of comparable or greater value? Are the streets and public services well-maintained? Is it close to major industrial or commercial centers of the area? All these factors make the location a good one and the growth potential similarly good.

If there is a gain when you sell your residence, you may be entitled to a tax exclusion on this gain. If you are 55 years of age or older, any gain up to $125,000 on the sale of your principal residence may be excluded from tax. This is a once-in-a-lifetime exclusion. Also, gain is not taxable on the sale or exchange of a principal residence to the extent it is used to purchase a new principal residence within 24 months before or after the sale.

Home Ownership:
The Cooperative Apartment

Individual home ownership is not the only possibility. Cooperative ownership has become increasingly popular. The lure of the cooperative apartment is that it seems to offer all the advantages of home owning, with none of the burdens. Is this really true? Let's take a look at the way a cooperative works.

In the cooperative arrangement a corporation builds or buys a building, then sells its shares together with a proprietary lease to each tenant. The tenant does not actually own his apartment. He is instead a shareholder and lessee. As such, he pays a share of the costs of operation, maintenance, repairs, taxes, mortgage, insurance, and other expenses for the whole building, and in addition decorates and maintains his own apartment. The tenants, as stockholders, elect the board of directors of the cooperative.

While annual costs vary widely from one cooperative to another, a cooperative apartment will usually cost less than a comparable rented apartment. Since the cooperative is a non-profit organization, there is no landlord's profit to be added to the rent. In addition, the cooperative owner gets the same tax deduction as the owner of a private home. The carrying charges paid by the tenant are applied partly to the amortization of the mortgage on the building and partly to his share of the mortgage interest and real estate taxes. Payments toward the amortization represent an increase in his equity interest. The mortgage interest and tax portion, which can run as high as 40 or 50 per cent, allows him considerable tax savings since they are deductible from federal and in some cases, state income taxes. However, mortgage interest is deductible only to the extent it is attributable to loans not exceeding the cost of the residence plus improvements.

Here, for instance, is a man in the 28 per cent tax bracket paying $7,200 rent annually. He has $20,000 to invest in a residence. If he puts it into securities, he will net, after taxes about $800 annually. Suppose, instead, that he buys an interest in a cooperative or a condominium with the $20,000. Let us say he pays $7,200 annual carrying charges on this. Often, $3,600 of this amount will be deductible for his share of interest and taxes. This would mean a savings for him of $1,000 annually, or $200 more than he would realize renting and investing his $20,000.

Then, too, there is the fact that the cooperative or condominium owner has no maintenance and repair responsibility (these are taken over by a manager or management firm) and also that he is usually not personally liable on the bond and mortgage.

The picture is not entirely rosy, however. If real estate values decline, so will the value of the cooperative. Carrying charges are not fixed. They can rise as well as decrease. Moreover, if the tenant cannot meet the carrying charges, he may have to sell or sub-lease. If he is unable to find a buyer or lessee, then he must vacate the apartment and surrender his stock. This places a greater burden on the other tenants, since assessments will have to be increased to pick up the tab for the defaulting tenant. This can be a serious problem, as cooperative owners discovered in the thirties when many cooperatives snowballed their way to foreclosures.

Other disadvantages? The cooperative owner does not have the freedom of the sole owner. He is responsible for his own maintenance but he usually can't make alterations without the approval of the board of directors of the cooperative. His interest is also less marketable than a home because he can't sell or assign his apartment without the board's approval. And usually he cannot assign his stock as security for a loan. Thus, he cannot use this asset as a collateral security.

Home Ownership:
The Condominium

This is a popular new type of ownership which is also cooperative but has certain advantages over the original type. The condominium owner actually owns his own apartment; he is taxed on it as a separate entity, and he can mortgage it. He also owns the common parts of the building (halls, land, stairways) jointly with the other owners, and pays a proportionate carrying charge for these facilities.

Unlike the cooperative owner, the condominium owner usually has the right to sell the apartment, although here, too, he may need consent or may have to offer it first to the other owners. He is responsible for the taxes and mortgage on his own apartment, and if he defaults in the payment of these, his interest may be foreclosed. The other owners' apartments are not substantially affected, however. There is also more mortgage money available to the condominium since each apartment is considered a separate private home. Mortgages on homes are available up to 90 per cent of their value while those on cooperative buildings usually do not exceed 75 per cent, if any.

TRUE REAL ESTATE INVESTMENT

Home ownership is only a peripheral form of real estate investment, of course. True real estate investment implies investment for investment's sake. It can take many forms. Let's take a brief look at the two major areas of opportunity: unimproved and improved real estate.

Unimproved Real Estate

As an investor in unimproved real estate, i.e., in vacant land, you are not buying the property for the purpose of improving it but for its own sake. You get no income from it, and except for the deduction for mortgage interest and taxes, realize no tax savings (since land is not a depreciable asset). You are conducting a holding operation, betting on the possibility that the land will increase in value over a short or long period of time. This is risk investment and usually it is long-term investment. It is commodity bought for the purpose of resale.

Whether it is to be famine or fortune depends again on that hallmark of real estate investment, location and the movement of the real estate market. With hindsight we can see what Mr. Astor saw in Manhattan. With foresight, today's investor can select locations which offer—if not the same prospects—quite favorable ones.

The wise investor of today looks to the patterns of living

and the movements of people to find the favorable locations. Our population is moving to the West and the Southwest. With the growth of industrial areas in these states, real estate is going to increase in value there. But there is still potentially valuable vacant land in the highly populated areas of the Northeast, and other built-up areas, as the boundaries of suburbia widen and what was once open country becomes a part of the metropolitan center.

With the growth of leisure time, the need for recreation and vacation areas steadily increases. Vacant land at the beaches, lakes, or in winter sport areas becomes valuable as people go farther and farther from the cities to find space. The rise in popularity of a single sport, such as skiing, can make land acquisition in hitherto desolate areas a valuable property. Property in sparsely populated resort areas has an additional advantage. Taxes are low since the community does not have to provide schools, fire protection, roads and public buildings. The investor can afford to wait.

Improved Real Estate

Investment in improved real estate—whether it is a parking lot or a large office building—involves two major considerations: how to manage the property and how to finance its purchase. Later on, we will be going into the management problem in connection with various types of real estate ownership. At this juncture, let's examine only the financing situation.

The usual method is through mortgages; they play an important role in making these investments attractive. First of all, the investor does not have to put up the full purchase price. Second, if the value of the property increases, the entire increase belongs to him. Here's Ms. Investor. She buys an apartment house for $200,000. She puts up $50,000 in cash, takes a mortgage for the rest. Later she sells the property for $250,000. That increase of $50,000 belongs to her. In other words, she realizes a gain of over 100 per cent on her original $50,000 investment, a gain made possible by the $150,000 mortgage.

Mortgage financing also means tax savings. The interest is fully tax deductible, thus reducing the cost of borrowing by the amount of tax savings.

Further, the depreciation allowance on the property means

additional tax savings. This is an important tax shelter. The depreciation is on the entire value, not just your equity. The tax-sophisticated investor looks for mortgage financing which provides a depreciation allowance in excess of his payments for amortization of the principal. Accelerated depreciation is a tax preference item and may be subject to the 21 per cent alternative minimum tax. Except for this, he is using tax-free income to pay off his mortgage. In effect, he increases his equity in the property with untaxed income from the property. However, he'll pay income tax on his gain when he sells.

OWNERSHIP: SOLE OR PARTICIPATING?

For the investor who has the time, the experience, the money, and the necessary skill, sole ownership of a real estate investment can be a worthwhile venture. But few part-time investors possess these attributes. For them the answer lies in some kind of participating interest. A number of opportunities are open.

Partnerships

Here is a typical investment situation. A person with a small amount of capital to invest wants to buy a small apartment building. He has sufficient capital to make the purchase. His problem, however, is management. Even a three-story apartment building requires continuing professional administration if he is to realize a good income from it. His solution is probably to join hands with a partner—someone he knows and trusts, and who has some capital and real estate experience. Pooling their capital and experience, the investment has a greater chance for success.

This is especially true where a fairly substantial investment is to be made. Here, a group of people with limited capital (including one experienced manager) can join forces. With their combined capital and available outside mortgage financing, profitable and productive opportunities can be developed. If you are interested in local real estate investment this method is highly effective. It has proved to be one of the more successful ways of entering the real estate investing field. It makes possible the establishment of a substantial fund for the investment; mortgage financing is usually available because of personal relationships between the participants and lending agencies; management is supplied by experienced personnel within the group itself on a low-cost owner-interested basis.

The Syndicate

The syndicate is the real estate market's equivalent of mutual funds. In essence, it is a partnership in which a large number of investors pool their funds for large-scale investment, a further development of the small partnership group. The investments can be limited to special types of real estate or to certain geographical areas. The syndicate might, for example, be set up specifically to seek high income or capital gain. On the other hand, syndicates can be widely diversified in type of operation or investment.

The investor in a syndicate owns a fractional share of the total syndicate investment. Usually he is a limited partner, not personally liable beyond his own interest for the debts and liabilities of the partnership.

Most syndicates are concerned only with single properties. Some, however, are more broadly based: these give the investor an opportunity to spread out his investments with a limited outlay.

There are other advantages too: high income return and income tax deductions for depreciation, mortgage interest, and real estate taxes are chief among them. As with individual real estate investments, if tax deductions exceed income, investors are allowed to deduct their proportionate share of any excess against their other income. However, the deduction for investment interest is limited to the amount of net investment income. Tax deductions are usually greater in the early years of the life of the syndicate, thereby increasing the actual yield. But even though they go down later, the gross income may increase as the mortgages are amortized.

Drawbacks? The same as for most real estate investments, that is to say, the problem of liquidity. When the syndicate is doing well, the investor usually has no difficulty in finding a buyer for his interest. In bad times, however, he may run into a good deal of trouble if he wants to liquidate.

Syndicate management offers some problems, too. The success of the enterprise depends on the managers. They are given a percentage of the profit as an incentive. But while this helps to ensure professional management, it can also take off a lot of cream at the top.

Very careful consideration should be given to the reputation and competence of the syndicators. Conflicts of interest between syndicators and the unit investors can occur. In some cases marginal properties have been syndicated at inflated values.

The Real Estate Corporation

The real estate corporation is similar in form to any other corporation. Its major business is the buying, selling, and ownership of real estate. Being a corporation, its income is subject to double taxation. The corporation is taxed first on its profit, and then the distributed dividend is taxed again in the hands of the stockholders.

This treatment tends to eat away much of the profit. Ordinarily this is a great drawback to the corporate form of organization. The rule doesn't always apply to the real estate corporation, however. Since its assets are in real estate, it has large deductions for depreciation which, together with real estate taxes, interest, and operating expenses, can reduce the tax bite. Its taxable income is lessened or offset by these deductions so that it may end up with no taxable earnings or profits, or even have a loss for tax purposes. Since distributions to stockholders are taxable dividends only if the corporation has earnings and profits, if there are none, payments to stockholders are not considered dividends, but a return of capital. This reduces the basis of their stock; on later sale of the stock these distributions are, in effect, taxable income.

It sounds strange to say that investing in a corporation with tax losses can be profitable unless you realize that tax losses are a form of tax shelter. A corporation is allowed to carry its excess losses forward (and back), and thus reduce present and future earnings for tax purposes.

Added point: the real estate corporation is one of the few types of real estate investment which offsets to some extent the problem of lack of liquidity. Like other corporate stock, its stock is traded on exchanges and over the counter, and can readily be sold at the prevailing quoted prices.

Some real estate corporation stocks have recently been selling below their asset values. Their returns have been comparatively low, but one advantage they do have is that their values and returns will move with the general stock market trends, and thus act as an inflationary hedge. Remember, too, that with public issues in real estate corporations, the investor is often not so much concerned with the income return as he is with the potentiality they represent for capital appreciation.

Real Estate Investment Trusts

An REIT is a taxable corporation, trust, or association investing primarily in real estate and mortgages, which elects preferred tax treatment. It has the corporate features of limited liability, centralized management, continuity, and transferability of interests. It is managed by one or more directors or trustees for the benefit of the investors who are shareholders or beneficiaries. In order to qualify for its preferred tax treatment, there must be at least 100 persons holding a beneficial interest and five or fewer persons cannot own more than 50 per cent of the REIT. However, entities created after 1986 can have fewer than 100 shareholders.

The entity must distribute at least 95 per cent of its income. The income of the REIT which is distributed is only taxed once, as opposed to corporate income which is taxed first to the corporation and then to the stockholders.

This is all good, but not quite as good as the tax treatment given to the syndicate. The partners of the syndicate can use excess tax losses against their other income but the REIT's excess losses are not available to the beneficiaries or shareholders.

Master Limited Partnerships

This is a relative newcomer to the real estate investment scene, and is one of the few real estate packages that continue to have tax advantages after the 1986 Act. It is a hybrid that has characteristics of stocks, bonds, and traditional real estate investments. It is traded like a stock, has partial tax-exempt yields like those on municipal bonds, and is subject to depreciation benefits and appreciation of property values as with any other real estate deal.

The master Limited Partnership is a group ownership of specific collections of properties, such as a shopping center, an office building, a mobile home park, senior citizen residential complexes, etc. Once the package is put together, you can buy shares of the partnership and later sell them like stock. The yields in the form of dividends are generally quite reasonable, and are generally 50–60 per cent tax exempt. There are also depreciation benefits.

In real estate this investment is a unique phenomenon. Its sell-out capabilities offer you liquidity in what is traditionally a non-liquid investment. The danger in this, however, is that because real estate values can fluctuate, you may be tempted by a slow market to sell out and cut what appear to be losses before the property has a chance to reach or even exceed its project values. If you decide to hold onto the investment, you are in until the properties are sold—hopefully at appreciated values.

Mortgage-Backed Securities

Most people know these investments by their trading names, Ginny Maes, Fannie Maes, and Freddie Macs. What they represent are home mortgages that are purchased from various banks and then pooled. These are then resold in the form of shares in the pool to investors. The mortgages are guaranteed by agencies of the federal government, meaning that if a home owner defaults on his home loan, the federal agency guarantees continuing payment on the loan, and forecloses on the owner.

Earnings come from the interest rates charged on the mortgages, minus a management fee. For instance, if the interest rate on a mortgage was 9¾ per cent, the investor may be getting 9½ per cent with the ¼ per cent going to manage the pool.

A SPECIAL CONSIDERATION: WHERE TO GET ADVICE

The prospective real estate investor has some special problems. Expert advice and help are not freely available to him as they are in the securities market. There are no market letters; reliable and independent analysts are usually not available. Where does he go for help in selecting a property investment?

If he is to go it alone, his solution must be the real estate broker. He is undoubtedly the most informed person he can find. But when he goes to him for advice, he should remember that, like the stockbroker, this broker is not a disinterested party; his object is, after all, to sell real estate. The best course is to seek out a well-established broker, one who enjoys a good reputation, get submissions on property within a selected type and financial range, and then ask your lawyer or accountant to review them.

If the investor is to participate in syndicates or trusts, then the information has to come from prospectuses and offering bulletins. Unless you have an expert ability to assess this type of literature, we would recommend you have an experienced real estate broker or perhaps your banker or attorney review it for you.

LOOKING AHEAD

The past two decades have been a time of boom in real estate. The growth of cities, the increase in our population, the expansion of industry, and the increase in private housing have sent real estate prices soaring. Few equities, not even the much publicized growth stocks, have increased in value at the same rate as real estate.

What is the outlook for the next decade? No one can tell with any certainty whether this boom will continue or begin tapering off. One thing is certain. Real estate values have always been tied to the movement of the general economy. If our economy in the long run continues to be prosperous and to expand, then real estate will reflect the gains our economy makes.

The estate planner's role is to make long-term judgments and assessments which evaluate the permanent character of various types of investments, not their cyclical fluctuations. Viewed in this manner, real estate well selected and managed will continue to be a form of investment which can yield high income and capital returns.

CHAPTER 9

The Day the Work Stops: Disability and Retirement

If you are 35 now, you have just about a 3 to 1 chance that you will live to 65. If you reach that age, you can add almost 17 more years to your life expectancy—17 years, probably, of retirement from your active earning career.

But if you are 35 now, there is also a 1 to 3 chance that you will at some time in your life become disabled for a period of 3 months or more. Moreover, the chance that you will have a long-term disability before 65 is greater than the likelihood that you will die before that age.

Does your estate plan take any of these events, fortunate or unfortunate, into account?

DISABILITY

A young executive whom we know is an indefatigable do-it-yourselfer around the house. Independent, strong, and somewhat self-willed, he has a tendency to take on jobs that are too much for him. One time, he decided to install a 300-pound staircase to an upper terrace. He hoisted the staircase onto a 2 by 4, and then onto his shoulders. In the process the staircase tipped and fell, missing his back by a fraction of an inch.

This near disaster had a sobering effect on him. He stopped his work and went inside and had a beer. His hands were trembling so that he could hardly open the beer can. What unnerved him so, he said later, was the thought, not that he might have been killed, but that he might very easily have been disabled for life.

As he sipped his beer and gazed out the window, contemplating the fallen staircase, he realized that he didn't even have the faintest idea what kind of income, if any, he could expect if he ever became permanently disabled. Did his life insurance cover disability? Were there any company benefits—after all, he'd been working on his own time, not the boss's. Would the government give him anything? If he got anything out of these sources, would it be for life or just for a short period of time? What on earth, he wondered, happened to people who had accidents of this sort?

Mr. Do-It-Yourself was not alone in his quandary. Most people today have no more than a vague notion of what kind of protection is available to them if they become disabled either through sickness or an accident. They don't know that there are different meanings of disability as the law or various agreements define it. They are at a loss as to what kind and what amount of protection to buy—that is, if they think about buying any at all.

All of this represents a serious default in estate planning. Disability, while not inevitable, is certainly a possibility.

Mr. Do-It-Yourself had an unusual experience that dramatically illustrated this, but the fact is that the possibility of disability looms in the foreground for everyone. What's more as life expectancy increases, so do the chances of contracting debilitating diseases which maim but do not kill.

Planning for support to cover disability, then, is just as much a necessity as planning for support to protect one's family at death or for a retirement income.

The Disability Picture:
What Is It?
Who Gets Protection?

The Estate Planning Worksheets will help you analyze the income which you can expect if you become disabled. It is probable that the disability income column will be the one which shows the greatest gap between what will be available as against what you will need. You will undoubtedly find that you are covered by some type of government or employment disability program. But will this be enough? Will it, together with unearned income from all other sources, be sufficient to support your family for an extended period of disability?

The answer will depend on the type and amount of coverage you have. What will be the amount of the payments? After what length of disability does it begin? How long does it last? What type of disability does it cover?

Only when these questions are answered is the true disability-income picture revealed, and the directions of its improvement indicated.

If you think of disability as an inability to work, caused by an accident or sickness, that's simple enough. But the plans or laws providing coverage include a number of variations within that meaning. Some define disability as an inability to do any kind of work at all. Some broaden it to cover an inability to work at your regular occupation. Some limit the definition to an impairment which is "reasonably certain" to last for life; others to one which is merely "expected to continue indefinitely." Some will give you coverage for a limited period of time, others permanently.

The point is to know what you can expect and from what sources.

Source Number One: Federal and State Governments. There are five prime sources of government protection against disability—state workmen's compensation, state sickness disability, social security, veteran's benefits, and government insurance policies for people in the armed forces or veterans.

Most of these will not provide anyone with more than a subsistence level of support, and some of them are limited to those with low incomes. Nevertheless, it's as well to know just what you can expect for them—for you must take them into account in your disability estate planning.

WORKMEN'S COMPENSATION—STATE: This is limited to accidents or diseases that occur as a result of your job. Generally it provides benefits to compensate for your loss of earning power. The compensation is awarded by a board or hearing officer and is based on the extent of the disability, its estimated duration, and incurred medical expenses.

SICKNESS DISABILITY—STATE: A few states also have compulsory coverage for disabilities that occur as a result of non-occupational injuries and sicknesses. Under the New York State disability law, for example, a worker is entitled to a monthly allowance if he is unable to perform the regular duties of his employment or any other employment at his regular wage. He receives an amount equal to one-half his average weekly wage up to a maximum of $145 per week, for a maximum period of 26 weeks. This is really coverage for a short-term disability, and although $145 per week isn't enough for support, it is of some help to the person who has a savings account reserved for just such an emergency.

SOCIAL SECURITY DISABILITY BENEFITS—FEDERAL: You can get a monthly allowance for a long-term disability under liberalized provisions of the Social Security Law. Previously, there was a minimum age limitation, which has now been completely removed. To be eligible, you must have been covered by social security for varying periods, depending on your age, before you become disabled. Lesser periods of coverage are required if you are blind.

There is a five-month waiting period before benefits are available, but they continue as long as the disability does. The monthly allowance is based on average monthly earnings and is the same as the amount which you would receive as old age benefits at age 65. There is a dependency allowance for unmarried children under 19 who are attending school full-time, and totally disabled children over 18 who become disabled before that age. There is also one for a spouse of any age if she has children in her care who are eligible for dependents' benefits, as well as for a spouse 62 years old or older.

The protection is designed for long-term disabilities. The law defines disability here as an illness or injury so severe as to make the applicant unable "to engage in any substantially gainful" occupation for a long and indefinite time.

VETERAN'S BENEFITS—FEDERAL: These are important, because so many people may qualify for them.

If your disability is service-connected, you are entitled to a compensation either from the Veterans Administration or from your branch of the service. You can get this no matter what your income is. Amounts for a disability whether wartime or peace time vary from $69 per month to $1,355, depending on the degree of disability, with specific rates to $2,360 in severe cases. If the disability is rated 30 per cent or more, there is an additional allowance for dependents.

If your disability is not service-connected, you can get a pension, provided your income is not above $5,963 (for a single person with no dependents) or $8,562 (a married person with dependents).

If you already get social security disability benefits, you still qualify for the service-connected compensation, but if it is non-service-connected, your social security above what you paid in will be counted as part of your income, and therefore may affect your eligibility.

G.I. INSURANCE—FEDERAL: There are two types, United States Government Life Insurance policies for those who served before World War II and National Service Life Insurance for those who served during and after World War II.

If you carry USGLI, you can get payment for a total and permanent disability that keeps you from working in "any substantially gainful" occupation and that seems "reasonably certain" to continue for life. The proceeds will be paid out in monthly installments of $10 per $1,000 of coverage for the duration of your disability. If you die before 240 installments have been paid out, the balance is paid out as death proceeds.

Does your policy have a Total Disability Income Provision? If it does and you incur a total (but not necessarily a permanent) disability before you are 65, you will get $10 per month for each $1,000 of insurance in force. These payments do not reduce the amount of the insurance.

If you carry National Service Life Insurance, your benefits are somewhat different. These policies provide for a waiver of premiums if you become totally disabled before the age of 65. This doesn't give you any income, of course, but it does remove the burden of keeping up the life insurance premium payments.

NSLI also has an extra premium provision which gives you disability income payments. It's for total disability prior to age 65 (defined here as the inability to follow "any substantially gainful" occupation without injuring your health). It provides for $10 a month for every $1,000 of insurance in force. Payments do not reduce the amount of your insurance.

You can see what this melange of government benefits add up to. They provide only a minimum income, unquestionably, not sufficient to meet the support needs of your family. For that, we must turn to other sources of disability income.

Source Number Two: Your Occupation. For the corporate

executive, his job offers other opportunities for disability protection, most of them available in the corporate compensation package.

VOLUNTARY EMPLOYER AID: Generally employers will continue an employee's salary for a period of time during disability. Others will supplement existing disability payments which are paid by state or federal governments. But since such employer aid is not required by law or an employment contract, it is apt to be short-lived. Most such benefits are limited to a short-term salary continuation, usually for a few months, or at most, a year.

GROUP HEALTH INSURANCE: Depending on the type of program your company offers, you are likely to find that your group health plan covers all or part of your hospital expenses and your medical and surgical care. Some plans also include disability income provisions which pay a percentage of salary. For example, a policy might pay monthly benefits of 75 per cent of salary for the first year of disability, 50 per cent for the next 2 years, and 25 per cent from then on. Another type of policy pays a straight 50 per cent of salary for 20 years or until age 65.

What about taxes on these disability benefits? Often it may be possible to avoid any income taxation at all.

Thus:

1. If the employee pays the premiums, there are no taxes on the benefits.

2. If the employer pays the premiums, the premiums aren't taxable to the employee, but the benefits are. However, the exceptions are very broad. Thus, there is no income tax to be paid on benefits which reimburse an employee's actual medical expenses or on payments based on certain types of illnesses or injuries such as the loss of a limb.

3. There is a maximum 15 per cent annual tax credit on $5,000 of income for a person 65 or over, or under 65 who is retired and permanently and totally disabled. This amount is reduced dollar for dollar by his adjusted gross income in excess of $7,500.

PROFIT-SHARING PLANS: Disability income provisions are often included in these qualified plans. They may take the form of a payout in weekly installments. They can, however, provide for a lump sum distribution of the vested account. If paid out in a lump sum, then the distribution receives special income tax treatment (see page 49).

PENSION PLANS: Some pension plans pay out retirement funds if the disability is "permanent and total." Payout plans vary. They are usually connected in some way to the vested pension rights which have accrued before the disability. Some of them reduce payments if you are getting social security or state disability benefits. Other plans, however, separate disability benefits from retirement funds, and the amounts bear no relation to each other. This can be advantageous, for in some of these plans both retirement and disability benefits are paid. The same tax treatment applies as in the profit-sharing payouts.

SELF-EMPLOYMENT RETIREMENT PLANS: Under the retirement act for the self-employed, funds can be withdrawn upon disability. The withdrawals will be taxed in the same way as retirement distributions.

Source Number Three: Your Own Plan. After you determine what you will receive from all sources for disability, as well as all sources of other unearned income, you may find that additional income will be needed. Except in rare cases, some form of additional disability insurance protection is required—particularly in younger years when the estate has yet to be created.

Disability insurance policies vary widely. You should know precisely what you are getting, and be aware of the many nuances, exceptions, and definitions contained within these policies. Your support will be affected by such details if you ever become disabled.

INDIVIDUAL DISABILITY INSURANCE: This can be a separate policy, or a rider to your regular insurance. In either case, since policies vary greatly from company to company, you should be sure to compare the following key points:

1. What type of disability is covered, total, or partial, or both?

2. How does the policy define disability? Some policies consider it to be an inability to perform the duties of your regular occupation; some say it's inability to work at any occupation; some define it as the inability to work in any gainful occupation for which you might be considered "reasonably fitted" by education, training, or experience. Still

others combine one or more aspects of these various definitions.

3. What is the "elimination period"? Will you start getting benefits immediately, or is there a period of waiting before they begin coming in?

4. What is the duration? Will you get them for 1 year, 5 years, or until you reach 65? (Few policies pay out for life except in cases of disability caused by an accident.)

5. Is there a cancellation clause? Can the insurance company cancel at will? If there is such a clause, the company can terminate your policy, or refuse to renew it, or increase the premium rate.

6. Is there a waiver of premiums during the period the monthly indemnity is being paid?

7. Can the company increase or reduce the monthly indemnity payments during the "guaranteed renewable" period?

8. Is there aviation coverage?

9. Must you be confined to your house in order to qualify for disability payments?

10. Is there a liberal "recurrent disability" clause?

GROUP DISABILITY INCOME INSURANCE: We are not referring to corporate group insurance but to insurance offered by many associations to their members. This type is common, for example, among county or state medical and bar associations as well as other professional groups. The premiums are lower than individual coverage, and it continues so long as you remain a member of the group and meet the age requirements. Don't substitute it for individual insurance, however. The insurance company, as well as the group, can terminate the policy at any time.

DISABILITY EXPENSES POLICY: Are you a self-employed professional or an independent proprietor? Then you might consider this kind of insurance. It covers your overhead expenses while you are disabled, paying up to a stated amount a week for validated expenses. However, this kind of policy is not common; the premiums are quite expensive.

WAIVER OF PREMIUM ON LIFE INSURANCE: During a period of disability, all fixed obligations should be reduced to a minimum. You should therefore consider having waiver of premium riders added to your life insurance policies. It is precisely during the period of illness when the need for the life insurance protection may be greatest that the funds for continuing the policies may not be available. We have always felt that the small extra premium to buy this rider represents a worthwhile investment.

RETIREMENT

Disability is a misfortune. It has to be planned for, but one hopes that it will never come about. Retirement is different. By all rights it should be viewed as the goal toward which one works, the fulfillment of an active life, a time when serenity replaces struggle, and aspirations give way to contemplation.

Frankly, there seem to be fewer people in this day and age who look at retirement as a time of good fortune. For a variety of reasons—some self-engendered, some inbred in the society itself—to the average person, particularly the average *successful* person, the thought of retirement is distasteful. The very word conjures up stereotype images which do not fit into the pattern of American life—the oldster in the rocking chair (useless and inactive), the determinedly cheerful white-haired couple in their little garden (lonely and isolated), the spectacled grandma by the telephone (unwanted and dependent).

"Not for me," says the successful person of today. "I'd rather die with my boots on."

This may be a laudable ambition, but chances of it being realized are slim. If you work for a large corporation, your retirement at age 70 is usually mandatory. If you are self-employed or an independent professional, you are going to find the demands of your work too great a physical strain in your later years. Like it or not, retirement is a fact of modern life. Far better to accept it and plan for it.

Personal Planning

The plan should be both personal and financial. By personal, we mean deliberately preparing yourself psychologically for your inevitable retirement. This can mean all sorts of things—preparations for continued work of some sort, either as a part-time worker in your field, or perhaps in a "second business" which you have built up during your active working years; decisions on where and how to live; most important, the building up of a backlog of interests, hobbies, and lifetime purposes which can enrich your mind and occupy you fruitfully in your later years.

This is where most people fall down, incidentally, a default of personal planning, which can be just as serious as the financial default we have been stressing so much. The high rate of heart attacks and disease among the retired is no accident, according to American Medical Association studies; it is a direct result of an inability to readjust to life in retirement, a psychological blow which takes its physical toll.

Financial Planning

Let's return for a moment to the Worksheets in the Appendix. There are three income columns which need to be filled in, if you remember: your family's income after your death; your own and your family's needs in the event you are disabled; and when you retire.

We are concerned now with the column dealing with your retirement financial needs. How can this be calculated? It takes a bit of figuring and planning. Assuming you are 65 at retirement and that your children are grown up, married, and on their own, presumably your income can be smaller.

But how much smaller? There is the standard of living to be considered. People who have been accustomed to a comfortable mode of life for many years find it especially hard to adjust. It may be more difficult for them to lower their standard of living than it is for the young and adventurous person. Then there are the physical problems. Comfort isn't just a psychological matter; it's also physical. Substandard or cramped housing, rigorous weather, lack of domestic help—all this takes a physical toll on the elderly person. You may have additional problems as well—needy grandchildren, indigent relatives, a retarded or handicapped adult child of your own who will need your support for the rest of his life.

What does it all add up to? Only you can know that. Suffice it to say that you should make sure you do know as early as possible in your working life. The sooner you begin to plan for retirement, the better.

Sources of Retirement Income

There are four main ones—social security, corporate employment plans, commercial plans, and your personal capital.

Social Security. National elections were fought on this issue 48 years ago and will be again in the coming years. Today social security remains one of our country's most famous social welfare laws. Here are some of the main things you, as an estate planner, should know about it.

WHO IS COVERED BY SOCIAL SECURITY? Almost all employed and self-employed persons are covered for old age benefits. The only major exceptions are federal employees, who are covered by a federal retirement system.

WHAT DOES SOCIAL SECURITY PROVIDE FOR? Basically, it provides a monthly retirement income for a person over 65 who has received social security credit for the required number of quarters; or a reduced amount from age 62. A dependent spouse is also entitled to benefits, even though he has never worked, if he is 62 or older; or at any age, if he is caring for a child eligible for dependents' benefits. A widow or widower age 60 or over is also entitlted to benefits. There are also additional allowances for unmarried children under 18, over 18, if they are disabled, or full-time students between 18 and 19, or surviving dependent parents at age 62.

HOW ARE THE AMOUNTS DETERMINED? Retirees get a fixed amount, depending on their average yearly earnings before retirement. A spouse gets one-half the worker's benefits.

SHOULD A WIFE WAIT UNTIL SHE IS 65 TO CLAIM BENEFITS? This question usually arises because wives are generally a few years younger than their husbands. Which is better? Claim benefits when the wife reaches 62, or wait 3 years in order to get the higher rate?

I'd say the first, because of the simple mathematics of the situation. A wife entitled to the maximum wife's benefit at 62 will get $69.50 less per month than if she waits until she is 65. But during the 3 years between 62 and 65, she will accumulate a total of $10,818. In order to equal or exceed that amount of income at the higher rate, she will have to live just about 13 years after 65.

CAN I STILL EARN MONEY AND GET SOCIAL SECURITY? If you are over 70, yes, any amount of earnings. Between 62 and 70, however, you must sacrifice social security benefits if you earn over certain prescribed amounts annually. Under current rules you lose $1 of benefits for every $2 you earn over $7,800 if you are 65 or over or earn over $5,670 if you are under 65. Losing social security dollars for earned dollars is not always wise since benefit dollars are tax-free.

There is one important exception about earnings, however. You can still qualify for social security benefits in any month in which you don't earn wages of over the amount of your monthly social security benefit or perform substantial services in self-employment during the calendar year in which you start drawing your benefits. After the first year, however, you are back to the general rule which covers loss of benefits when earnings are in excess of the annual allowable limits as described in the previous paragraph.

A word of advice: in order to get full benefits, it is necessary that your social security records be complete and correct. It is therefore important that you check your account to make certain all contributions in your behalf have been fully credited to you and that your qualifying periods have been correctly adjusted. You can get a record of your account and have any questions on social security answered by writing to Social Security Administration, P.O. Box 57, Baltimore, Maryland.

Corporate Employment Plans. A lot has already been said in this book about the retirement aspects of these plans. Let us only add that such things are deferred compensation agreements and qualified retirement plans should prove the *bulk* of retirement funds for the corporate executive. The person who bargains well and wisely for these should have no difficulty with retirement income.

You can depend upon your payments from a pension plan because the amount is actuarially determined. The payout on a deferred compensation agreement is normally a set amount and depending upon the solvency of the corporation can also be relied upon.

But profit-sharing plans and stock benefits, while important and usually reliable, cannot be counted upon to provide a fixed income. You can only estimate how much these will eventually bring in. Time and the economic cycle have a way of altering your estimate radically. There may be no profit for the corporation to contribute into the plan. The plan's investments, as well as the stock of a corporation, may also decline in value and in their ability to produce income.

The method of payout, however, is in any case an important factor in retirement planning. The plans usually offer a lump sum or a variety of installment payments. The means you select will depend on your own retirement picture. For example, how many and what dependents you will have to support; and important, how to receive the income so as to minimize erosion from income as well as estate taxes. The proceeds, for instance, may be rolled over in an IRA to defer taxation until later withdrawal. It's best to make these decisions before you retire. If you leave it to the last minute, you may find there are limitations on your choice.

Self-employed Retirement Plans. In Chapter 6, we dealt with the tax shelter and retirement opportunities of these plans. Here, however, we want to emphasize that the withdrawal of the retirement fund should be made in the years of your lowest income. This is so because the taxable portion of this payout will be subject to income taxes at your bracket. It is especially so if you make a lump sum withdrawal of the entire fund because the same tax treatment (capital gains phasing out and 5-year averaging) accorded the corporate employer is also available to the self-employed retiree.

Commercial Sources of Retirement Income

1. *Annuities and retirement income insurance* offer a guaranteed annual income from the time you retire to the day you die. This income represents both interest and a return of principal; its unique aspect is that the principal is never used up while you live but continues to provide income to you for as long as you live.

Thus annuities function chiefly as an alternate or substitute for personal investment which frequently cannot offer the same security. Suppose, for example, that after age 65 you find that your income from investment and/or other resources isn't enough to support you. You begin to use up your principal. But how can you be sure that this principal will last all your life? You may live past your life expectancy and outlive your capital. The risk as to how long you will live is something you cannot afford to take. If you buy an annuity policy, the insurance company takes that risk for you.

You can buy one of several types of annuities. If you want to guarantee security for your spouse as well as yourself, you might consider the *joint and survivor* annuity. This pays income to you during your life, and when you die, the income is continued for your spouse for the rest of her life.

Or there is a *period certain annuity*. This pays income for your lifetime but also guarantees payments for a minimum period of time, usually 10 or 20 years. Thus, if you die before the period is up, your beneficiary gets the fixed income payments for the balance of the period. Your return is a little less, but you are not running the risk that your early death will cause a complete loss of the annuity fund.

Even if you have sufficient retirement income from investment sources, it's a good idea to consider putting some of your assets in annuities. The security they offer is psychological as well as economic. You are relieved of the strain and effort that an investment program involves. Beyond this, a program that balances annuities with growth stocks operates as a hedge against unpredictable changes in the economy. The stocks are there to meet an inflationary trend; the annuities, a possible deflationary situation.

Retirement income policies (already discussed in Chapter 3) combine annuities with life insurance. If you die, your beneficiary gets the face amount of the policy. If you live, to retirement, you have the advantage of an annuity for yourself.

2. *Ordinary life insurance* can be used for retirement purposes. Let's assume that on retirement age, you find you don't need all the insurance coverage you had previously carried. Most policies contain annuity options for the payout of the cash values. This right to convert to an annuity is an extremely valuable one. The annuity rate used is based on the one in effect at the time you bought the insurance and is included as a provision of your policy. Since life expectancies have increased, you'll get a better return by converting than if you bought a new annuity at the time of retirement.

3. *Endowment insurance* is a classic example of life insurance that can be used for retirement purposes. If you die before the time of endowment, the face amount of the policy will be paid out as a death benefit. If you survive to the time of endowment, the amount is paid to you in a lump sum, or it can be paid out as a retirement fund.

A point to remember about endowment policies: be sure to select the right endowment time. If you make it too early, you may find yourself coming into the retirement fund before you have actually retired, and thus be adding additional income to earned income, with a consequent increase in taxes.

Personal Investments

If over a term of years you have followed a systematic program of personal investments, by the time you retire, you should theoretically have accumulated a substantial amount of capital—enough to produce income for you during your retirement. That is the significance of investment income. It takes over for you when you are no longer an active earner.

When you reach retirement, however, you should take a fresh look at your investment pattern. You may find that the time has come to alter it. If, for example, you have used your investments for capital growth, you may want now to switch to safe, fixed-income investments. On the other hand, if you own annuity policies or other fixed-return investments, then perhaps you will want to put a part of your assets in growth stocks. Or perhaps you were heavy in tax-free bonds during your high-earning, high-tax years. Now that you are in a lower income bracket, you may want to choose higher income producing securities. In any event, this is the time to get together with your financial adviser for a complete reappraisal of your financial portfolio.

A LAST WORD ON RETIREMENT: DECIDING WHERE TO LIVE

Change of residence is common among retired people. Many of them move to the warmer, retirement states of California, Arizona and Florida. Before you join the trek, however, you should check on the various estate and income tax situations in each of these states. If your estate is sizable, the tax situation can make quite a difference.

ARIZONA: The income tax goes up to 8 per cent on net income in excess of $7,000. The estate tax, however, is relatively low, beginning at four-fifths of 1 per cent on the first $40,000 of the net estate. There is a maximum rate of 16 per cent on any amount over $10 million.

CALIFORNIA: The income tax goes as high as 11 per cent on net income above $14,400. The estate tax is equal to the maximum credit for state death taxes under federal estate tax law as discussed above.

FLORIDA: There is no income tax and no estate tax. The federal estate tax allows a credit for death taxes paid or to be paid to a state, according to a schedule. Florida will receive the amount of this credit as the death tax due to it. There is, however, a tax of 0.001 per cent on the value of the intangible property (stocks and bonds) that you may own.

PART TWO

Conserving and Transferring Your Estate

CHAPTER 10

Estate Transference: The Problem and the Goals

In 1962, Robert S. Kerr, United States Senator and former governor of the state of Oklahoma, died. The Senator was not only a zealous and determined public official; he was, while alive, a zealous and determined estate builder. During his lifetime he put together an estate which has been estimated at somewhere between $35 and $50 million.

At the time of his death, Senator Kerr had been discussing the making of a new will with his attorneys. One had even been drawn for him but was not executed. The old one, made in 1939, was obviously outdated. It failed to take advantage of the important tax savings offerd by a law passed in 1948—the estate tax marital deduction. As a result, the taxes on his estate could be $25 million if his estate proved to be $35 million—almost $37 million if it turned out to be $50 million.

Because the Senator, like many other successful and hard-working people, pressed from every side by demands on his time, never did get around to revising his will, it stood as his instrument of transfer.

With a will using the marital deduction, estate taxes of from $13 million to $19 million could have been saved. In fact, the utilization of a variety of techniques—lifetime gifts combined with charitable bequests and the full use of the marital deduction—could have resulted in even greater tax savings and possibly an estate transfer without any taxation at all.

This story is a dramatic illustration of the need to keep a will up-to-date. But it is more than that; it illustrates one of the basic laws of estate planning. When you have created an estate, you have completed only half of the job. Unless the creation is accompanied by a well-designed plan of transfer, much of what you have so painstakingly built up runs the danger of being dissipated, and with it the goals and objectives you have sought to achieve.

ESTATE CONSERVATION

A person plants a stand of trees. His idea is to eventually build for himself a nursery which will be a going business. The trees are his resources that supply the business with its product. When they reach maturity the nursery is completed, but his work is not. Now he must preserve and maintain those trees, and allow for their future growth as well. It is the job of a lifetime, of several lifetimes if the nursery is to continue. This is what we mean by conservation.

Conservation—the preservation of what you have—is an indispensable element of estate transfer, indeed almost a synonym for it. Substitute the capital that makes up your estate for the trees that make up the nursery and you see its relation to the transfer program. If you want to conserve your family resources for the future use and benefit of your beneficiaries, then you must find ways to prevent erosion of these resources, just as you would have to find methods of halting soil erosion in your forest.

THE PROBLEM OF EROSION

Halting erosion is indeed an important problem which faces the estate planner in this second phase of his program. Its threat is omnipresent throughout the estate building process, but is most likely to happen at the time of transfer of resources, when the estate owner passes all or some of his property on to his beneficiaries, usually his spouse, children, grandchildren, or parents.

The agents of erosion are several. There are the costs of transfer and administration; the liquidation losses which occur when assets have to be sold to meet the need for cash to pay estate costs. Then there is poor management, a personal factor which can dissipate capital just as surely as taxes and estate costs can. And finally there is taxation—usually the most powerful and vigorous erosive force. In property transfer it is estate taxation primarily, but gift and income taxation play their parts as well.

Tax erosion is not inevitable. It can be enormous, sizable, minimal, even non-existent, depending entirely on the methods you use to transfer your property and the modes of ownership you set up for it. There is a great variety of these methods available to you, so many in fact that the choices presented sometimes seem to resemble a labyrinth. The job of finding your own right path through the labyrinth is tedious and challenging but the stakes are large; the outcome is of great personal and financial importance to every estate planner.

In the course of the second half of this book, we will discuss the ways of reducing erosion and of achieving estate objectives. We will explore the concept of lifetime giving, examine the living trust, see how to minimize taxes, set forth the principles of charitable giving, point up the need for a will, and explain how to assess your estate in order to make that will. Finally, we will look at the question of estate management: how to choose the people for this job and how to find the experts who will help you plan your transfer.

ANALYZING YOUR OBJECTIVES

Do you remember the definition of estate planning set forth in the beginning of this book?

"The creation, conservation, and utilization of family resources to obtain the maximum support and security for the family during the lifetime and after the death of the planner."

These goals—family support and security—are basic objectives of practically every estate plan. They operate just as strongly in the conservation and transfer phase of the planning as they do in the creation. In that earlier phase the struggle to achieve these objectives, while dynamic and challenging, was a comparatively short-term one. Now the character of the problem changes. It is long-term; its impact reaches out beyond the span of an individual life and covers future generations. Now you are planning for the happiness of your family, not only in the present but in the future.

PLANNING FOR YOUR BENEFICIARIES

When you begin to plot your transfer program you must think of the specific people who will receive your property. You will have to assess their needs, both future and present; determine whether this person or that one can handle property; predict as well as you can what problem may crop up in his life that you would want to prepare them for or help them cope with. How else can you make a fair distribution or decide who gets what, and how?

Your children, for example. The needs of an adult child are different from those of a younger one. So are those of a handicapped child versus an able one. One child has different abilities and capabilities than another; one has different needs and desires. All this will have to be taken into account when your distribution pattern is charted.

When you come to your spouse—the person who you probably think of as the focal point of concern in your transfer plan—you must think in terms of the meaning of widowhood, of the problems and situations your spouse will encounter. Does a man subject his wife to the bewildering details which administration of property often involves if she has had no experience with it? Does he cast her into a position where she will be in conflict with her own children over the distribution of that property? Or perhaps at odds with and defenseless against his former business associates? Does he want to involve her in situations where relatives, his or her own, make continuous financial demands on her?

Your goal in this case is not only your spouse's financial security; it is also her peace of mind. This, too, you can help create for her by proper methods of transfer.

Finally, there are your other dependents. Somehow you must fit them into this fabric that you are to wave into a harmonious pattern. These can include your own parents, relatives, even people outside your family. Sometimes these people are forgotten in a transfer plan with unforeseen consequences. We remember a situation where a man who had been the sole support of his own elderly parents left his entire estate to his wife. The wife re-married. The man's son, with an already inadequate income, took over the entire burden of their support. Certainly the father never intended this to happen. Like so many people, he simply never conceived of the possibility that he would die before his parents.

To all, or nearly all, of these beneficiaries, you have another responsibility too; the responsibility to educate them to handle their property during your life and after your death. Family education is essential to the success of both property conservation and transfer. Property is inanimate; whether or not it grows, shrinks, is preserved, passed on, or is dissipated depends in large measure on the abilities of the people who administer and use it. When you are gone, this will be your family's task. It is up to you to see that they are prepared to assume it.

More than property values are at stake here. If human beings can affect the eventual fate of your property, remember that the opposite is also true. The money that you pass on can bring happiness to your family or it can bring disaster. It can build character and it can destroy it. If you transfer your assets in trust in such a way as to prevent your children from developing into responsible, stable adults, you may be setting the stage for unhappiness, helping to create dependent instead of self-sufficient people. On the other hand, if you transfer it so that your children are encouraged to take on responsibility and to use their money wisely, you are building the environment for their future well-being and maturity.

SECONDARY OBJECTIVES

Most people have other motives beyond the primary ones of security when they struggle for success, or work to accumulate capital. These may be called secondary objectives, motivations of the planner which are not family-oriented.

For some there is the hope of achieving personal immortality—the estate they leave behind them represents for them a concrete symbol of a lifetime of accomplishment. They may die, but their estate does not die with them. For others the building of the estate is motivated by an all-too-human ambition, the desire to attain power through the accumulation of capital.

What else? Family obligation and duty—the responsibility felt by many possessors of inherited wealth to pass on the estate intact to the next generation. Or business loyalty—

the desire of a person to make sure that his business and those who helped build it will not suffer on his death. The wish to help a good cause or a charity is another important objective. In fact, there are probably as many individual goals as there are individual planners.

The point: motive—both family and personal—is at the core of conservation and transfer. Behind all the legalities and the technicalities, it operates as a driving force. Determining your overall purpose is the first step in planning your estate transfer—and one that only you can take.

WHERE TO BEGIN

Like all elements of estate planning, conservation and transfer are continuous. They begin when your estate begins; end only when you die (and in a sense, not even then, for the conservation and transfer plan that you have structured will continue on after your death). But this point in your planning, the time when you assess what you have created and begin charting its future, is a particularly crucial one. As you marshal your assets and put them into place for orderly transfer, you are producing a master plan which (while it can be altered at many junctures and in many situations) will eventually control the financial lives of your family.

The Estate Planning Worksheets should be put to good use here. Working with them, the pattern of your estate and its transfer problems and potentialities become clear. Together with the general information contained in the following chapters, they should help you to set your house in order.

But where, specifically, to begin? With the first problem of estate conservation and transfer—understanding the new unified system of taxing lifetime gifts and transfers at death.

CHAPTER 11

The Unified Estate and Gift Tax and How It Works

QUESTIONS AND ANSWERS ON THE GIFT TAX

Prior to the Tax Reform Act of 1976, lifetime gifts were a way of transferring property to members of the family and saving substantial amounts in estate taxes. The gift tax law was very liberal. There was an annual exclusion of $3,000 per donee and we each had a lifetime exemption of $30,000 in addition to the annual exclusion, before any gift tax became payable. For every gift to a spouse, there was also a 50 per cent marital deduction. The gift tax rates were only three-fourths of the estate tax rates and moreover, the property was removed from the donor's top estate tax bracket and was taxed at the bottom rungs of the gift tax scale. With good planning, hundreds of thousands of dollars could be transferred with little or no tax.

When the donor died, except for gifts made within the last three years that were deemed to have been made in contemplation of death, the slate was wiped clean. The estate got a $60,000 exemption and a possible marital deduction of one-half the adjusted gross estate. The estate tax was applied to the balance.

Lifetime giving became such a widespread way of avoiding estate taxes that Congress decided do something about it. As of January 1, 1977, it set up a unified structure for taxing lifetime gifts and transfers at death. The reasoning behind it was that a person should pay the same tax whether he transferred his estate at death or before.

Congress decided not to tax small gifts and kept the

$3,000 annual exclusion. It replaced the former $30,000 gift tax and $60,000 estate tax exemptions with a unified credit, which was phased in from 1977 to 1981, when it reached $47,000 and was essentially equivalent to an exemption of $175,000.

Then came the "summer of '81." In the Economic Tax Recovery Act of 1981, Congress recognized the effects of inflation and tax bracket creep. It made sweeping changes in the estate and gift tax law but retained the unified structure for taxing them.

Let's look at the broad picture of the unified system of taxation of estates and gifts before getting into specifics.

As of January 1, 1982, the annual gift tax exclusion was increased to $10,000. This permits a person to give away as much as $10,000 a year to each of as many persons as he wishes without making a taxable gift ($20,000, if the spouse consents).

The unified credit was again increased to $192,800 which translates into an exemption equivalent to $600,000. So as to reduce the impact of the loss of revenue, Congress phased in the increase in the credit over a six-year period as follows:

For Transfer Made and Decedents Dying in	Unified Credit	Exemption Equivalent	Starting Tax Bracket on the Excess
1982	$ 62,800	$225,000	32%
1983	79,300	275,000	34
1984	96,300	325,000	34
1985	121,800	400,000	34
1986	155,800	500,000	37
1987 & after	192,800	600,000	37

The top tax brackets for estates and gifts was reduced from 70 per cent to 50 per cent and was phased in as follows:

For Transfers Made and Decedents Dying in	Top Tax Bracket	On Amounts in Excess of
1982	65%	$4,000,000
1983	60	3,500,000
1984–87	55	3,000,000
1988 & after	50	2,500,000

No gift tax is payable until the credit is used up. The gift tax is cumulative. Prior gifts are added to current ones in figuring the credit used and tax payable. The tax rate is the same for gifts and estates.

At death, all gifts made after December 31, 1976, except those coming within the $10,000 annual exclusions and those which qualify for the marital deduction, are called "taxable gifts" and are added to the taxable estate. A tentative tax is figured to the total, and then the unified credit plus any gift taxes paid on lifetime gifts are subtracted. The credits exemption equivalent works like a charge account. Taxable gifts are charged against this balance until it is exhausted. The unused balance at death is then applied against estate taxes. Here's how the unified system works: Ms. Donor, a widow, made taxable gifts to her children, above the $10,000 annual exclusions, totaling $50,000. She paid no gift tax because she hadn't used up her credit. When she died in 1983, she left an estate of $400,000. In calculating the tax on her estate, the $50,000 of gifts must be added back and the tax figured on the total. The tentative tax on $450,000 is $138,800. Against this the credit of $79,300 allowed in the year 1983 is subtracted, leaving a tax due of $59,500.

Suppose instead that Ms. Donor had given away $200,000 in 1981. She would have exhausted her credit that year of $47,000 and paid $8,000 in gift taxes. Her executor, in preparing her estate tax return, would have to add the gifts to her $250,000 estate and arrive at the same $450,000 taxable estate. Instead of paying $59,500 in estate taxes, though, he would deduct the $8,000 of gift taxes already paid and the total taxes in each case would be the same.

All lifetime gifts and transfers at death from one spouse to the other which qualify for the marital deduction are tax-free. All outright transfers qualify as well as transfers in trust if they meet specific requirements (see page 214 for discussion of the types of trusts which will qualify for the marital deduction).

Let's turn now from the general picture and get down to some questions and answers on the implications involved in making gifts.

Should I Make Gifts and How Much Should I Give?

Making gifts may be advisable from a tax point of view. But this does not mean that lifetime giving is always financially advantageous. There are other considerations besides taxes.

How much can you afford to give away? That is the heart of the matter. No one should ever give so much money away that he jeopardizes his own financial independence. A person transfers a large part of his estate to relatives and then comes up against a radically changed economic situation, a depression, or a recession. Or perhaps he suffers a reversal of personal fortune. What happens then? From an independent person of wealth, he has suddenly become a dependent person of limited means. A true gift is irrevocable. That is something that all would-be givers should remember. The gift once made is gone, often beyond recovery. Recipients are always grateful at the time the gift is made. But both the memory and the gratitude of donees are usually short-lived.

There is also the question of age. A person of 30 would obviously not want to give away as much as one of 70. It is not only that no one can predict the future; it is also that money given away is no longer available for investment and capital accumulation by the donor.

With these thoughts in mind, let's take a look at some of the workings of the gift tax.

What Does the Gift Tax Tax?

Generally speaking, the tax is imposed on the transfer of property by gift during a person's lifetime. The tax applies to all gifts except gifts between spouses and charitable donations. Also excepted are payments made on behalf of anyone for tuition or medical care directly to an educational institution or a provider of medical services. The donor pays the tax, not the donee. But if the donor defaults on the tax payment, the government has the right to collect it from the donee.

How Is the Value of a Gift Determined?

In the case of any kind of property other than cash, the

value of a gift is considered to be its fair market value on the date the gift is made.

Thus, if the gift were securities, the value would be the current market price. The market value of real estate is usually arrived at by using expert appraisal, the assessed value, and the sale price of similar properties as guides. Business interests of closely held corporations represent a more complex problem. There are various methods and combinations of methods for arriving at the value of these: book value, capitalization of earnings, expert opinion, as well as many other criteria. The services of an accountant and attorney are required to make a proper valuation. You may also need the help of expert appraisers. (For a fuller explanation of the valuation of business interests, see Chapter 18.)

How Does the Annual Exclusion Work?

Any person may give away as much as $10,000 a year to each of as many people as he wishes without paying any tax at all. This exclusion is available to both a husband and a wife. They can therefore give away together as much as $20,000 per year to any person, even though it all comes from the property owned by the husband, for instance. In order to take advantage of this provision, called "gift splitting," a husband need only have his wife sign a consent to his gift on the gift tax return; it is not necessary for her actually to give any property of her own. The two exclusions then amount to $20,000.

The annual exclusion is applicable only where there is a gift of "a present interest," meaning that it can be claimed only when the recipient of the gift can immediately use, enjoy, or benefit from the gift. This has particular significance for gifts made in trust. When, for example, you make a gift in trust to a beneficiary who does not have the right to the income or principal of the property immediately, then you have made a gift of a future interest and it will not qualify for the annual exclusion.

Take the case of the person who makes a gift in trust to his daughter and grandchildren. The daughter gets the income during her lifetime and the principal is to go to her children at her death. The annual exclusion applies to *her* part of the gift (the right to the income) but not the grandchildren's part (the right to the principal). Since the right to the income during her life vests in her immediately, her interest is a present one. Since the grandchildren's right to the principal can be enjoyed only after their mother's death, their interest is considered a future one.

With minors, if your gift meets certain conditions, then the entire gifts in trust will qualify for the annual exclusion.

Suppose, for example, that you want to make a gift to your minor son, aged 10. If you put it in trust and provide that the income and principal could be used for his benefit now with the remainder going to him at 21 (or, if he died, to his estate or according to his will), then the gift would qualify for the annual exclusion. This is so even though the age of majority has been reduced to 18 in your state. Exactly the same applies to gifts made under the Uniform Gifts to Minors Act, which also qualify for the annual exclusion.

Many donors do not want trusts for minors to end at 21, but still want the tax savings of the annual exclusion. They can have both if the income may be used for the minor and any accumulated income is payable to him when he reaches 21. The value of his right to the income qualifies for the annual exclusion (although the remainder does not). If the trust principal is large, this right to income may exceed the annual exclusion.

How Are Gifts Made Before 1977 Treated?

Generally the gifts you made before 1977 have no effect on your estate. You get a fresh start but with exceptions. If you used part of your former $30,000 exemption between September 8, 1976, and the end of that year, your new tax credit is reduced by 20 per cent of the exemption used. Also, in figuring the tax on post-1976 gifts, prior gifts are added back, the gift tax is then computed and the tax on those prior gifts under the new rates are subtracted. The result is that it is possible that the pre-1977 gifts may put your post-1976 gifts into a higher tax bracket.

When Must a Gift Tax Return Be Filed?

No gift tax return need be filed for gifts that come within the $10,000 annual exclusion. If a spouse consents to a gift, though it may be $20,000 or less for the year, a return must be filed. A return is not required for interspousal transfers which qualify for the marital deduction. Returns are due on April 15th following the year in which the gift was made. However, if you have an extension for filing your income tax return, you get the same extension for filing the gift tax return.

What About Gifts Made Within Three Years of Death?

Before 1977 gifts made within three years of death were presumed to have been made in contemplation of death and taxed as part of the estate unless the executor could prove the gifts were made with lifetime motives. As of 1977 all gifts within three years of death were automatically included in the estate except for gifts that qualified for the annual exclusion.

Now only gifts of life insurance and certain other transfers where the decedent has retained or has been granted powers over the property are includable in the taxable estate. Other gifts made within three years of death that exceed the $10,000 annual exclusion, though not part of the taxable estate, are added back in calculating the estate tax and the unified credit. Since the latter are not part of the taxable estate, they don't get a step-up in basis.

Can Husband-Wife Gift-Splitting Be Used for All Gifts?

As described in connection with the annual exclusion, gifts can be made from the property of either spouse. If the other consents, the gift is taxed as though each made a gift of one half of the value of the property given. However you must be aware that the consenting spouse will be using up some of his or her unified credit if the gift is over $20,000.

Are Transfers by Sale Ever Taxed as Gifts?

Yes, when the sale price of the property transferred is less than the fair market price. In this case, the amount of the difference is considered a gift. For example, if you sold your daughter 100 shares of Blue Chip Corporation for $5,000 at a time when they were selling for $8,000, on the basis of a market price of 80, you would be making a gift of $3,000.

Are Gifts in Trust Subject to the Gift Tax?

Yes, the gift tax applies to gifts in trust as well as outright transfers, when the gifts are complete. If the trust is irrevocable and you have retained no power of appointment, or right to alter or amend it, it is a completed gift and it is subject to the gift tax.

What about Joint Ownership of Property?

What happens when you take property of your own or purchase property with your money and put the title into a form of joint ownership with another person? Is there a taxable gift? The answer is no, if he or she is your spouse, otherwise it depends on a number of things: the type of property involved and whether he contributed money or "consideration" toward the joint ownership; also whether or not the gift is considered to be a completed one—i.e., one in which the donor has given up any of his interests in the property. Thus:

Joint Savings Accounts. When you make a deposit of your own funds in a joint savings account with your son, for example, there is no gift until he makes a withdrawal. Then you have made a gift to him of the amount he withdraws, and that amount is subject to taxation.

Joint Ownership of U.S. Savings Bonds. Much the same principle applies. If you buy these bonds and list your son as co-owner, there is usually no gift until he cashes them in. At that point a taxable gift has been made.

Joint Ownership of Securities. Whenever you put stock, bonds or mutual funds into joint names and your co-owner doesn't contribute one half of its value, you are making a gift. Joint brokerage accounts are an exception to the rule.

Joint Ownership of Real Estate. Purchase or transfer of real property into joint names is ordinarily a gift where one does not contribute consideration. Thus, if you bought a house and put the title in the names of both your daughter and yourself, you would have made a gift to her of more than one half of the value of the house, based upon your respective life expectancies.

What Are the Estate Tax Rules on Joint Property? The basic estate tax rule is that property in joint names is fully taxable in the estate of the first to die, except to the extent that the survivor can prove his own contribution. So it is possible to make a gift, such as by putting stock into joint names, and still have 100 per cent of the property included in the donor's taxable estate.

However, there is a special rule for property held in the joint names of a husband and wife. Each spouse is treated as owning half. On the death of the first to die, only the value of half of the property will be included in the decedent's gross estate, regardless of which one paid for the property. There will be no tax on the property because of the unlimited marital deduction. However, only the half that is included in the gross estate gets a step-up in basis.

What about Gifts Made During Life but Not Payable Until the Death of the Donor?

Again, there is a distinction made depending on whether you relinquish control and interest over the gift during your life. U.S. Savings Bonds, for example, registered in your name but payable on your death to your niece, are not gifts, since she had no right to the proceeds until you die. At that time, ownership of the bonds passes to her, but they are includable in your taxable estate.

Gifts of insurance depend on how the insurance policy is written. If you make your niece the beneficiary of an insurance policy, you have not made a gift, provided you own the policy or retain the right to change the beneficiary. However, if you designate her as the beneficiary irrevocably or if you assign the policy over to her, then you have made a gift.

Are There Other Financial Advantages?

Making gifts not only saves on estate taxes, it also reduces the size of your estate and thus reduces the cost of the administration of your estate. These administrative costs can run as high as 5 to 10 per cent of the total estate, so it pays to keep the estate as low as possible.

Savings can often be obtained when a gift is made because the future income from the property may be transferred to a member of the family with a lower income tax bracket than that of the donor, and the future appreciation in the value of the property is removed from the donor's estate with a consequent savings in estate taxes in his estate.

Is There a State Gift Tax as Well as a Federal One?

The states of Louisiana, New York, North Carolina, Oregon, South Carolina, Tennessee, and Wisconsin, as well as Puerto Rico, have gift taxes. The rest do not. If you, as a resident of a non-gift tax state make a gift of real property which is located in a gift tax state, however, then you are subject to both the federal gift tax and that of the state in which the real property is located.

that a decedent only rarely owns property when he dies—most of it (during life, that is) having been transferred to persons who would eventually become beneficiaries under a will.

. . .

Let me relate an incident which happened to me shortly after I hung out my shingle. A frightened woman in her mid-forties appeared in my office one day. She had just lost her husband and was facing her first experience in handling money. Shortly after his death and to his everlasting financial shame, she went through the papers that she knew were now in a lower drawer of her desk. Although she was devastated with grief when she read the papers she found, she was also consoled to learn that her husband's estate had provided so generously for her needs. After discussing the situation, she decided to come to . . . .

THE PERSONAL SIDE

People who suddenly inherit large sums of money often do not understand the dynamics of money in our society. Because the amount is substantial, it seems to them as if it will last forever. After all, my grandparents, my parents, or my spouse had it and managed to hang onto it over a period of years, why shouldn't I be able to do the same? So the reasoning usually goes.

These innocents—and innocents they truly are—realize too late how ephemeral money really is, how rapidly it can disappear whether invested or merely spent. It takes experience to walk the tightrope of economic planning. Even the most sagacious of administrators is sometimes hard put to know how best to handle investments in a fluctuating market. How is it that we expect inexperienced people to do it then?

This is where lifetime transfer comes in. It prepares and

educates the family—spouse and children both—in all the problems and skills needed in the management of property. It provides learning's most priceless asset, experience.

The Spouse

Let's use as an example a widow whose estate, inherited from her husband, included a block of stock worth $200,000 in a blue chip corporation. She knew little about the world of investment, but learned rapidly. Or so she thought.

Shortly after her husband died, the company announced a stock split. Seeing in the papers that the stock was now listed at a lower price, she got panicky, thought she was losing money, and sold off her stock, all $200,000 worth.

Next, she put the proceeds into a speculative stock (recommended by a friend she met at a cocktail party). Within 2 years, the value of the stock dropped from $200,000 to $50,000. Had she kept her investment in the original firm, it would have been worth $250,000.

It's easy enough to criticize or ridicule the unfortunate heroine of this little drama, but in doing so, we miss the point.

Was it her fault she acted so foolishly? After all, she never handled or owned any sizable amount of property in her life. Her husband had never "bothered her with money matters."

The "Male World of Finance"

Many men (and their wives, too) consider the management of property and investments to be exclusively the prerogative of the male. According to this philosophy, women don't understand the world of finance; they're not interested in it; they are incapable of grasping its fine and more subtle aspects.

But if women receive a higher education, if they vote, if they hold down jobs, if they play responsible roles in the community, if they can become politicians, scientists, engineers, doctors, and laywers, does it make sense to presume that they cannot tell the difference between a stock and a bond? The world of finance may be a mysterious one, but it's not as mysterious as all that.

What's more, the presumption is not only illogical but

dangerous. We know from the actuarial tables that most wives outlive their husbands. Twenty per cent of all married women become widows by the time they reach the age of 55; almost one-third by 65; and two-thirds by 75.

It's a fact that most women in the United States are going to be faced with the problems of administering property, sometimes large amounts of it. What happens then to the "mysterious male world of finance"?

The woman whose husband has entrusted her with the ownership *and* management of a share of his property during his life is far luckier than the average widow. She can tell the difference between sound and poor investment advice. She isn't likely to fall prey to "hot tips" gleaned at the hairdresser's or proffered by well-meaning friends. If her husband dies, she will have to surmount the shock of his death, but it will not be heightened by fear and panic about money matters.

The Children

When it was suggested to a client that he start making gifts of property to his 21-year-old son, he looked skeptical. "Give him money? Why, he'll go right out and buy a sports car with it. He thinks money grows on trees."

Not knowing his son, we don't know whether he was right or wrong, but we do know that if the son is going to buy a sports car with the $20,000 his father gives him now, he may spend the one million he will inherit at his death just as unwisely.

But isn't it true that you can get around this problem by leaving all your property in trust for a child for the rest of his life? It is. Have you ever come across any of these trust-sheltered children?

We have, and the picture they present is not a pretty one.

One "trust baby" that comes to mind was 50 years old, married several times; at this juncture single once again. He didn't work. His life was made up of two important monthly dates. On the first of each month he received his stipend from the trust. By the fifteenth he had succeeded in drinking it up and began borrowing against the next payment.

The man who gives money to children during his life cannot guarantee that they will handle their inheritance wisely, but he has done far better than either the parent of the prospective sports-car owner or the parent of the trust baby.

Through judicious giving, he has guided his children, helped them plan, taught them responsibility. When the time comes for them to take over, they may not be financial wizards, but they will certainly not be neophytes.

Let us make clear, however, that when we say "Give to your children and let them take responsibility for the gift," we're not speaking of young children. We are referring to young adults.

The pattern of lifetime transfer should be planned, and carried out in installments: so much at one age, another amount in 5 years, and so on. About 18 is a good age to begin, with a small gift, say, a few thousand dollars. Once the gift is given, you should back it up with advice—but if the young person doesn't want to follow it, we recommend letting him have his way and making investments as he wants. He may lose—but win or lose, he will surely have gained in experience.

The Donor

It is not only the spouse and children who learn from the experience of receiving gifts. The donor has a good deal to gain too. If he has the opportunity over a period of years to see what his children and his spouse do with the property he has given them, he will be in a much better position to make the always difficult decisions on the distribution of his property after his death.

Will this child be able to handle his bequest? Or should the money be put in trust? Is this one capable of taking over the business? Would he be enthusiastic about it? Or do his interests lie elsewhere? Does the spouse take an intelligent interest in her property? Or is she genuinely and permanently not interested?

All these questions are much better answered in the framework of lifetime giving.

The Economic Side

Lifetime giving opens up opportunities for saving, from which both the family and the individual estate planner can benefit. These opportunities are many and varied, but they can be summed up in a single phrase, tax savings.

Income Tax Savings

Spreading ownership of property among the family not only saves taxes, it increases the spendable income available to the family unit after taxes, in many cases by a substantial amount.

This is particularly true when unearned income is piled on top of earned income. At this point taxes become so heavy that the added income does not actually add very much cash to the family exchequer.

But if the high-bracket individual who is receiving all this money divests himself of some of his income-producing property and gives it to a member of his family who is in a lower income bracket, or not previously a taxpayer at all, total taxes will be lowered and more after-tax money will be left. In short, it is axiomatic that one of the ways to save income taxes is to create new taxpayers or to level out income among the family members.

Thus, a person who is in the 28 percent tax bracket will ordinarily pay $280 in taxes on each added $1,000 of taxable income. But if he transfers property producing $1,000 of that income to his son, who is in the 15 per cent tax bracket, the son will only pay $150 on the same income return. The donor has, in effect, added $130 to the family's spendable cash. These tax savings apply to any family gifts except to the spouse. Since most married couples file joint returns, there is no point in diverting income from husband to wife. For tax purposes, what's hers is his and vice versa.

The income tax savings factor has a number of other applications as well. Often it can help a family meet obligations that would otherwise pose heavy burdens. If you have a dependent parent, for example, why not make a lifetime gift to him? In this way he will be paying taxes on the income return in his low tax bracket. With income thus spread, the after-tax money available for the support of your parent will be increased.

Estate Tax Savings

This is important, in spite of the unified estate and gift tax.

The principle is simple: the more an estate is depleted by lifetime transfers, the smaller it becomes and the less taxes have to be paid on it. The results are often quite dramatic.

Take, for example, the mythical (but nonetheless typical) case of two women: Ms. A and Ms. B, who happen to have identical estates of $750,000. Both are widows and both plan to leave all their property to their children.

Ms. A keeps everything until her death in 1987. Her children pay an estate tax of about $37,000 plus administration expenses of $45,000, and end up by receiving $668,000 from their mother's estate.

Ms. B, on the other hand, makes tax-free gifts of $10,000 to each of her two children over a period of years amounting to $100,000. When she dies, she leaves an estate of $650,000, subject to tax of approximately $8,000 and with administration expenses of $32,000.

In all, Ms. B's children have received $710,000 from their mother, or $42,000 more than Ms. A's children got.

WHAT TO GIVE
AND HOW TO GIVE IT

The would-be donor of lifetime gifts has a wide choice as to the kind of gift he makes. It can be almost anything of value—cash, jewels, fine art, or stocks and bonds. But some gifts are better to give than others; tax savings can be greater depending on a number of factors. Gift giving, in fact, is a fine art. It takes a good deal of information and knowledge to make the proper choice in the proper circumstances.

Here are some general rules about what kinds of property to give.

Give Income-Producing Property

You save on income taxes; the future profits follow the gift, not the giver.

Give Appreciated Property

You can save income taxes if you give property that has increased in value. As a matter of fact, if you are in a high tax bracket, you should always consider the possibility of giving appreciated property instead of selling it.

Take the case of the man in the 28 per cent tax bracket who wants to take his profit on a stock which has risen in value from $4,000 to $10,000. If he sells the securities, he will have to pay a 28 per cent tax on his $6,000 profit, or $1,680. But if he gives the stock to his daughter who is in a 15 per cent bracket, she can sell it and pay a tax of only $900.

Give Property Which Has a Potential Increase in Value

If you expect certain property will greatly appreciate in the future, a gift of this property will permit the donee to take advantage of the appreciation. Insurance is ideal for giving. It is taxed only at its cash value at the time of the gift. The recipient gets the face value when the donor dies, but does not have to pay estate taxes on it. If the cash value of the policy when originally given is less than the $10,000 annual gift tax exclusion, and subsequent premium payments by the donor do not exceed the annual exclusions, nothing would be includable in the estate of the donor, unless he dies within three years of making the gift of the policy.

Gifts of insurance, however, have to be absolute (meaning that the ownership of the policy goes to the recipient, with no strings attached). If you retain any kind of control over the policy, the insurance will be considered part of your estate and therefore subject to estate taxes.

OTHER TYPES OF TRANSFERS: SALES, SALES AND LEASE BACKS, ANNUITIES

Sometimes it is wiser to sell than to give. This is especially true since the amount of a gift over the $10,000 annual exclusions is included in figuring the taxable estate at death.

Gifts can cause family difficulties too. Often one member

of the family will resent the fact that the gift goes to someone besides himself. Finally, you may not be able to afford to give property away.

The answer in all these cases is usually some form of sale. The sale, however, must be a true sale, for tax purposes; that is, it must be sold at its fair market price. If it isn't, you may have to pay gift taxes on the value of the property in excess of what is paid for it.

Installment Sales

When you substitute a sale for a gift, however, you may be bypassing the Scylla of the gift tax, only to fall prey to the Charybdis of the regular income tax. If you are in a high tax bracket, or if your profit on the sale is substantial, then you will have to pay 28 per cent in income taxes. If you receive only part of your profit in cash, and the balance in notes, you would have to pay the entire tax in the year the sale is made, perhaps paying in tax more than the cash you received from the sale. However, the installment sale provisions of the tax law allow you to spread the taxable income over the period the installments are to be paid.

Thus, on a sale of an asset which was originally bought for $12,000 and is now sold at a price of $20,000 there is taxable income of $8,000. The tax on it would be a maximum of $2,240.

But if the sale were an installment sale, payable, say, over a 10-year period at $2,000 per year, the law allows you to consider 60 per cent of each payment, or $1,200, as a *return of capital* (the price originally paid for the asset). The other 40 per cent, or $800, is treated as taxable income. The spreading of the income over a period of years reduces the total annual income, and thus you avoid paying a large income tax on a lump sum. This may reduce the overall taxes you have to pay on the profit of the sale. Moreover, your tax savings can be greater if the installment payments are received in low-bracket retirement years.

Sale and Lease Back

This device is often used by business enterprises, but it is just as applicable to the family group. A father who owns business property, for example, can sell it to his son. The son then leases it back to his father. Both parties save on taxes in this kind of arrangement. The father can take a deduction for the rent or royalties he pays. The son also has deductions for depreciation and operating expenses.

The Private or Family Annuity

Although rarely used, it occasionally can be a useful form of lifetime transfer.

The private annuity is similar to a commercial annuity except that the transaction occurs among members of the family group—usually between a parent in a high income bracket and his children, or between the donor and a family-controlled trust.

The idea of the private annuity is that in exchange for an outright transfer of an income-producing business or property by the parent to the children, they agree to pay him a reasonable annuity for the rest of his life. When the parent dies, the payments stop and the children have no further obligation to his estate. Thus a valuable estate is transferred to children but there are no estate taxes to be paid.

The private annuity also has a number of unique income tax advantages. Usually it reduces the parent's income taxes without reducing his income return. It can also allow the parent to transfer appreciated property in exchange for the annuity without paying an immediate income tax; the tax on the gain is deferred and spread over the parent's life. It gets special annuity tax treatment; most of each payment is considered a return of capital, and the remaining portion is taxable income.

The private annuity probably has as many disadvantages to a child as the obligee, as it has advantages to the parent annuitant. First of all, the child is taxed with the income from the property. He receives no deduction for the payments he has to make to his parent. Furthermore, the annuity payments may greatly exceed the income on most property so that the child will have to use his own resources to pay income taxes, as well as make up the difference between the property's income and the annuity payments. If the child sells the property, he may be eventually liable for substantial taxes because his final cost basis amounts to only the annuity payments paid by him to his parent.

Lastly, the private annuity must be an unsecured transaction to qualify for the favorable tax treatment to the annuitant. Although a parent may trust his child, he does run the risk of the child's untimely death, and as a result may have to enforce the obligation on his child's estate if he leaves any.

No rule of thumb as to the usefulness of this device can be stated. Each case must be evaluated on the basis of its unique circumstances.

GIFTS TO MINORS: A SPECIAL PROBLEM

There are many instances when it is advisable to make a gift to a minor child. If you want to do this, be sure that you make the transfer properly or you may find yourself restricted in the use and transfer of your child's property at some future date. The minor's freedom to deal with his property is limited by law. In addition, the income tax consequences of transferring income-producing assets must be considered.

Cash gifts of U.S. Savings Bonds usually pose no problems. A minor can deposit and withdraw money from a bank or redeem savings bonds, if he has reached an age of sufficient maturity.

The trouble arises when the gift is one of securities or real estate. In both cases, a court-appointed guardian will be needed to deal with the property owned by the minor. This is burdensome and costly.

A friend of ours ran into this situation a few years ago. He had been a foresighted estate planner in that he had been transferring property to his son ever since he was born, anticipating the high cost of education in the sixties. But when the boy entered college and the father tried to sell some of the stock he had put in his son's name, he found it couldn't be done without going through all the red tape and expense of having a guardian appointed. The father ended up by borrowing the money.

You can avoid this kind of transfer problem by setting up a trust for your minor instead of making an outright gift. Trustees can be given broad powers to manage, to buy and to sell, without being tied down by judicial supervision.

If you plan to give securities or cash, a simpler solution is to utilize the Gift to Minors Acts which now exists in all states. This permits you to give securities and cash (and in some states, insurance and real property) to a minor by transferring them to a custodian. The custodian has broad powers similar to those of a trustee. He maintains control of the property until the minor reaches 18 or 21, depending upon your state's law, and can use the income and principal for the minor. When the child reaches 18 or 21 the property is turned over to him.

If income producing assets, such as real estate or securities, are transferred to a child under the age of 14, unintended tax consequences may result. The Tax Reform Act of 1986 provides that for a child under 14 years of age unearned income over $1,000 will be taxed at the rate of the parent (if higher). If the minor is over 14 years of age, the income will be taxed at the child's rate.

To avoid this problem, children under the age of 14 may be given non-income producing assets, such as EE bonds or growth stocks, in order to defer the recognition of income until the child reaches 14. These gifts will still provide important transfer tax benefits by reducing the parent's taxable estate.

FAMILY PLANNING

Earlier, we spoke of the estate planner and his obligation to provide for his family. But there is another parental responsibility which enters into the picture—that of his own parents who may themselves possess a substantial estate.

If you have expectations of inheriting property from your parents, the planning of their estates is an integral part of your own estate plan. Whatever the size of their estates, the manner of disposition may have an effect on your plans for your family's security and on your tax picture.

If your parents are in the top income tax bracket and they make gifts of their property to you (assuming you are in a lower tax bracket), there will be, of course, an overall income tax savings. In addition, there will be an eventual estate tax savings when they die, since their estates will have been reduced to the extent of the subsequent income and appreciation thereon.

If your income tax bracket is higher, or just as high, gifts to your children rather than to you would be more advantageous. If your children are minors, the gift can be made in trust and the income accumulated until needed. The trust is a separate tax entity, so this income is taxed to the trust or to your children at rates lower than yours or your parents' in certain circumstances. Here is a means of creating a fund with a minimum cost in taxation which will be available for future use in educating your children. Not only has the property been removed from the erosion of estate taxes in your parents' estates, but by bypassing you, any estate tax which would have been imposed on the property in your estate is avoided.

If your tax bracket is low or you need additional income, it still may not be advisable for your parents to make outright gifts of property to you, but rather to make them in trust. The trust can specify that the income, and as much of the principal as the trustees consider necessary, be paid to you and that after your death (or at some specified time), the trust property be paid to your children. In this way you have use of the income, and as much of the principal as you need. Because of the generation-skipping provision, however, the value of the trust may be taxed as though it were a part of your estate at your death, subject, however, to a lifetime exemption of $1,000,000 (see page 181 for generation-skipping transfers).

You should also discuss with your parents the inheritance you expect to receive from them. They might be conferring a burden instead of benefit. Remember that any property you inherit becomes part of your estate, and the income earned on it will be taxable to you. Inheritances can be renounced. But the renunciation creates the possibility of gift taxes, problems in estate administration, and could disrupt your parents' estate plans. Further, if your own estate plan includes a program of annual gifts to your children, an unwanted inheritance can frustrate the accomplishment of that program.

When there is bad planning (or no planning), the sins of the parents can be visited on successive generations.

Here is a classic example of this maxim. A man had a substantial estate of his own. When his father died, he inherited $100,000 from his estate. He didn't want to give up the inheritance, but on the other hand, he didn't want this additional property increasing his own taxable estate.

Moreover, the income on the property meant little to him because of his high tax bracket.

Obviously, his father should never have left him that property. Better to have transferred it to his grandchildren. Better still, in trust for them.

Family Communication

Unfortunately, the case we have just cited is not unusual in the annals of estate planning. It is the exception rather than the rule when two generations enter wholeheartedly into a mutual plan that will benefit everybody all around.

Yet such plans are a necessity. And furthermore, the planning has to be on an individual family basis because the circumstances to each family are different. What to give and who to give it to (children versus grandchildren, for instance) depends on the various estate and income tax positions of the two generations. All sorts of variables are possible.

Behind the failure of most families to do planning for lifetime transfer is the old problem of communication between generations. On the one hand, the children are reluctant to bring the matter up; it involves asking their parents to give them money; it sounds grasping, selfish, a bit morbid. On the other hand, the parents hesitate because—and this is a common failing—they still tend to look on their children, whatever their ages may be, as children. There is also an all too human tendency to hang on to what you have while you are still alive.

Somehow, perhaps through an impartial third person such as the family lawyer, perhaps by reading a book like this, perhaps through general discussions which lead to specific ones, the problem must be broached and the family communications barrier breached. For family planning is the essence of lifetime transfer and sound estate planning.

CHAPTER 13

The Living Trust

Ms. Thrifty has heard that her estate will have to go through a costly and time-consuming probate proceeding after her death. She wonders whether she can pass a large part of her estate directly to her beneficiaries, in the shortest time and least expensive way, by avoiding a court proceeding.

Mr. Successful has a unique problem. At age 57 he controls a number of corporations and travels all over the United States and abroad handling their affairs. This leaves him little time to manage his own sizable portfolio of investments. He knows that he isn't giving them the attention he should, but what can he do?

Mr. Disappointed Father has four grown children. Three of them have turned out to be all that a parent could wish, but one, his middle son, is a true black sheep: a spendthrift and an ingrate. Mr. Disappointed would like to cut the Black Sheep off and leave the bulk of his estate to his other children. But he shrinks from the idea of all the publicity such a will would receive and the embarrassment it would cause his family. He is looking for some way to disinherit his son without having everyone know about it.

Ms. Cautious Parent would like to distribute some of her hard-earned and considerable wealth amongst the various members of her family while she is still alive. For one reason or another, she doesn't feel that any of them are capable, at this point, of assuming responsibility for large sums of money. What should she do?

Ms. Plan-Ahead's oldest child is now only 7 years old. Nevertheless, Ms. Plan-Ahead is already thinking about his college education. She has started a savings fund for that purpose, but is having a difficult time increasing it. In her 28 per cent bracket, a great deal of income is being drained away in taxes. Isn't there some way she can get the income of the fund out of her taxable income?

Mr. Dutiful Son supports his aged mother to the tune of $6,000 per year. Since he is in the 28 per cent bracket, he must use over $8,300 of gross income each year to provide this support for her. Giving her a large amount of income-producing property in order to have the income taxed to her is a poor solution; chances are that she will die before him, and the property will come back to him, reduced by estate taxes and administration expenses. He needs to find a way of having the income taxed to his mother without giving her the property.

Mr. Worried is not sure that he has made the right plans for disposing of his estate after his death. Sometimes he wishes that he could repeat Tom Sawyer's famous adventure, get a chance to attend his own funeral, and see how his estate plan would work out. He supposes that is a silly idea, but is it really?

Ms. Real Estate Investor is concerned about a different aspect of after-death estate transfer. Her estate consists primarily of large real estate holdings scattered all over the country. When she dies there will have to be a proceeding in each state where the property is located. If only all these administration proceedings could be dispensed with!

All of these problems and many more—some of them commonplace, some of them unique—can be solved by a marvelously flexible device for lifetime transfer, the living trust.

If you transfer your property to a trust you can avoid the problem of having your estate administered in the courts (Ms. Thrifty and Ms. Real Estate Investor); get professional management for it (Mr. Successful); keep the transfer private (Mr. Disappointed Father); protect your beneficiaries against their own inexperience (Ms. Cautious Parent); preview the management of your after-death estate (Mr. Worried); and realize greater after-tax income in order to achieve important objectives such as providing a fund for education, or support of dependent parents (Ms. Plan-Ahead, and Mr. Dutiful Son).

In short, of all the devices for lifetime giving, one of the most useful is the living trust. It can do almost anything that the grantor can do with his property—and yet still have additional advantages which are not open to him.

WHAT IS A TRUST?

The device dates back to feudal times but the basic concept has remained the same over the centuries. When you give property in trust, you give it to another person (or group of persons or institution) to be used and administered for the benefit of a third person (or group of persons or institution) or yourself. In other words, you are trusting somebody else to handle your property for the benefit of your beneficiaries.

Trusts are two types, *testamentary* and *living* (the latter, in legal parlance, called "inter vivos"). Testamentary trusts are those you create by will which become effective at your death. Living trusts are created during your lifetime by an agreement but may, and often do, continue on after your death. This chapter is focused on the uses of the living trust, but much of what we will discuss also applies to the testamentary trust. (For more on testamentary trusts, however, see Chapter 16.)

HOW IT WORKS

Here's a simple example of how a trust works. Uncle Bountiful gives his best friend, Mr. Trustworthy, 1,000 shares of Top Grade, Inc. Trustworthy agrees to hold and invest the property for the benefit of Bountiful's nephew, Peter, and for Peter's children.

The trust agreement provides that Trustworthy will pay all the income of the trust to Peter so long as he lives. When Peter dies, the property will be turned over to his children.

Bountiful is the *settlor* of the trust, or he may be called the *grantor, trustor*, or *donor*. Trustworthy is *trustee* and he becomes the legal owner of the trust property. He is Bountiful's personal representative, empowered to carry out Uncle B's objectives. Bountiful could have had more than one trustee, and he could also have designated substitute or successor trustees to take over in case Mr. T becomes disabled, resigns, dies, or cannot act for any reason.

Peter and his children are the *beneficiaries* of the trust. Peter is called the *life tenant*, because he has the right to the income of the trust for the duration of his life. His interest is called a *life estate*. Peter's children are called *remaindermen*, meaning that their interest is a remainder one—the right to the property when the life estate ends.

Unborn or unknown persons may be beneficiaries of trusts. If, under Bountiful's trust, the remaindermen were to be Peter's children, living at his death, the beneficiaries might include children as yet not born. If instead the remainder were payable to Peter's wife (without naming her personally), the remainderman might be unknown or unascertained, since his wife will be the woman to whom he is married at the time of his death.

The stock which Bountiful gave to his trustee is called the *trust fund*, or *corpus*, or *principal*. In this case the fund was stock, but it might have been real estate, cash, insurance, or even a business. A trust fund may be composed of any kind of property which can be owned or assigned. It can also change as new investments are made.

Two factors dictate what the trust does and how it will operate: state laws and the terms of the trust agreement.

State Laws

The laws governing the operation of a trust vary from state to state. They are concerned with placing various limitations on the powers of the trustee and on the length of time the property can be held in trust. No state will allow a trust to operate indefinitely (except in the case of charitable or employee trusts). A trust can be created to last a long time, in most states for a period measured by the lives of a reasonable number of living people, plus 21 years.

In one famous case, for example, a trust created in 1926 to continue until 21 years after the death of all the lineal descendants of Queen Victoria who were then living was held valid. There were 120 lineal descendents of the Queen at the time.

When creating a living trust you usually have some choice as to which state you want your trust to be governed by. The only rule is that the trust have some material connec-

tion with the designated state. It could be the location of a
piece of real estate, for example, or the residence of either
the settlor or the trustee.

Trust Agreement

Except for the limitations of state law, the settlor can
make his own rules about how the trust is going to operate.

Thus, the settlor designates the purpose of the trust; he
determines the amount and type of property it will contain;
he sets the length of time it will last; he picks the beneficiaries; he directs how much they get and when they will receive
it. Further, he can set forth conditions that a beneficiary
must meet in order to receive income or principal. (Uncle
Bountiful might have said, for example, that Peter's children weren't entitled to the principal until they had reached
certain ages, or had earned a certain income themselves.) He
can provide alternate dispositions in case his conditions aren't
met or the circumstances change.

Moreover, he can set the rules which the trustee has to
follow, and he can make these as broad or narrow as he
wants. His trustee can become his alter ego, possessed of
powers both of management and disposition, which will
permit him to handle the property as changing circumstances
require, and dispose of income and principal according to
his own discretion.

The settlor's ability to set his own rules makes the living
trust not only an important instrument of lifetime transfer,
but also a means of estate creation and death transfer. The
rules the settlor lays down will depend upon what the trust
is to be used for. One trust may play many different roles in
an estate plan. Though a trust may be principally created for
one purpose, it can achieve other objectives at the same
time.

Much, in fact all, of the ability of a trust to accomplish
these aims, however, depends on the ability of the settlor
together with his lawyer to devise the proper rules. For a
would-be trust creator, professional advice is a must. In
addition, he should have a general understanding himself of
the many paths of trust creation that are open to him;
equally of the many opportunities for income and estate tax
savings.

The Generation-Skipping Transfer Tax

As demonstrated by the trust created to last until 21 years afer the death of all of the lineal descendants of Queen Victoria then living, it is possible to have a trust that can last 100 years or more. Before the Tax Reform Act of 1976, this meant that property could be used by successive generations without it being subject to estate taxes as it passed in trust from one generation to the next.

The 1976 Act gave birth to an entirely new transfer tax, separate and apart from estate and gift taxes. It is a tax on generation-skipping transfers and applies to trusts—living and testamentary—and to similar arrangements designed to last for more than one generation. This might apply as well to insurance proceeds paid under an installment option.

In its simplest terms, the tax was originally imposed on a trust having younger generation beneficiaries (that is, beneficiaries in generations below the testator's or grantor's) if they are in more than one generation. An example of such a trust is one for the life of the grantor's daughter Able that goes on her death to her child Baker. Here there are two younger generations: Able is the first tier and Baker the second. On Able's death, there is a generation-skipping transfer.

The Tax Reform Act of 1986 expanded and imposed the generation-skipping transfer tax on "direct skips." A direct skip includes an outright transfer to a beneficiary at least two generations younger than the grantor. An example would be a transfer from grandparent to grandchild.

The tax is payable on Able's death and is computed as if the value of the trust property at that time were added to his estate. It is designed as a substitute for the estate tax Able's estate would have paid on that property if her father had given it to her outright. However, it's the trust that pays the tax.

An important feature of the generation-skipping transfer tax is the grandchildren exclusion. This is an exclusion of up to $2 million per grandchild of the grantor for direct skips made before 1990. After 1990 there will be no extra exemptions for transfers to grandchildren. However, each grantor is allowed a lifetime exemption of $1 million for generation-skipping transfers of any type.

The test of whether a trust will be taxed is the number of

tiers of younger generation beneficiaries. Many commonly used trusts won't be caught because they have only one such tier. Here are some examples of trusts not subject to the generation-skipping tax:

A Trust for a Wife and Children Which Goes to the Children at the Widow's Death. There is only one tier of younger beneficiaries, the children. A grantor's spouse is always treated as being in same generation as the grantor, regardless of age.

A Trust for a Child, Then to His Children But if There are None, to the Grantor's Other Children. If the grantor's child dies without offspring, the property goes to his sisters and brothers. Then all the beneficiaries will be in the same tier.

THE IRREVOCABLE TRUST

An irrevocable trust is one that cannot be revoked or terminated. Why make a living trust irrevocable? For two reasons: the irrevocable trust—if properly set up—can result in both income and estate tax savings.

Income Tax

If you set up an irrevocable trust, you will not have to pay any income tax on the trust fund's income, provided that (1) you do not receive any of this income; (2) it is not used to support someone you are already legally obligated to support (e.g., your minor child); (3) it is not used to discharge your legal obligations; (4) it is not accumulated for you or your spouse; (5) the income is not used to pay premiums on an insurance policy on your life or your spouse's life; and finally (6) the assets of the trust will not revert to either you or your spouse.

Under such conditions the irrevocable trust can be a prime means for the high-income estate planner to avoid high income taxes, while still keeping the property within the family. The trust operates here just as the lifetime gift does: taxes are saved by diverting income to lower-bracket taxpayers or by creating new taxpayers.

Estate Tax

The unified estate and gift tax has discouraged many from making large taxable gifts, because the value of the gift when made is added back in figuring the estate tax on the donor's estate when he dies. However, donors desirous of eliminating future income and growth on estate assets are able to transfer large amounts of such assets before they have to pay a gift tax on it. Each donor or spouse, who has not used any of his or her unified tax credit in prior giving, can make gifts up to $600,000 without having to pay a federal gift tax. This large exemption in effect comes about because it is the amount which is equivalent to the unified credit allowed. This credit is $192,800 in 1987 and thereafter. Remember, this is the amount which can be given without paying gift tax. Thus, by making substantial gifts, larger amounts of income from and appreciation on such assets will be removed from the donor's subsequent estate.

One can also remove such income and growth from the impact of estate taxes by transferring the underlying assets to an irrevocable trust. But in order to do so there must be no strings attached. The donor may not have any right to the income or retain any power to alter or amend the trust or control the enjoyment of the property. He can be a trustee, but his power as trustee must not go beyond the standard administration of the trust as distinguished from any power which could alter or modify the beneficiaries' interests. Moreover, he cannot retain any voting rights in stock of a corporation he controls.

In setting up a trust designed to remove income and appreciation on assets from the settlor's taxable estate, the settlor is making a completed gift. He is not only giving up the ownership of his property, he is also losing its uncontrolled use and benefits. Therefore, before taking the step, he should carefully and thoroughly weigh the gift as he would any other type of irrevocable transfer of property.

Let's assume a grandfather sets up a trust for his son and three grandchildren, which at creation in 1987 has a value of $600,000, which uses up his unified credit that year. Let's assume that the trust appreciates to $900,000 when grandfather dies. What did he remove from his estate without the imposition of any tax? First, he removed all the income from the property, which was paid to his son or grandchildren in a low income tax bracket. Second, since only $600,000 was reported in his estate as a taxable transfer, then the $300,000 difference, representing the appreciation, escaped estate taxation.

Let's take the example a generation further. Assuming at son's death 30 years later, the trust has appreciated in value to $1,000,000, the value of the trust would be taxed to the trust as though it was part of the son's estate, as a generation-skipping transfer. However, there is a $1 million lifetime exemption for generation-skipping transfers. Therefore, the entire $1,000,000 has been excluded from the son's estate.

Non-tax Benefits

In addition to tax savings, grandfather has achieved another result. He has controlled the disposition of the property to be made at his son's death. If he had given the property to his son outright, it might have been dissipated, reached by his son's creditors, or given to the son's wife when he died with the ever-present possibility of its reaching the hands of a second husband or children of another marriage.

Powers of Appointments

If grandfather is more concerned with giving maximum flexibility to the trust than with controlling its ultimate disposition, he can give someone, the son or grandchildren, for instance, power to change or direct the flow of distribution of property without adverse tax consequences.

He confers what is called a *power of appointment*. This allows the recipient of the power to select or change the beneficiaries or their interests. So long as the person who holds the power of appointment cannot exercise it for his or his estate's benefit, the trust property will not be taxable in his estate. Grandfather could have given his son a non-taxable power by providing that the son could appoint the trust property among his children.

Suppose then that 10 years after the trust was created, the family situation was such that one child needed more than the others or that one was greatly more deserving than the others. At that point, the son could bequeath that particular grandchild all the trust property or a large share of it.

Such a power of appointment gives more than mere flexibility; it also has a psychological value. It is the prerogative of grandparents to spoil their grandchildren, but no grandparent wants to destroy parental authority. The grandchild who can count on a substantial inheritance from his grandfather's trust at his father's death may flout parental control, if he chooses. But with the use of a power of appointment, the father controls the disposition of the trust and maintains his authority as head of the family.

THE REVOCABLE TRUST

A trust is revocable if the trust agreement provides that the grantor can revoke, alter, or amend it at any time. This permits him to terminate the trust and take back the property if he wants to. Or it gives him the right to change the terms of the trust, including the names of the beneficiaries and the amounts, and the manner in which they are to get their shares.

Revocable trusts have no tax advantages. Whether or not the grantor receives income from it, he must pay income taxes on the trust income. The principal is taxable in his estate.

But there are many non-tax reasons for creating a revocable trust. It ensures professional management, guarantees privacy, saves administration expenses, gives a preview of the after-death estate, provides, in short, all the inherent non-tax advantages of a trust.

Take the case of Mr. Successful; he wanted to be relieved of the burden of managing his property, if you remember. He places this property in a revocable trust, with himself as the beneficiary, and makes a person he had confidence in or a professional institution, such as a trust company, the trustee. The trustee will take over the property, manage it, invest it, and do all the day to day things necessary to conserve and increase its value. Mr. Successful will have all the advantages of his property without the headaches connected with management.

Revocable trusts of this type (where the donor is also the beneficiary) are often profitably used by independent entrepreneurs or owners of small businesses. Here the owner transfers his business to a living trust. While he is alive, he continues to receive income from it. After he dies, the trust remains in force with the family as beneficiaries. This ensures the continuance of professional, experienced, management for the business without interruption when the owner dies or if he becomes incapacitated.

THE SHORT-TERM TRUST

A trust can last as long as the grantor wants it to within the legal limits described before. We have seen that if the trust is revocable, the income from it will be taxed to him. Even if he makes it irrevocable the income will be taxed to him.

Prior to the Tax Reform Act of 1986, in the case of a trust that lasted 10 years or more, or for the life of the beneficiary, the income was not taxed to the grantor but to the beneficiary who received it, or to the trust if it was accumulated. This was called a *short-term trust* (also known as a Clifford trust). A short-term trust offered high-bracket grantors important tax advantages.

A person in a high tax bracket could divert income on some of his property to members of his family who were in much lower tax brackets. He may not have wanted, however, to give his property away completely, recognizing that at a later time he would need the principal and its income for himself.

His solution: to set up a trust which lasted at least 10 years. He could provide that the income be paid out to whatever person he selected, or conversely, that it be accumulated in the trust. At the end of the trust term, the property itself, together with any capital appreciation, was returned to him, and the accumulated income, if any, was paid to the beneficiary.

Remember Mr. Dutiful Son's dilemma? If the trust was created prior to March 1, 1986, a short-term trust could be used to transfer the income to his aged mother. For trusts created after that date, however, the law eliminates the tax benefit by taxing the person who funds the trust. In this case, Mr. Dutiful Son would still be subject to tax on the income of the trust, even though his mother received the money. A short term trust, unless created prior to March 1, 1986, is no longer useful to transfer income from one person to another for tax purposes.

ACCUMULATION TRUSTS

This is a method of setting up a trust so that the income is not paid out to a beneficiary but allowed to accumulate within the trust. The purpose is to save income taxes by taking advantage of the fact that the trust is a separate tax entity.

Income received by a beneficiary from a trust is taxed to the beneficiary at his bracket. If this income is not paid out but is instead allowed to accumulate in the trust, the income will generally be taxed to the trust. But when the accumulated ordinary income is finally paid to the beneficiary, he is taxed on it under a special method designed to tax the income as if it had been paid to him in the years it was earned. He receives a credit for the taxes paid by the trust up to his computed tax liability. This is known as the throwback rule. Even though the beneficiary ultimately pays, the growth of the fund, while accumulating income at the trust's lower brackets, is greater than it would have been had the grantor tried to build a fund at his own bracket.

However, there is a very important exception to the throwback rule. Income accumulated while the beneficiary was under 21 or before he was born is not subject to the throwback rule. It is only taxed to the trust.

For example, a parent wants to provide for her minor child's education. When the child is young, say 7 years old (as in the case of Ms. Plan-Ahead), she takes $30,000 of securities which produces an annual income of $2,400 and places them in a term trust to last for 11 years. The income may be accumulated or paid out and when the trust ends, the accumulations and principal will be used by the child for his college education.

On the $2,400 of income, the trust will pay a tax of only $360, leaving a net return of $2,040. In Ms. Plan-Ahead's 28 per cent bracket, she would have netted only $1,728 on those same investments.

LIFE INSURANCE TRUSTS

When you set up a life insurance trust, the trustees will either own the policy or be its beneficiaries.

Life insurance trusts (like all trusts) can be either irrevocable or revocable.

The Irrevocable Insurance Trust

Irrevocable life insurance trusts are generally created for two reasons: to avoid estate taxes and to lessen overall income taxes. They avoid estate taxes because the proceeds are not included in the estate of the settlor when he dies. The cash value, if any, of a policy at the time it is assigned, together with subsequent premium payments, are considered as gifts. To the extent they do not qualify for annual exclusions of $10,000, these gifts will be added to the settlor's estate in computing his estate tax.

Irrevocable insurance trusts can also help lessen income taxes if they are funded.

A funded trust is one where the trust principal consists of property in addition to the insurance. This property realizes a greater net income after taxes because of the lower tax bracket of the trust. The trustee uses this income to pay the premium. The increases in net income means that greater insurance coverage can be obtained.

Can a settlor achieve this tax savings by funding a trust of insurance on his own life? No—generally the income will be taxed to him if it is used to pay premiums on insurance on his own life. However, if an "adverse party" such as a beneficiary (or the guardian of a minor beneficiary) must consent or approve the use of trust income to pay the premiums, then this income will not be taxed to the settlor but to the trust.

The funded insurance trust may be used in a variety of situations. A parent could use it to create an education fund for his child by the purchase of endowment insurance. By beginning an insurance program for his child at an early age, he can take advantage of the low premium rates for children. One could use a trust to finance a retirement income policy on the life of a dependent relative.

Funded insurance trusts are also a means of saving estate taxes in successive generations. Grandfather wants to pass on a substantial sum of money to his grandchildren free of estate taxes on his and his child's estate. He also wants to protect his grandchildren in case their father dies prematurely. He transfers $50,000 of securities to an insurance trust for the purchase of insurance on the life of his 30-year-old son. The grandchildren are the beneficiaries of the trust. The net income after taxes of $1,700 would buy $85,000 of insurance coverage. At their father's death, the grandchildren will have the $85,000 of insurance, plus the $50,000 of securities, a total of $135,000, tax-free.

The $50,000 in securities represents a taxable transfer (gift) by grandfather and will be added in figuring grandfather's estate taxes. It will bypass his son's estate. However, upon the son's subsequent death the $85,000 in insurance will pass to the grandchildren completely free of taxation in grandfather's or his son's estate.

The Revocable Insurance Trust

This is the usual form of life insurance trust. While the revocable trust does not have the income and estate tax saving advantages of the irrevocable trust, it is a more flexible device. Being revocable, it can be changed by the grantor any time he wishes or at any time his objectives should change.

At the same time, it is an excellent instrument for making sure that his objectives *will* be carried out when he dies and his life insurance proceeds are paid into the trust. Suppose, for example, that a husband feels that his wife should be protected against the risk of her poor management of money after he dies. He assures this by putting the property in trust for her, as we have seen. But unless he also puts his life insurance proceeds, which may constitute a large part of his estate, in trust, he may end up by defeating his original purpose. Hence the importance of the life insurance trust.

But what if he had the insurance payable to his estate and then provided for trust distribution under his will? Wouldn't this method accomplish the same result?

Yes, but this method lacks certain other advantages of the living insurance trust.

Thus:

1. Insurance proceeds paid to a living trust are generally

not subject to the claims of creditors. This is not true when they are paid to the estate.

2. In many states insurance proceeds payable to a living trust are exempt in whole or part from state inheritance taxes. This may not apply to proceeds which go to the estate.

3. Insurance proceeds in a living trust are not part of the probate estate, hence not subject to administrative costs. Not so when the estate is the beneficiary.

4. The living insurance trust has the advantage of immediate liquidity. Insurance paid to an estate is subject to the delays and costs of probate. The trustee of a living trust presents his proofs of death to the insurance companies, collects the proceeds, and begins the administration of the trust.

In some states insurance paid to a testamentary trust will enjoy some of the advantages which the living trust enjoys.

Insurance Owned by the Wife. The revocable insurance trust can take care of another common problem. What happens when a wife has been made the owner of insurance policies on her husband's life in order to prevent their proceeds from being included in the husband's estate? How can trust protection be gained for her then?

Enter the revocable living trust again. Here the wife and not the husband creates it, and all the same advantages pertain. Such trusts are made revocable only during the insured's life. Once he dies, the trust becomes irrevocable and the wife is thus protected for its duration.

A word of warning here, however. If the wife makes the policy on her husband's life payable to a person other than herself (the trustee is such a person), even if she is the income beneficiary of the trust, she makes a gift of a part of the proceeds of the policy when it is paid. This gift is subject to the gift tax. To avoid this, she should retain the right to the income of the trust and a power of appointment to provide for the distribution of the remainder of the trust when she dies. This prevents the gift from being completed, and hence avoids the payment of gift taxes. The trust principal remains subject to estate taxes in her estate, however.

Pouring Over. A final word on revocable insurance trusts. They are frequently used as the basic after-death transfer instrument, a depository for most of the estate assets. In most states an estate owner who wishes to do this can provide in his will that all his probate property on his death be "poured over" into the trust. The trust then carries out all his estate-transfer objectives. The will becomes merely a subsidiary vehicle for bringing all his property together into the living trust. It is possible to do this, of course, with any kind of living trust, but commonly it is the life insurance trust which is used as the receptacle for the pour-over.

The Contingent Insurance Trust

A common problem in estate planning is what to do with insurance which a husband owns on his own life if his wife dies before him, or if they die in a common disaster. His wife is the beneficiary of the insurance and he wants her to receive it outright, if she survives. But what does he do about his minor children if she doesn't survive? Normally they are named as contingent beneficiaries. Lump sum payout to them is not advisable. There are settlement options available under his policies, but rarely can they approach the flexibility of a trust.

What he needs is a trust which will receive the insurance proceeds if his wife doesn't survive him. In other words, a contingent insurance trust to handle the proceeds on behalf of his children.

THE SMALL TRUST

Many people have the mistaken idea that trusts should be limited to use by large taxpayers and large estates. This isn't necessarily true. The advantages to be gained from a trust still exist for the smaller estate although perhaps reduced proportionately. There will be initial costs in the creation of the trust and the transfer of securities or other property, yes. But if the long-range benefits are important enough, and cannot be attained in any other way, then the costs are worthwhile.

What about finding trustees? And the problem of commissions? For one thing, relatives or friends will often serve without commission. And while corporate trustees generally will not take the administration of small trusts, they will undertake them when they can be combined into a common trust fund. Under a common trust fund, the bank administers a group of trusts as one fund. This keeps down the costs of administration and permits the bank to charge standard commissions.

PROTECTING YOUR BENEFICIARIES

Up to this point we have been talking about trusts as if they were primarily tax-saving devices. But in the long run this aspect, important as it is, is only a subordinate one. The true importance, and the chief reason, for setting up trusts is to transfer property in such a way that it will be most useful for one's beneficiaries. The trust, both living and testamentary, often does this better than the outright gift or bequest for two reasons. First, it can be made as flexible or as rigid as the grantor wants to make it. A well-planned trust is able to take care of the needs of each beneficiary according to his station in life, his age, and his abilities.

Second, there is the unique function of the trustee: someone who, in effect, carries on for the estate planner, protecting his family and meeting their needs, acting as he would, in accordance with the changing conditions and situations that arise. This makes of the trust a unique instrument of protection.

The Wife

Many women feel insulted or hurt if their husbands leave property in trust for them. A woman may feel that it shows a lack of confidence or faith in her. If she has not had previous experience, however, she may not be prepared to handle large sums of money. If this is true, she herself would not want to be burdened with administration of the property. Or perhaps she may be capable but not interested. Perhaps she's too busy with her career to have time for financial matters. The ability is there but not the inclination. In this case, too, outright gifts could be a burden to her.

Beyond all this, a trust acts as a buffer against the demands and pressures that a widow is frequently subjected to. When one comes into substantial property, it is difficult to resist requests for loans or gifts—especially when they come from relatives; more especially, from one's own children. We know of one widow who was left $300,000 outright. She lent $100,000 to one son, then felt guilty toward her other son. When he demanded a similar loan to buy a house, she lent him an equal amount. The sons realize their obligations; they both pay interest on their loans, but just the same she is left with only $100,000 of ready cash available. If she needed the money in an emergency, or if they stopped paying the interest, what could she do about it? She would have been happier if the money had been put in trust for her.

We're not saying that all bequests or gifts to wives should be made in trust. Many women have both the ability and the willingness to handle property and end up by doing a better job of it than their husbands did. Such a woman has no need of a trust. We are saying, however, that a trust implies no lack of faith, or even a desire to restrict a woman's freedom. Its purpose is protection.

The Children

Here is certainly an instance where the elasticity of the trust device comes into play. It can be used to cover all kinds of situations which require special handling. Obviously, minor or incompetent children need the protection of a trust. It obviates the necessity for a guardian of property (for the minor) or a conservator (for an incompetent), and at the same time it permits greater flexibility in the management of the beneficiaries' property.

As we have said, a trust can be used to protect irresponsible adult children against themselves. If you do have such a child—one who simply cannot handle money in any way except to spend it—you might consider setting up a "spendthrift trust." This prevents the beneficiary from assigning or selling his interest in the trust and places it beyond the reach of his creditors. The very existence of organizations that specialize in buying trust and estate interests for as little as 15 or 20 per cent of their potential value testifies to the need for this kind of trust provision.

Trusts which have "spendthrift" provisions usually provide that the trustees, instead of giving the beneficiary large sums outright, are free to use the money in his behalf as they see best and exercise their own discretion. For example, a trustee could pay the person's rent and provide him with the necessities of life, but otherwise conserve his money for him.

On the other hand, your adult child (or other young beneficiary) may be unpredictable at this juncture. There is no way of knowing if he will eventually be able to handle his property wisely, but you don't want to restrict him forever with a rigid trust. The answer might be to set up an "incentive trust." For example, the amount of income payable to him could be gauged to his own earned income. Or payments of principal could be conditioned on a minimum amount of earned income over a specified period.

In many families the problem is not with the children, but with their spouses. A donor may be worried about the possible effect of a large gift of property to a child; they too may be subject to pressures from their spouses. He wants to protect his child against this, to make sure that the property his child receives from him will remain within the family, and not go ultimately to the child's spouse. The trust is again the solution. He can use it to assure final distribution to grandchildren or other members of the family or to carry out some other family purpose.

A Special Device: The Sprinkling Trust

But suppose you have no way of knowing precisely what your family's future needs may be? After all, no one is omniscient. Who can tell whether there might not come a time when one beneficiary will need an extra amount of money, another time when his share should be less?

Enter the trustee. You can give him the power to use his discretion in such instances by setting up a trust which allows him to "sprinkle" or "spray" income among a group of beneficiaries. Not only does this give the trust flexibility, it can also aid in keeping family tax costs at a minimum.

Suppose, for example, that a grandmother creates a trust with the income payable to her children and grandchildren in such amounts as "the trustee may determine." Some years later, the settlor's oldest grandchild enters law school. It will take about $10,000 per year to pay for his higher education. If his father called on the trust for help, he would have to receive about $14,000 from the trust in order to pay the $10,000 fee, since he is in a 28 per cent bracket. But because the trustee has sprinkling powers, he can pay the money to the grandchild instead. Then he need take only about $12,000 of the trust fund to produce the $10,000 at the grandchild's tax bracket.

GUARANTEEING PRIVACY

All of the above applies to both living and testamentary trusts. But the living trust also provides another protection for the settlor and beneficiaries: it guarantees privacy. Mr. Disappointed Father, if you recall, wanted to cut one son out of his will but shrank from the idea because of the publicity the will would engender. Not everyone has such exotic problems, but no one likes to have his dirty linen washed in public. A living trust ensures this won't happen. It is a personal agreement between the settlor and his trustee. It is not a matter of public record as the will is, because it doesn't have to go through the courts.

Mr. Disappointed Father, for example, could set up a living trust which contains almost all his property. Three of his children would be the beneficiaries of the trust; the trust property would pass to them at his death. His will, however, could leave all his remaining property (of which there would be little left) to his four children equally. As far as the outside world would know, he had treated all four children equally.

PREVIEWING THE AFTER-DEATH ESTATE

The living trust has one final advantage. When it is created consciously as the after-death transfer plan, there is a unique opportunity to give the entire estate-transfer program a dress rehearsal. The planner can work with the trustees to acquaint them with the problems and duties he wants them to assume. He can familiarize his family with the trustee. He has ample opportunity to see how his plan will work while he is still alive. He may be able to correct weaknesses or oversights before it is too late. In his estate plan he gets what most people want but few ever get: a second chance.

CHAPTER 14

Why Everyone Needs a Will

Everyone?

But what about the young person whose estate consists primarily of a few stocks and bonds, a little insurance, and a house that isn't paid for? What good would a will do his family? Surely his spouse is bound to inherit everything, including the debts.

Or the husband and wife who own everything jointly? What's the point of a will in this case? The survivor gets everything, doesn't he?

And the wife who owns little or no property in her own name? Does she need a will if she has nothing to pass on?

The truth is, they all do. The wife of the young man with the "little estate" is not going to get it all; state laws provide that children or relatives are entitled to a portion. Death in a common disaster may upset the plans of the couple with joint property. The wife with "nothing" forgets that someday she may inherit property from her husband and that wills not only dispose of property but also provide for the guardianship of children.

By means of a will, a person exercises the right which the law says is his, to express his post-mortem objectives: to provide for the welfare of his family, to distribute his assets as he thinks best, and to secure the efficient management of his property. Implicit in these rights also is an opportunity— the opportunity to save taxes by means of a well-drawn will which takes advantage of available tax shelters.

For the estate planner who does not make lifetime transfers, his will is his entire property transference program. It is the sole expression of his intentions and the only way he has of carrying out his ultimate objectives. Without a will these objectives will not be met. Without a properly designed will the desired results will not be achieved.

The underlying aspect of a will, then, is the maker's *intention*. Though the planner's attorney draws the will, it is the planner who must determine what he wants his will to do. He is, after all, the only one who knows his family needs and how he would like to see them met.

If the planner does not use his right to make a will, the law will step in and make one for him—but the results may be quite different from what he had envisioned.

THE STATE OF INTESTACY

If a person dies without leaving a will we say he died *intestate*. The law takes over and directs how his property will be distributed; in effect, writing the will he failed to make. The law's writing is as fair and equitable as possible; the major trouble is that it is done blindly.

It is based on general principles regarding the disposition of property; general principles for the guardianship of children; general principles as to the rights of relatives; and general principles as to who shall manage the estate. It is therefore impersonal and by necessity rarely coincides with the particular interests and objectives of the individual who has died.

The law in question is the law of the state in which he had his domicile and the state where his real property was located. It varies from state to state but there are certain general patterns of distribution in all the intestacy laws.

If you die without a will, what happens?

Your Wife's Share of Your Estate May be Smaller Than You Intended

Many people think that a husband or wife automatically inherits everything when the other spouse dies. This is not so. Depending on the state in which you live, your spouse will be entitled to from one-third to one-half of your estate. In some states, the widow's share is equal to a child's share. What she gets depends on the number of children. If there are five children, the widow only gets one-sixth. For example, the wife of a man with a net estate of $300,000 who had five children would get only $50,000. Is this what her husband would have wanted?

When the average man disposes of his property, his chief aim is usually to ensure the protection of his widow. But the laws of intestacy may run counter to that concept. When they prevail, a widow may not have enough to support herself; she maybe become dependent on her children. While the estate owner is alive his wife enjoys a standard of living which matches her husband's $300,000 estate. After his death she can't live on the income from her $50,000 capital. How long will the income and principal last when she has to dip into this fund year after year to meet her financial needs?

Moreover, she is restricted in her freedom to use her minor children's inheritance to provide and care for them as she thinks best. This means that the children can also suffer from their father's intestacy.

The hardship may be greater if the estate is a small one. The young father who doesn't make a will because he hasn't much to leave is a husband and parent who is not facing up to the problems his surviving family will have. His wife will need the entire estate to support herself and the children. If he were to leave an estate of $75,000, he would probably want her to have it all and not just one-third, for example. In the absence of a will, his widow, in some states, would get only $25,000. The balance of $50,000 would go to his children, but his wife would not have free use of it.

But what if there are no children? Many childless couples assume that each will automatically inherit everything from the other in the absence of a will. They should be aware of the fact that under the intestate distribution laws of many states, the survivor shares the estate with the deceased spouse's parents or brothers and sisters, or even nieces and nephews. The results are sometimes appalling.

One of the saddest victims of intestate distribution we can recall was the husband who, in order to save estate taxes before there was an unlimited marital deduction, had put most of his property into his wife's name, assuming she would survive him. She died before him and without a will. Her parents and her sister had predeceased her, but she had a niece whom they hadn't seen in 20 years. To whom did this property go? Her husband received the first $10,000 of his wife's estate and shared the balance of what had once been his property equally with her niece.

Children Get Equal Treatment

Except for what goes to the surviving husband or wife, the children will be treated alike. If there is no surviving husband or wife, they share the entire estate to the exclusion of all other relatives. Children of a deceased child inherit the share their parents would have taken.

This equal treatment may be equitable when a fixed standard has to be set, but it cannot and does not take into consideration the needs and deserts of the individual child. One child may be disabled and entirely dependent on his parents, but his share will be the same as his healthy brother's. One daughter may have cared for her parents through illness and old age, but she will receive no more than her sister who had deserted the family.

Inheritance by Minors Will Be Affected

If you do have children and they are minors you have even greater need for a will.

Property which minors inherit belongs to them, but its use is restricted until they reach their majority. An outright inheritance by a minor, as occurs in an intestacy, results in the need for appointment of a guardian to deal with the minor's property. This involves the trouble and expense of a bond for the guardian, periodic accountings by him, and judicial proceedings for authorization to act or for approval of acts already performed. The mother who has been appointed guardian of her children by the court may be indignant to discover that in order to use their funds for tuition, she must bring a court proceeding for authorization. She may, as their mother, know best, but as their guardian she is subject to judicial supervision.

Sometimes a guardian of the person of the minor (as distinguished from the property of the minor) must also be appointed. A parent, as a child's natural guardian, has the primary right to both these appointments. However, if the surviving parent is unfit to be guardian or dies before the child reaches adulthood, someone else has to be selected.

In one celebrated family, a father of considerable wealth

died. His estate passed one-half to his wife and one-half to their 2-year-old child. A court proceeding was brought for her appointment as guardian of the person and property of her child. A few years later she died in an auto accident. Another proceeding was necessary in order to have her executor account to the court for her acts as guardian and to have a new guardian appointed. Each grandmother sought the appointment to the exclusion of the other, and a bitter fight ensued. The issue was finally resolved by their appointment as co-guardians, but the dissension remains to this day.

Expenses Will Be Greater

The cost of administering an estate may be greater when there is no will. The administrator of an intestate estate must furnish a bond in most states. The bond protects the beneficiaries and creditors of the estate, but the cost of the premiums must be paid either out of the estate or out of the administrator's fees.

The administrator is also limited in his actions by the laws of the jurisdiction in which he is appointed. In order for him to sell property, compromise claims, or distribute the estate, he may need juidicial authorization. The cost of each proceeding for authorization or approval is paid out of the estate.

The Administrator Is Not a Free Agent

The limitations set upon the administrator are again for the purpose of protection—in this case, protection of the estate. But, in fact, they can be a hindrance to sound management. For example, administrators may be restricted to specified percentages and types of investments. The estate may consist solely of high-grade common stock but if the law of the state does not permit full investment in common stock, the administrator must sell some of them or risk personal liability. If the asset that must be disposed of is a business, people other than the members of the family may also suffer.

An unfortunate case was brought to us by the surviving partner of a growing business. He and his late partner, whom we shall call Joe, had started the business on a combined capital of $10,000 and had built it into a successful enterprise. When Joe died, he left a wife and three young children but no will. His wife inherited one-third and his children two-thirds. The attorney for the estate had informed the surviving partner that, by law, he had to liquidate the assets of the partnership and pay Joe's share to the estate. He didn't believe it. We could only confirm the fact that liquidation was required by existing partnership law.

Although provision could have been made for continuation of the business, this hadn't been done. Since Joe's children were minors, they could not agree to continuation. The liquidation meant an economic loss to all involved. As a going business it had provided each partner with a minimum income of $50,000 a year. The operating value, of course, would not be realized on liquidation.

The Law Picks Your Administrator

The law—and not you—selects the administrator of your estate if you die without a will. As a general rule this means that the surviving husband or wife has the first right to be appointed. But is this always desirable? How about the man whose wife gets one-third and whose children by an earlier marriage get two-thirds of the estate? Would the husband— even if he were to agree to this disposition—want the wife to administer it? It would hardly make for family harmony.

If the surviving spouse doesn't want to be the administrator or if there is no surviving spouse, what happens then?

The general rule is that the children have an equal right to be appointed. But would all parents of all children want this? Supposing there was an irresponsible or spendthrift child?

Sometimes the court will appoint all of the children jointly. We know of one case in which this happened. The children (there were four of them) had never liked each other, never got along together. Now they carried their jealousies, their bitterness, and their petty quarreling over into the administration of their father's estate. Every step taken, large or small, meant a family quarrel resulting in the inefficient and costly administration of the estate.

There May Be Unnecessary Taxes

Intestacy is the opposite of planning. It means leaving things to chance—the chance of what the law will be in the state in which you are living at the time of your death, the chance as to who will survive you. It may cost your estate unnecessary taxes because your spouse receives less than the full amount she could have been given tax-free. If your spouse receives more than the amount needed to eliminate tax on your estate, the excess amount may be needlessly taxed in her estate.

If your parents turn out to be your heirs, they may not welcome an addition to their own estate that causes an increase on their estate taxes. The child with a substantial income of his own may realize only a small net return on his inherited property after the bite of income taxes. Instead of savings there is waste.

Tax savings is a prime ingredient of estate planning. As we will see in the following chapters, the carefully planned estate can minimize losses from unnecessary taxes, both income and estate, simply by taking advantage of existing laws. But little can usually be accomplished toward this end without the aid of a will.

With a Will There's a Way

So much for intestacy. Let's look at the other side of the picture, and examine some of the advantages to be gained through a will.

A will is a plan or a design for the distribution of property. It is custom-made, created by one individual for the benefit of his family. That is its great advantage. With a will you can:

Choose Your Beneficiaries

Instead of letting the law select the people who will share your estate and determine their respective shares, you can choose those upon whom you wish to confer your bounty. Take the situation of the widow who received only one-sixth of her husband's $300,000 estate—the income of which was not enough to support her. By means of a will, her husband could have left her a larger share of the estate and could have made provisions for a trust for the rest. This would give her sufficient income for a continuing comfortable support.

Only by means of a will can a parent provide for the special financial security of a dependent, disabled child or compensate the worthy child in preference to the undeserving.

What's more, the person with a will can determine not only *who* his beneficiaries will be, but *how* and *when* they will receive this inheritance. If he wants, for example, to leave his spouse's share in trust, he can do this through his will. If he wants one person to have the use of the property for a certain period of time, and then to have another succeed him, this can best be done through his will.

Leave Property to Minors the Better Way

If minors are to receive property it should be set up so that it can be most efficiently and economically administered for them. The trouble with their inheriting property by intestacy is that they become outright owners. The fact that they are underage limits their ability to deal with their property and requires that it be handled by a guardian in their behalf.

A will can dispense with the need for a guardian of the minor's property and the bond, accountings, and judicial supervision which accompany it. If a guardian of the minor's person is needed, he, too, can be designated in the will.

Take the case of the struggle between the two grandmothers we cited before. A will could have prevented family friction as well as needless expense. If the father had left the child's share in trust, the trustee could have managed the property for the minor without the need for a guardian of the property. The mother or any other person could have been designated as trustee and a successor named in the event of her death or resignation. Furthermore, to ensure continuous management, uninterrupted by possible death, a trust company could have been selected as trustee or co-trustee.

Save Administration Expenses

A person who makes a will can generally dispense with

bonds for his executor and trustee. In an estate of some size, the savings may be thousands of dollars. In a small estate, even the few hundred dollars saved is meaningful. By giving your managers broad power to deal with the property, you may enable them to administer the estate without having to resort to court proceedings for authorization and approval. One sentence in a will, for example, giving the executor power to sell real estate can save the costs of a proceeding for judicial approval of such a sale.

Set Your Own Rules for Managing Your Estate

Again, with some limitation the person who makes a will can make his own rules. He can confer extensive powers on his executor or trustee in the administration of the estate or trusts. On the other hand, he may want them to have more restricted powers than the law would otherwise allow. In any event the powers that he gives them should enable them to deal effectively with property he leaves. They should be flexible enough to permit changes as the needs of the surviving family and economic conditions change.

A partner in a business, such as Joe, should give his executor and trustee power to allow the business to continue and permit the estate to participate as a partner. The executor is in that way free to choose his course of action in the light of the best interests of Joe's family and the economic conditions then prevailing.

You Choose Your Own Managers

The person you name in your will to administer the estate is your executor or executrix. The one designated to manage the trusts is your trustee. The court will accept the person or persons nominated by the testator unless he is a felon or lunatic. Some states have restrictions on the appointment of non-residents.

One member of the family may be designated by the testator to the exclusion of all others. Co-executors or co-trustees might be advisable for soundest management or family harmony. The person with an irresponsible beneficiary can prevent him from running the estate. The person with an irresponsible family can put the estate into the hands of competent, reliable outsiders.

WOMEN AND WILLS

The number of male intestacies may be great, but it is surpassed by the female intestacies. Unless she possesses wealth of her own, the average woman just doesn't think about making a will, and usually her husband doesn't either.

Remember the man whose wife died without a will, leaving him to share the property which had once been his with her niece? He learned about this problem of estate planning the hard way. His oversight was in not seeing to it that he would get the property back if his wife predeceased him. A will could have done this.

It can solve just the opposite problem too—situations where the husband already has a large estate which will be subject to high estate taxation at his death, and doesn't want to inherit additional property from his wife. Often it is better for her to leave it directly to the children or grandchildren.

This problem crops up most frequently in families where the wife owns insurance policies on her husband's life. He has transferred them to her in order to keep the proceeds from being included in his taxable estate. But if she dies without a will, he could find himself the owner of the policies. This can be avoided by having her will transfer the policies to the next generation. When the husband dies, the proceeds will come tax-free to the children (or to a trust for them).

As the possessor—potential or actual—of property, then, a woman has, just as does her husband, the problem of disposing of this property in the most effective manner.

For women who are also mothers, the responsibility is especially strong. If there are minor children, the necessity for their property being left in trust and for making provisions for guardianship is doubly important. A husband's will may provide all this, it is true, but ordinarily his will would pass all or most of his estate to the wife if she survives him.

If she dies without a will, then the original plan for the distribution of the entire estate is defeated. The property which she has received from her husband will go outright to the children and not have the trust protection which they require. In addition, her opportunity to nominate a guardian of her choice for them will be lost.

Can't she wait to do all this until she is a widow? This is playing with fire. There is no assurance that if she neglects it now, she won't neglect it then. Nor does she have any sure way of knowing that she might not become incompetent to make a will. Moreover, the threat of death by common disaster (husband and wife both dying in an accident, such as a plane or automobile crash) is always present, particularly in today's society. If it can be established that he died before her (even minutes or seconds before her), then she is the survivor—a survivor who may have died intestate, with all that that implies.

WILLS AND JOINT PROPERTY

What happens to joint property when both owners die simultaneously? Many people mistakenly think that if all their property is jointly owned with their spouse, there is no need for them to make a will; the survivor will take it all. This holds true, but not in a case of simultaneous death, as in a common disaster. If there are no wills, the joint property is divided in half and each half distributed according to the laws of intestacy. Is this what the husband and wife wanted? If not, a will could have provided for this situation and disposed of their property as they wished.

BEWARE OF JOINT AND MUTUAL WILLS

A joint will is *one* instrument executed by two people as their respective wills. Mutual wills are separate instruments executed by two people as their respective wills, but the wills are similar or reciprocal. Husbands and wives execute joint and mutual wills in the mistaken belief that it makes things simpler. Or they believe that it guarantees that the survivor ultimately has to dispose of the property as the first to die would have wished. They want to be sure where the property will go after the deaths of both of them.

A joint will—one document executed by both—doesn't simplify matters. It should be avoided if for no other reason than the fact that the probate on the death of the survivor is needlessly complicated—particularly if the survivor dies in a state other than the one in which the will was first probated. The simplest method is by separate wills.

Both joint and mutual wills are ambiguous things. Take

the question of whether the survivor has the right to make a new will. Sometimes the courts have held that if there is no agreement not to revoke, the survivor is free to go ahead and dispose of the property as he or she chooses. On the other hand, sometimes the mere making of a joint or mutual will has been found to imply sufficient agreement not to revoke. Then the provisions are binding on the survivor whether or not they are intended to be.

Thus, if you do decide to make a joint or mutual will, you should be sure to spell out your agreement, whether it is to allow revocation or to prohibit it.

Moreover, you should not make agreements not to revoke without the fullest consideration of the pros and cons. The husband who is convinced that after his death his wife will give his property to a second husband, or the wife who fears the same thing in reverse, can both achieve their objective through other means—a trust, say, or an annuity. Moreover, even if the will is irrevocable, the survivor might be able to circumvent or violate the agreement by using up the property, wasting it, or giving it away.

If both have faith and confidence in each other, then tying the survivor's hands is certainly unwise. Circumstances may change radically after one of them dies and call for a different disposition. The survivor, however, would be powerless to make it.

And finally, joint and mutual wills can be invitations to litigation. If the survivor rightfully or wrongfully makes a new will, the stage is set for a court battle between the beneficiaries of the old will and the beneficiaries of the new.

So it was in the case of the estate of Grace Oursler, widow of Fulton Oursler, the noted writer and editor. At the time of his marriage to Grace in 1925, Fulton had two children by a prior marriage. He then had two more children by his marriage to Grace.

In 1951 Grace and Fulton executed wills at the same time which were identical in the disposition of Fulton's property. His will provided that his residuary estate go to his wife, but if she did not survive him, then to the four children. Grace's will provided that her residuary estate go to Fulton, but that if he died before she did, then property she received from him passed on to all four children.

Fulton Oursler died the following year and his wife inherited his residuary estate. She made a new will leaving everyting to her two children and nothing to the others. She died in 1955. The two children of Fulton's former marriage went into court to get their half of his property. They won in the higher courts, but after years of litigation the highest court of the State of New York dismissed the suit. By a vote of four to three, the court determined that a promise not to revoke the earlier will was not proved or implied. It said that "Grace may have had a moral obligation to give the property which she inherited from Fulton to all four of the children, but a moral obligation is not enough. . . ."

Don't Procrastinate

Intestacy seems to be a universal failing. The person who doesn't make a will is in illustrious company; Abraham Lincoln, to name one famous instance. No doubt the millions of people who followed in his footsteps and died without a will never meant this to happen. They were procrastinators. They meant to make one some time soon, maybe not tomorrow, but soon.

But a will should not be put off like this. There may not be time to do the job later. Or conditions may change, and the prospective testator become incompetent to make a will. The will should be made now—as if death were imminent—to cover present needs and foreseeable future ones. It can always be changed. A will is ambulatory. It has no effect until death. When a situation alters, it can be altered. But if it is not made now, it may never be. That is the point.

CHAPTER 15

An Ounce of Prevention: Meeting the Problem of Tax Erosion

In the course of estate planning, it may sometimes seem to the planner that the primary beneficiary of his estate is the Internal Revenue Service. A feeling of frustration develops. One elderly lady, on being informed of the estimated amount of estate taxes her executors would have to pay, indignantly said, "If the taxes will be *that* much, I'd rather not go."

If death and taxes are inevitable, unnecessary tax erosion is not. Unnecessary tax erosion is the wasting of estate assets through the payment of taxes which, with proper planning, could have been avoided. The prevention of tax erosion, or, in other words, tax savings, is an essential element of estate transference.

At the risk of being repetitious let us emphasize again that the purpose of estate planning, whether it be in the creation or transference stage, is not tax savings. The purpose is security for the family. Planning which keeps taxes at a minimum, leaving as much as possible for the family, helps to achieve that goal. Tax savings then, is not an end in itself but a means.

Even if a planner doesn't care about tax savings (although we have yet to meet one who didn't) he must know what the tax on his estate will be in order to determine how much he will actually be leaving to his beneficiaries. His gross estate and his estate after taxes may be two very different things. He must work with the net figure if he wants to have a true picture of what he is actually transferring.

WHAT ARE THE TAXES

In tax planning there are various taxes which come into play. The major one is, of course, the federal estate tax. Other death taxes must not be overlooked, however. The state in which you live at the time of death will impose a tax which may be called an "estate" or "inheritance" or "succession" tax. Real property located in another state may also be taxed by that state. Property in a foreign country, even stock of a foreign corporation, may be subjected to death duties of that country.

The variations among these state and foreign taxes is so great that it is not feasible to discuss them here. As a rule, state taxes are small in comparison with the federal estate tax, and they may be allowed in part or wholly as a credit against the federal tax. They should be considered, however, in any final calculations.

Proper planning also calls for consideration of income taxes, that is, the taxes which the beneficiaries will have to pay on the income from the property they receive from your estate (when added to their other taxable income). The ultimate figure which determines whether your sought-after objective, family security, has been achieved is, in the end, the net income your beneficiaries will have after the payment of all taxes.

WHAT THE ESTATE TAX TAXES

The federal estate tax is a tax on the transfer of property at death. The tax is imposed on the "taxable estate." Since the taxable estate is arrived at by calculating the gross estate and subtracting from it the allowable deductions and exemptions, your first step is to determine what will be included in your gross estate.

A person normally considers the property which he owns, or the property which will pass under his will, as being the assets of his estate—the stocks, bonds, real estate, business interests, cash, and personal effects which he thinks of as his. However, his gross estate for tax purposes may include other property—property he owns together with someone else, property he once owned, and even property he never owned.

f the survivor of the money that would otherwise have paid out in taxes for producing additional income. is why the marital deduction is easily the most valuable available for alleviating estate tax erosion.

w to Qualify Property for It. This deduction isn't an matic one. It is allowed only for property which does ally (1) pass to the surviving spouse (2) under conditions ch make it includable in her taxable estate when she , if she still has it.

ou must know what kind of property transfers qualify the marital deductions and what kind don't. Otherwise, stand to lose its great benefits.

Property which qualifies for the marital deduction in-des property passing outside your will as well as under ur will so long as it is includable in your gross estate. Thus, surance proceeds payable to your spouse which are part of ur gross estate will qualify. So, too, does the half of the int property which she takes by right of survivorship and includable in your gross estate. This is property which she ill receive outright.

Property given to her in trust can also qualify provided e trust provisions meet specific requirements set down by e tax law. In order for a gift in trust to qualify, the rincipal of the trust must pass to her estate at her death (an tate trust) or she must receive all of the income of the ust (a qualified terminable interest trust).

The estate trust is useful in the cases of large estates or ere the surviving spouse has large income from other urces. The estate trust, unlike the qualified terminable erest trust, does not require that all of the income be paid the survivor. It can either be accumulated in the trust or d to the survivor in the discretion of the trustees. The ult is that the trust income is not piled on top of other able income and thereby taxed away. The income being ained in the trust is taxable to it. The only requirement is in order to qualify the trust for a marital deduction, the cipal and accumulated income must pass to the survi-s estate at his or her death and be subject to distribution art of the estate.

ith a qualified terminable interest property trust, popular-own as a "QTIP trust," not only must the surviving spouse ntitled to all the income, but no one can have a right to t the use of income or principal for anyone other than

Here are some items which a planner may not know are includable in this gross estate for tax purposes or items which can be easily overlooked.

1. *Gifts Made at Any Time Under Any of These Circumstances.*

If you retain the right to the income or a power to designate who shall enjoy the income, or

If possession or enjoyment of the property can only be obtained by the beneficiary if he survives the donor and there is a possibility that the property may return to the donor or his estate, or

If you have retained a right to change the beneficial enjoyment of the property by a power to alter, amend or revoke.

2. *Transfers Made Within 3 Years of Death.* Gifts of property made within 3 years of death are generally no longer includable in the gross estate with the major exception of life insurance. In addition, if the decedent set up a trust or similar arrangement but retained a life estate or power to revoke or which didn't become effective until his death and he released his rights in the property within 3 years of his death, the property is taxable as part of his estate. The same rule applies if he released a general power of appointment (see page 212) within that time.

3. *Annuities.* The value of an annuity payable to a survivor is includable to the extent of the contributions made to it by you or your employer.

4. *Jointly Held Property.* Each spouse is treated as owning half of the property in their joint name, so only 50 per cent of the value of the property will be included in the estate of the first spouse to die. The total value of property held jointly by you and another person or persons with right of survivorship will be included in the gross estate of whoever dies first. There are two exceptions. If the survivor can prove he contributed to the purchase price, then the part represented by his contribution will be excluded. If the property was received from a third party by inheritance or by gift, then the survivor's percentage of interest in the property is not included.

5. *Insurance on Your Life.* It will be includable in your gross estate if it is payable to your estate or if it is payable to other beneficiaries and you had any incidents of ownership in the policy. Incidents of ownership may be something less

than what one commonly thinks of as ownership. They may be the right to change the beneficiary, to surrender or cancel the policy, to assign or pledge it, or to borrow against the cash surrender value.

6. *Insurance on Another's Life.* This is an asset like a stock or bond or any other piece of property, but it is frequently overlooked. Generally speaking, the amount of the cash surrender value of the policy will be included in your gross estate.

7. *Income Payable After Death.* At the time of death there is generally some income which has been earned by the decedent and will be paid to his estate or beneficiaries. It may be salary, commissions, royalties, or a share of partnership income. While it is sometimes difficult to forecast what unpaid salary or uncollected fees at the time of death will be due, there are income items which can be estimated. These include renewal commissions, installment payments under a contract or other agreement, and employment benefits paid under a non-qualified plan.

8. *Power of Appointment.* Strange as it may seem, property which you never owned may be included in your gross estate. This will happen if you are given a general power over property—that is, a right to designate who the property will go to including yourself, your estate, your creditors, or the creditors of your estate. If the power was created after October 21, 1942, the property will be included in your gross estate whether or not you exercise the power. If it was created on or before that date, however, it will be included only if you exercise it.

9. *Distributions from Pension and Profit-Sharing Plans.* Such distributions are now fully taxable for estate tax purposes.

While the following items are not truly part of your gross estate, they will enter into how the tax on your estate will be computed.

10. *Taxable Transfer Made After December 31, 1976:* Post-1976 gifts that exceeded the annual exclusions, other than gifts which qualified for the marital or charitable deductions, are taxable transfers and are added to your taxable estate. However, you may have a credit for gift taxes you paid.

11. *Generation-Skipping Trusts.* If someone a generation older than you established a trust for your benefit by will or trust agreement and such trust eventually passes to benefici-

aries a generation younger than yourse[ ] nieces, or nephews), the trust might be ta[ ] assets were added to your taxable estate [ ] skipping taxation on page 181).

DEDUCTIONS

Expenses and Debts

Once having arrived at the gross estate the n[ ] determine your deductions. The costs of your [ ] the expenses involved in the administration of [ ] such as executors' commissions and attorneys' f[ ] ducted from the gross estate.

These generally average from 5 to 10 per cent [ ] estate, depending on the size of the estate, the co[ ] allowed by the particular state to your fiduciarie[ ] problems which may arise in connection with the [ ] administration of your estate. A will contest or tax[ ] can run up the cost considerably. To have a figure [ ] with, we recommend taking 7½ per cent of your es[ ] your estimated administrative expenses.

In addition, your debts, whether it be the mo[ ] your home, unpaid taxes, or an electric bill, [ ] deducted.

When expenses and debts have been subtracte[ ] gross estate, the figure arrived at it is the adj[ ] estate. Next comes the most valuable deduction [ ] marital deduction.

The Marital Deduction

Under the unlimited marital deduction, any [ ] by a husband or wife to his or her spouse w[ ] for the marital deduction passes tax-free. Bef[ ] maximum marital deduction was limited to [ ] the adjusted gross estate or $250,000, whichev[ ] In the Economic Recovery Tax Act of 1981 [ ] cided that a married couple should be trea[ ] nomic unit and to permit them to postpone [ ] their estates till the death of the survivor. [ ] tax until the second death, the family has th[ ] the surviving spouse during his or her lifetime. A provision, for example, permitting the trustees to use the principal for the support of someone else would disqualify the trust for the marital deduction.

On the survivor's death the property can pass to the beneficiaries designated in the will or trust agreement. Alternately, the surviving spouse can be given a power to appoint the trust principal, but the planner should provide for the disposition of the trust principal should the survivor fail to exercise the power.

The Charitable Deduction

A deduction is allowed for property included in the gross estate which is given to charity. Unlike the income tax law, there is no percentage limitation (although the state of your domicile may limit the amount you can leave to charity). The gift need not be exclusively for charity. For example, you might have a trust with the income payable to your children, and the remainder to charity. The value of the remainder interest will qualify for the charitable deduction. (This important deduction has many ramifications. For a full examination of them, see Chapter 17.)

THE FEDERAL UNIFIED CREDIT

Because of the unified credit, which is equivalent to $600,000, an estate of that amount or less is no longer liable for any federal estate tax and no estate tax return need be filed. A married man or woman with an estate greater than that could leave his or her children, relatives, or friends an amount up to the exemption equivalent or put that sum into a non-marital trust and leave the balance to his or her spouse. No matter how large the estate, the combination of the unified credit and use of the unlimited marital deduction for the balance in excess of this exemption makes it nontaxable.

FIRST STEP IN TAX PLANNING:
THE DRY RUN

The first step in tax planning is to determine how much your estate taxes will be. This calls for a bit of pencil work. Your Estate Planning Worksheets have the necessary forms and instructions for you to estimate the amount of these taxes.

This estimate, of course, includes only federal estate taxes, not state inheritance taxes. There may also be credits for state and foreign taxes which your attorney can calculate for you and certain credits which can't be determined beforehand. But the figure you arrive at in the Worksheets is your starting point for any estate planning you will want to do.

SECOND STEP IN TAX PLANNING:
REDUCING TAXES

If the figure is higher than you would like it to be, the next step is to see what can be done to bring it down without sacrificing your basic objectives. Estate planning being an individual matter, what can and should be done depends upon your particular circumstances.

Here are some suggestions for ways and means of bringing down the tax bill.

Reduce Your Gross Estate

The major way to reduce your gross estate is by making lifetime gifts. However, as indicated in Chapter 11, taxable lifetime gifts and estate assets are taxable under one unified tax system. Nonetheless, by making maximum use of annual exclusions and available deductions, some portions of gifts otherwise taxed can be eliminated from all taxation. In addition, large taxable gifts if timely made can exclude a good amount of subsequent capital growth and income from taxation even though the value of the gift itself is taxable. If you have already made gifts where you have retained some right or power over the property, such as a right to revoke a trust, you might release that right or power. This should only be done after careful consideration, however. Giving up a right or power can mean a taxable gift.

If you have a general power of appointment under a trust which was created on or before October 21, 1942, in order to keep the value of the trust out of your gross estate you must be careful not to exercise it or else take steps to release it.

Make Full Use of the Marital Deduction

Unless there are strong non-tax reasons against it, it is wise to take full advantage of the marital deduction when your combined estates—both husand's and wife's—will be less than the amount of the exemption. That is obvious. But what about the case where both husband and wife have approximately equal and sizable estates?

One theory has it that the marital deduction should not be fully used. Following this logic, whereas use of the deduction reduces taxes on the husband's estate, for instance, it ends up by piling his property on top of his wife's (i.e., adding the property which qualified for the marital deduction to the wife's estate). So when she dies, her estate will be in higher estate tax brackets and her estate taxes greatly increased. The combined taxes on the estates of husband and wife may be larger than if the husband did not use the marital deduction.

One cannot quarrel with the logic of this reasoning. But it does result in a situation where taxes are not postponed, but instead are paid out immediately. On the whole, we think this is inadvisable. Here is a case where taxes should be postponed, for two reasons:

First, when taxes are postponed, additional money is available for investment. This can produce income for a widow and/or family over the period of the wife's lifetime. If the wife is 50 years old when the husband dies, this could mean 25 years or more of capital appreciation and income production on money which otherwise would have been paid out in taxes.

Second, why assume that the wife's property is going to be conserved in toto until she dies? It may well be that she will give some of it away, or be forced to spend a large part of it on living expenses. Also, no one can foresee what the course of the economy will be over such a relatively long period of time. A depression or severe recession could shrink values to the point where the property left at her death would be subject to less estate taxation than can now be anticipated.

Get Maximum Mileage from the Unified Credit

However, it is still important to get maximum mileage from the unified credit in the estate of the first spouse to die, because the estate of the second will be subject to tax on everything above the exemption. An amount equal to the exemption can be "sheltered" by using a non-marital trust, so as to give the survivor the full benefit of the estate without all of it being taxed in his or her estate.

Take a couple with assets of $1,200,000—$800,000 in his name $400,000 in hers. The husband could leave all $800,000 to his wife and there would be no tax on his estate because of the marital deduction. But then, let's look at hers. She has a potential $1,200,000 estate. Since the unified credit was fully phased in by 1987, the tax on her estate will be $239,000.

If instead of an "everything to my wife" will, this husband shelters the $600,000 exemption equivalent in a non-marital trust and leaves the balance of his estate ($200,000) to his wife, there will be no tax at his death. However, now his wife's estate will be only $600,000—her original $400,000 worth of assets plus the $200,000 she inherited from her husband. Thereby there will be no tax on either estate.

Save Taxes Through "Wasting"

You can realize even greater tax savings, both estate and income, and assure adequate support for your spouse with a "wasting" marital deduction trust. This is done by creating two trusts, one of which qualifies for the marital deduction. Support for your spouse is provided by using both the income and principal of the marital deduction trust for her benefit. The income of the other trust is accumulated and this second trust is not used until the marital deduction trust is exhausted.

Case history of a wasting trust arrangement: Mr. Green will have a net estate of $900,000. His main objective is to make sure that his wife will receive $50,000 a year in addition to the income from her own substantial assets.

Under his will, he creates two trusts. The first, a marital

deduction trust, will have a principal of about $300,000 and the second, the non-marital deduction trust, the balance of $600,000. The marital deduction trust pays her $50,000 a year, first all of the income, then principal as needed to make up the balance. She will pay tax on the income. The amount she receives from principal is not taxed. Over the years, as the principal of the trust is used up, the portion of the $50,000 annual payments which comes out of the principal will increase while the income portion of it will decrease. This means that her income taxes will continually decrease.

Meanwhile, the income of the second trust is accumulated, income taxes are paid on it, by the trust as a separate tax entity. If and when the marital deduction trust is exhausted, the income and principal of this second trust are used to make the $50,000 annual payments.

When any accumulated income is paid to Mrs. Green from the second trust, it will be treated roughly as though distributed to her in the year it was accumulated. This is done through a short-cut averaging method. She will be liable for any increase in tax that would have resulted had that income been distributed to her in those prior years but with a credit for the tax that the trust paid on it. Therefore, because her taxable income will be continuously decreasing while the marital deduction trust is being exhausted, use of the averaging method could result in a situation in which she will have to pay little or no additional tax on the distribution, after using the credit for taxes paid by the trust. Moreover, in spite of the additional tax that may be due, the family benefits from having the use of the deferred tax monies until it actually becomes payable.

At widow Green's death, whatever remains of the second trust passes to the beneficiaries under her husband's will without being taxed in her estate.

What has Mr. Green accomplished? First of all, he has provided the support that he wants for his wife. Second, there is no estate tax at his death. Third, his wife's support is backed by the property of his entire estate. Fourth, there can be an overall savings in income taxes. Fifth, this plan will help reduce the estate tax on his wife's potential estate by using up the property of the marital deduction trust (which would be taxable in her estate) and preserving the property of the second trust (which is not taxed in either estate).

Provide for a Marital Deduction in Case of Common Disaster

To get the marital deduction there must be a surviving spouse. What happens when the couple dies in an accident or disaster so that the order of deaths cannot be established?

As we know, generally the laws provide that each is presumed to survive the other. Therefore, neither will inherit from the other, and so no marital deduction.

It is possible, however, to change this presumption. The change should be made if the two estates are disproportionate in size. By a simple provision in the will, trust, or insurance contract, the beneficiary can be presumed to have survived and the property will pass to him. When one spouse has little or no property and the other has a substantial amount, such a provision in the latter's will can mean considerable tax savings in their combined estates.

Take the case of Mr. and Mrs. Brown. He has an estate of $1,000,000, but she has no property of her own. His will "shelters" the amount equal to the exemption and leaves the rest outright to Mrs. Brown. If they were to die simultaneously in a common disaster, under the law of their domicile, Mr. Brown would be presumed to have survived his wife and she would inherit none of his estate. Without a marital deduction, the federal taxes on his estate would be $153,000 if they died in 1987 or after. If he were to insert a provision in his will that if they were to die in a common disaster, she is presumed to have survived, then $400,000 of his estate would pass to his wife tax-free under the marital deduction. There would then be a $600,000 and a $400,000 estate—both of them exempt from federal tax. Tax savings: $153,000.

Save Income Taxes by Spreading

Some items may be taxed on your beneficiaries as well as being subject to estate taxes. Pensions, annuities, renewal commissions, fees, royalties, and salary continuation payments all fall into this category. There is, however, an income tax deduction allowed for estate taxes paid on any income items. By dividing these benefits and other forms of income among a number of beneficiaries and other forms of income among a number of beneficiaries or trusts, income taxes can be saved. In addition even greater savings can be realized by giving them to low tax bracket ones. Give other assets to those in high brackets.

Save Income Taxes by Sprinkling

If you have a number of beneficiaries, it may be advantageous to have the trustees or some other person determine how much income is to be paid to each. Ms. White has, let us say, three daughters, each of whom has children. She creates three separate trusts, one for each family group, and provides that the income of each trust shall be paid out among the members of the particular family in such amounts as the trustee shall see fit. The trustee can then "sprinkle" income within each group according to individual needs and tax brackets.

THE NEED FOR TAX PLANNING

Many people do their tax planning in a hit-or-miss fashion. That is not the approach to this chapter, as you can see. It calls for a conscious and continuing effort. It's worth it, however, for the most elementary of reasons. The stakes are high, the possible savings to be realized—for large estates—in the millions. For small ones it is perhaps not as dramatic. But to the family of the person with a modest estate, each dollar saved can be of greater importance than to his wealthier counterpart. This is the point to remember: tax savings are always important; tax planning is for everyone.

CHAPTER 16

Assessing Your Estate: What to Leave and How to Leave It

One way to look at estate planning is to view it as a jigsaw puzzle. Here is one piece called "taxes," another known as "lifetime transfers," others labeled "investments," "charitable giving," "corporate benefits," and so on. As a planner you yourself have dealt with these pieces and so created your estate and prepared it for transfer.

Almost, but not quite. The pieces of the jigsaw puzzle are still separated from each other, and until you fit them together, you will not have a coherent picture of your estate or its transfer plan—no real way of knowing what's going to happen to it after your death.

A preview or dress rehearsal of the estate transfer is basic to all estate planning. It is as if you were to give a piece of machinery a trial run. You note its defects and its strong points. You prepare it in the best of all possible ways for its eventual use: by testing it.

The test is often focused on one element in the estate transfer plan, your will. The will is the fundamental instrument in most plans of after-death estate transfer. On how well you make your preparations for it will depend the success of your particular plan.

Previously we have talked about the need for making a will. Now we want to discuss *how* to make it.

Contrary to the usual procedure, the making of a will should not be simply a matter of consulting your attorney, listening to his advice, and then signing a document. A lawyer's function in estate planning is not to tell a client what he should do with his property. It is to advise him on what can be done and to create the means for carrying out the wishes and objectives the client wants to achieve. The initial preparation for a will must be undertaken by the client himself. This is best done before his first conference with his attorney.

THE "DISTRIBUTABLE" ESTATE

You should begin by examining exactly what you will have to distribute. Before you can decide on what property or how much property you want to give to any particular member of your family or to your family group, you must first find out what your *distributable* estate will amount to.

Distributable estate means the property which will be left after taxes, funeral and administration expenses, debts, and any losses or costs incurred in the liquidation of assets to meet these cash requirements. Most people do not realize that, both in volume and content, the distributable estate is not the same as that which a person may have enjoyed during his life. The only way to know what it really will be is to subject your estate to a hypothetical administration: a trial run.

This is also the time for you to crystallize your objectives; to determine what they are generally and specifically; to decide which ones are primary and which are secondary. Unless your estate is large, you will not be able to accomplish everything you might wish to. As in other phases of life, the more important things must take precedence over the less important, and compromise may have to be made. This aspect of preparation necessarily involves analyzing your beneficiaries and weighing their needs against what you are able to provide for them.

Only when you know what you have to work with and what you want to accomplish can you begin to chart the "distribution flow" of your estate—what property is to be distributed to whom, and how.

Outside Taxation But Inside the Estate

If you have done your homework and filled out the Estate Planning Worksheets you already have a list of the assets which are includable in your gross taxable estate.

To find out what your distributable estate is, however, you must now do some additional calculating. The distributable estate includes anything which will pass to your beneficiaries at your death, *whether or not it is then subject to taxation.* If your plan has focused on steps to reduce tax erosion, you may find that this non-taxable but distributable property is quite substantial. Property in your distributable estate but not in your taxable estate could include:

• A living trust which has been designed to remove the property from estate taxation.

• Your spouse's half of your jointly held property.

• Insurance on your life which you do not own and over which you have no incidents of ownership.

• Property over which you have a limited, not a general, power of appointment.

In order to formulate a plan of distribution you must include all such items. You may not have the power to direct the disposition of some of these, it is true, but they do affect your overall plan and must be incorporated within it.

Inside Your Estate But Outside Your Will

The inventory for your trial run is different in another respect. Property which passes under your will constitutes your *probate estate* and is controlled by the directions in your will. But as we have seen, the will is not the only means by which property passes at death. Property can also pass outside of the will by right of survivorship or by contract. Your will does not control the disposition of these assets, unless, as we shall shortly see, they become payable to your estate.

In almost every estate there will be some property which will not pass under the will. In fact, often the value of the nonprobate assets exceed that of the probate estate.

Your inventory, therefore, must separate the property passing *outside* of the will from the property passing *under* it, for two reasons.

First of all, you must know what and how much property is controlled by your will. Otherwise some of its provisions may fail.

For instance, a widow plans to have her estate go to her children, but she wants her sister to have payments under a deferred compensation agreement. She makes her will accordingly, bequeathing the deferred compensation to her sister and the rest of the estate to her children. She knows that the value of her deferred compensation contract will be in her taxable estate and so mistakenly believes it will pass through the probate estate.

Ms. Widow has forgotten that the terms of the contract provide for payment to her children. At her death, what happens to the bequest to her sister? It has no effect. The terms of the contract, not her will, determine the disposition of its proceeds.

In an extreme case the will may turn out to be nothing more than an empty shell, because nothing passes under it. If this is what the planner intended, fine. The estate plan may have been designed to have everything pass outside the will. In that case the will is made to take care of certain events which may occur such as the premature death of a beneficiary. It is also drawn to take care of nominal or miscellaneous property which has not been otherwise provided for.

But if the will was designed to transfer substantial properties and it turns out to be such an empty shell, then the estate plan will necessarily fail.

The second reason for separating property into "outside and inside" the will is the need for an integrated master plan. Where it is possible to do so the disposition of non-probate assets can be altered to fit into the plan. For instance, the beneficiary of an insurance policy can be changed. But this is not always possible and so the will must be drawn so as to compensate for, or coordinate this factor into the plan.

Take the case of Mr. Equalizer. He had set up trusts for his two older children but never created one for his youngest child. His financial affairs are such at present that he is unable to create a trust for the youngest. He believes in equal treatment but the living trusts can't be altered or amended. He must compensate for this imbalance by means of his will so that the total property received by his children, both the living trust and his probate estate, will be equally divided among them.

Therefore, it is important to know how each item of your property will pass. Let's look at some of the assets which commonly pass outside the will.

Jointly Owned Property. Property in the names of two or

more persons, where there is a right of survivorship, passes by operation of law. This means that on the death of one owner it automatically goes to the survivor or survivors, and is unaffected by the decedent's will.

Take a certificate of stock which is jointly held. The registration will read something like "John Shareholder and Jean Shareholder, as joint tenants with right of survivorship, and not as tenants in common." The one who outlives the other takes all. Note, however, that if you have a stock certificate or deed or other certificate of ownership which reads "as tenants in common," there is no right of survivorship. Each owner controls the disposition of his share of the property and it passes under his will.

Most people put the family home in the joint names of the husband and wife. This form of ownership is known as a "tenancy by the entirety" but it is simply a joint tenancy with right of survivorship between husband and wife. The principle is the same. The survivor takes all.

People often rent safe deposit boxes in joint names. This does not generally affect the ownership of the property in the box. In a few states, however, the property in the box may pass by right of survivorship.

One other type of property commonly held in joint names is U.S. Savings Bonds. If a bond is registered "Peter Patriot or Polly Patriot," the survivor automatically becomes the sole owner.

Savings bonds can also be registered in the name of "Peter Patriot P.O.D. Polly Patriot." The initials P.O.D. stand for "payable on death." This isn't a joint ownership. Peter is the sole owner while he lives. But if Polly survives, the net result is the same. She becomes the owner of the bond.

Living Trusts. The trust instrument, not the settlor's will, controls the disposition of the trust. But if the settlor reserves a power of appointment over the trust property exercisable by his will, or if the trust by its terms specifies that the property returns to him, then the will takes over and determines the disposition of the property.

Bank Account Trusts. Bank accounts are frequently opened in trust for children or grandchildren. On the birth of his heir, the proud sire opens an account in the name of "Donald Depositor in trust for his son, Donald Junior." If this is a true trust, it is controlled by trust law and by the terms of the signature card. But often these accounts are not true trusts because the agreement with the bank (the signature card) permits Donald Senior to use the funds for his own benefit.

In this case, when Donald Senior dies, there may be a question as to whether the trust passes to Junior or goes to his father's estate. Many states have adopted the New York doctrine which permits the depositor to use the funds for his own benefit during his life, and at his death, the balance to pass automatically to the designated beneficiary. If the beneficiary dies before the depositor, this pseudo-trust terminates and the account belongs to the depositor and not to the beneficiary's estate.

This is known as a "Totten trust," named after the case which established the doctrine. A planner with a bank trust account can find out how the account will pass at his death by inquiring at his bank.

Insurance. Your life insurance is an asset of major importance which passes outside the will (unless you have made your estate the beneficiary). This applies to annuities as well. The terms of the contract determine not only to whom it is payable, but also how it is to be paid—in a lump sum or under options.

Employee Benefits. Although they may be payable to your estate, specified beneficiaries are usually named to receive profit-sharing, deferred compensation, pension, or other benefits.

Business Agreements. Contracts for the purchase or sale of business interest, at the death of a partner or stockholder, frequently provide for payments to be made, not to the deceased's estate, but to specified people, such as the spouse or children.

Under the Will: The Forgotten Property

If it is important to know exactly what property passes outside your will, it is equally important to know exactly what is passing under it.

Too often certain items are overlooked. What will happen to the jointly owned property, the P.O.D. bonds, or the Totten trusts if your co-owner or beneficiary doesn't survive you? What happens if the beneficiaries of your insurance or employee's benefits die before you, and you haven't designated secondary beneficiaries? In all these cases the property passes under your will. Obviously, you can't predict who's going to survive. If your estate plan does not call for alternative dispositions in case a beneficiary dies before you do, then you must be sure to include this property in your calculations.

Suppose you have a distributable estate of $400,000. $300,000 of this is jointly held with your husband. You figure that only $100,000 will pass under your will. But if he dies before you do, then the figure jumps to $400,000. In planning your will you must take care of this contingency.

Remember that you need not specifically devise or bequeath property in your will in order to have the property pass under it. Your will includes a residuary clause which reads something to the effect: "all the rest, residue and remainder of my property, both real and personal, of which I may die seized or possessed or to which I may be entitled, I hereby give, devise and bequeath to . . ." Whatever you haven't disposed of before in your will passes under this clause.

In addition to property which falls into your probate estate because a co-owner or beneficiary doesn't survive you, there are certain items which are commonly overlooked, or which the planner doesn't realize he is bequeathing by his will.

Insurance on Someone Else's Life. A policy owned by you on someone else's life is your property just like any of your other assets and therefore is transferred by your will. The fact that a third person is a primary or contingent beneficiary has no effect on the ownership of the policy. Let's assume you own a $20,000 policy on your wife's life. Your children are the beneficiaries. Under your will, your wife receives your residuary estate. The insurance policy on her life will go to your wife at your death, not to your children.

Living Trusts. As we know the property will pass under your will in certain instances: if you specifically provide in the trust agreement for this or if the trust property is to be returned to you when the trust ends.

Employee Benefits. There is one type of employee benefit which is always controlled by your will, the restricted stock option. One of the restrictions is that it cannot be transferred except by will (or by the laws of intestacy).

Inheritances. Why is it people tend to think property isn't theirs until it is actually in their hands? Suggest to someone who has been left an inheritance that he revise his will to provide for his changed circumstances, and his answer is frequently, "Why should I hurry? I can wait until it's paid to me." In truth he should not wait. Whether or not he has actually taken possession of the inherited property, it is his by law and it passes at his death just like any other property he may own.

Powers of Appointment. So far we have been mainly concerned with powers of appointment from a tax point of view. Let's look at them now as they affect estate transference.

You give yourself a power of appointment when you create a living trust and reserve the right to change the disposition of the trust property. Usually, however, the power of appointment is given to you by someone else, either in his will or in a living trust.

Powers are of two types: general and special (or limited). Under a general power of appointment, you have the right to appoint the property to anyone you choose, including yourself, your estate, or your creditors. Under a special power you can appoint it to any one or group, but not to yourself, your estate, or your creditors or those of your estate.

If you have a power of appointment, you can control the disposition of the property and so you must include it in your planning. You must decide whether or not to exercise it from the point of view of your overall estate plan of distribution and its tax consequences.

There is a major drawback in having power of appointment. You can have a power without knowing about it and exercise it without intending to. This can throw an estate plan completely out of kilter.

Listen to the sad tale of a New York lady who evidently didn't know she had a power of appointment. She was a widow with a son and a grandchild and lived on the income of an $800,000 trust created for her by her husband. She thought the principal of the trust would pass to her son at her death.

She often visited her son and grandchild at their home in Texas. One day while there, she decided to make a will. She told the Texas attorney whom she consulted that since the principal of the trust would go to her son, she wanted to leave her own small amount of property to her infant grandson. The will was duly drawn and executed.

It was only after her death that it was discovered that she had a power of appointment over the $800,000 trust. Her will left everything to her grandson. Did this include the trust property?

The courts of New York, whose law governed the exercise of the power, said it did. In New York, then, as in many states, a residuary clause in a will automatically exercised a power of appointment unless the will specifically stated that it should not. Even though the evidence showed that she had believed her son would receive the trust property at her death and that she wanted him to, her will gave it to her grandson. Without knowing it, she had disinherited her only child.

Figuring Your Distributable Estate

If you have inventoried all your assets and have arrived at a grand total, you are now ready for the second step. This one involves not addition, but subtraction. Refer to the "Estate Cash Requirements Schedule" in the Worksheets and get the total of your debts, expenses, and estate taxes. These are subtracted from your grand total. You now have an estimate of your distributable estate, assuming, of course, that there will be no further losses caused by liquidation of assets in order to pay estate taxes and costs.

ESTABLISHING LIQUIDITY

At this point you know *how much* is available for distribution but not *what* is available. One task remains to be done on your inventory: establishing liquidity to pay the taxes, debts, and expenses. One or more of your assets must be used for this purpose. It may be that your inventory indicates that your estate will have enough cash to pay these items. If so, you have no problem. Make the appropriate entries in the column headed "Property to Be Liquidated" and are ready to go on to the next step.

But if there will not be enough ready cash, you must select assets which will have a ready market, such as savings bonds, or actively traded securities.

In Chapter 7, we pointed out that if your security portfolio contains U.S. Treasury Bonds, then your estate may be able to use them to pay the taxes and realize a profit on the transaction. This is because certain Treasuries (the Federal

Reserve publishes a list of them) owned by a decedent may be redeemed at par to pay estate taxes. If an estate contains these, they should be used for this purpose.

In addition, a planner (especially an older person who is about to make new investments) should consider the advantage of investing in such Treasuries in an amount up to his estimated federal estate taxes. Because their interest rate is below the going rate, they are currently selling below par. The planner can buy an issue at the market price and when he dies, the estate can redeem them at 100 by having the proceeds applied to the payment of the taxes. Though the estate realizes a profit, the difference between the purchase price and par, the profit will not be subject to capital gains tax. Since they can be redeemed at par to pay taxes, the estate's basis will be par.

It is important, in determining if there will be sufficient available cash or liquidable assets, to remember that the property listed on your inventory as passing outside your will does not go to your executor and so may not provide the needed liquidity. Suppose, for example, a woman has a $100,000 certificate of deposit which she figures will cover her estate expenses and taxes. However, the certificate is in her name and her son's as joint owners. On the death of the mother, the C.D. automatically goes to the son, who doesn't have to turn it over to the estate. The most the son could be required to contribute would be his share of the estate taxes on that $100,000. Establishing liquidity may call for changing ownerships of assets so that they pass to your estate instead of outside the will.

It may be, however, that your trial run shows that there will not be sufficient cash or readily marketable assets available to pay taxes and the other costs. A valuable property may have to be sacrificed to meet these obligations. This indicates a serious defect in your estate picture.

Now—while you have the opportunity—is the time to alter or re-organize your assets, to buy additional insurance, or to take steps to reduce taxes. Otherwise, your estate plan may run into difficulties.

REVIEWING YOUR BENEFICIARIES

Now that you know what you have to distribute, you are ready for the next phase in your analysis: a review of your beneficiaries and your responsibilities to them. This is the time to set forth your objectives as clearly and completely as you can.

If you have had an opportunity to judge your beneficiaries as to their ability and responsibility in handling property, either through lifetime giving or through other means, you have a guide to base your judgments on. If not, you must still decide on some pattern of distribution because you need a will now. You can't wait until you are sure. You devise the best plan for the present and change it if necessary when you have more knowledge.

Unless yours is a very large estate indeed, you will have to establish preferences among the various claimants to your largesse. You must choose your primary and secondary beneficiaries. The selection should be based primarily on two major factors: the needs of each and the resources of each.

Is the support of your spouse your primary concern, your major objective? Or does the fact that she has an estate of her own put her in the secondary beneficiary category? Is her estate so substantial that your wisest course would be to omit her entirely?

Should your children be treated equally, or is there a disabled or incompetent child whose welfare must be given special attention? Have you considered your grandchildren—present and future ones? Have you thought of the often neglected daughter-in-law who might need financial assistance on the death of your son?

Do you have dependent parents? Perhaps they don't need financial assistance now, but might they in the future? Are there other relatives who might be in need of support such as a widowed sister or invalid brother?

Your plan of distribution must be based first on the needs of these people who look to you for support and care. Don't forget bequests to friends and relatives, however. These tokens of affection and respect, albeit a financially insignificant part of your transfer plan, should also be taken care of.

At this juncture, gifts to charity also enter into the deliberations. You don't need to make large charitable gifts like those envisioned in Chapter 17. Even though your means are limited, you may still have charitable objectives.

When mulling over your list of beneficiaries, don't be so coolly rational that you neglect an important human element in estate planning: the preservation of family harmony. You may give more to one child than to another for reasons that are quite proper. But are you sure that the "neglected" child isn't going to resent it? These resentments can be amazingly strong. The hostility and passions they generate can last for years, pass from generation to generation even. You may find it wiser, in the long run, to treat all your children equally even though their needs and resources are far from equal.

If the possibility exists of creating resentment or disharmony over unequal treatment (or possibly equal treatment), it may be wise to scrap a sound plan of distribution in favor of one designed to promote harmony. Remember, it takes only one person in a family to create disharmony.

FREEDOM OF DISPOSITION

You may think that you can dispose of your estate pretty much as you please. While this is generally so, there are certain legal restrictions on what you can do.

Freedom within Reason. A few years ago, a man died in New York, leaving a will which he had drawn himself, with a number of unique provisions. Among them were directions for a fund to be set up to pay the salary of a uniformed guard to watch over his grave. The court refused to allow this provision to be carried out, failing to see the need for guarding the dead.

Your disposition must be reasonable or it will not be given effect. You might want your executor to dump your securities in the ocean, but the courts won't permit such waste. Nor would they permit a provision to be carried out directing that all your personal property be used for your funeral pyre.

Freedom Consistent with Public Policy. The law will not allow you to dispose of your estate in a way that offends the public policy or law of the state. Your estate can't be used to promote illegal or immoral acts such as gambling or insurrection or prostitution. A condition attached to a legacy which induces conduct contrary to public policy will not be upheld. If you make a bequest to a daughter on the condition that she doesn't marry or she divorce her husband, it won't hold. Restraints on marriage and promotion of divorce are generally deemed to be against public policy and so the testator's condition will be disregarded.

Freedom to Choose Your Beneficiaries: The Special Status of the Surviving Spouse. The major restriction on your choice of beneficiaries is your spouse's right in your estate.

In medieval days, when land was wealth, a widow automatically received a life estate (the right during her lifetime to the income from and the use of property) in one-third of all the land her husband had owned during their marriage. This is known as *dower.*

A husband on his wife's death received a life estate in all of the lands she had owned, not just one-third. The husband's right is known as *curtesy.* For the husband to be entitled to curtesy, however, there had to be a child born of the marriage and heard to cry "within the four walls." As a result, when the lady of the manor was about to be delivered of her first-born, the lord gathered his men to act as attesting witnesses to the birth. They listened outside the lady's bed-chamber for the wail which would give their lord his curtesy. The child only had to be born alive. Legally it made no difference whether he survived. The sound of the baby's cry signaled the start of the feasting and revelry in celebration of the lord's good fortune.

In some states, these feudal laws, though not the rituals, are still retained in modified forms. But in today's non-agrarian society where wealth is usually made up of personal property, dower and curtesy are of little protection to a surviving spouse. A millionaire domiciled in New Jersey, for instance, who owned no real estate could cut his wife off completely until as late as 1981.

Other states which have retained dower and curtesy give the surviving spouse a right to part of the decedent's personal property as well, or permit the spouse to relinquish dower or curtesy for a share of the entire estate.

In many states dower and curtesy have been completely abolished. The widow or widower is given instead an absolute right to a fractional share of the estate which is known as a "statutory share." If the decedent's will doesn't give the survivor a minimum amount set down by law, he or she may claim the statutory share.

In community property states the survivor automatically gets one-half of all the community property.

Although these rights are conferred by law, a spouse can relinquish or alter them by an ante-nuptial or post-nuptial agreement. In addition, these rights of one spouse in the estate of the other are lost on divorce, abandonment, and, sometimes, separation of the parties.

Freedom to Disinherit. With the exception of your surviving spouse, you can generally disinherit anyone else, including your children. There is one exception—the state of Louisiana. There the children automatically get a portion of the estate, their share depending on the number of children.

In order to exclude your children, however, you may have to spell out your wishes in specific terms. If a child is born after the execution of the will, he may be entitled to his intestate share (what he would have received if you had died without a will) unless it appears that after-born children were intentionally excluded. In some states this applies to living children who were not mentioned in the will. This doesn't mean that you can't exclude your children. It means that if you don't make your intentions clear, the law may assume that it was an inadvertent omission, and so remedy it.

Freedom to Be Charitable. Odd as it may seem in a charity-oriented society, there may be limitations on your right to give charity at your death. In some states, bequests and devises to charity are invalid unless the will was executed a specified time before death. This was to prevent a dying person from trying to buy his way into heaven at the last, desperate moment. Other states limit the portion or percentage of the estate which can be left to charity if you leave certain descendants or heirs.

These are vestiges of English feudal law, when church and crown were vying for power and the crown was trying to combat the church's increasing wealth. Nowadays, however, the motive is different. Protection of the family is the reason for these laws.

PREVIEWING YOUR TRANSFERS

Once you have determined who your beneficiaries will be and apportioned your estate among them, what kinds of testamentary transfers can you, and should you, make?

As with lifetime transfers, your after-death gifts may be outright or in trust. They may be:

1. *Bequests.* A bequest is a gift of personal property by will. It may be a sum of money—"$1,000 to Aunt Jennifer"—or a specific piece of property—"my automobile to my wife." It can be a share of the estate, such as "one-third of my net estate to my sister, Mathilda." Or a bequest might be in the form of a direction to the executor to sell certain property and pay the proceeds to a beneficiary.

2. *Devises.* When the property given is real estate, as, for example, when you leave your home to your spouse, it is called a devise. The devise might be made entirely to one person or it might be a gift to one person for use during his life, or for a period of years, with the property then going to someone else.

3. *Residue.* As we have already seen, the residue is the balance of your estate after all other bequests and devises. Every will needs a residuary clause. Although it is possible to dispose of everything through the prior bequests and devises, and have no residuary estate, there will almost always be some property which hasn't been taken care of. In addition, if any bequests or devises should fail because a beneficiary died before the testator, or for any other reason, the property falls into the residue. Without a residuary clause there would be a partial intestacy.

A typical will includes gifts to relatives and friends, the secondary beneficiaries. Caution must be exercised because the residue is only the amount left over after payment of the prior legacies. If your property should decrease between the time of the making of the will and the time of your death, your primary beneficiaries could be left with little or nothing.

Here's a case history in point: a man with a half million dollars made a will leaving a bequest of $5,000 to each of his nieces and nephews, and the residue to his children. When he died 8 years later, his estate was worth only $135,000. Each niece and nephew got $5,000. There were 19 of them in all. Thus his children were left with less than $40,000, while their cousins inherited a total of $95,000.

This planner should, of course, have reviewed his estate plan during those 8 years and made the necessary revisions. Even failing this, he could have protected himself against such a fiasco by including a simple provision in his will which limited the $5,000 legacies to a fixed proportion of his ultimate estate. Thus, his primary beneficiaries would have been assured of receiving the bulk of his estate.

The Testamentary Trust. After-death gifts by your will, including the residuary estate, need not be outright. They can be in trust.

Although the form of a testamentary trust, as well as the motives for creating it, may be different, it is similar in most respects to the living trust.

There is the same flexibility and variety of arrangements possible with both types. Income can be paid to one or more beneficiaries, be accumulated, paid out in the discretion of the trustee or a third person, or be sprinkled or sprayed among a group of beneficiaries. They can be an arrangement to have the trust pay the beneficiary an annuity, guaranteeing that he will receive a stated sum or minimum amount, regardless of the income earned by the trust.

As to the principal, it can be paid in specified sums, at specific times or ages, on the happening of certain events, in the discretion of the trustee or a third person, or at the demand of the beneficiary. Making the decision as to when and if principal payments should be made to beneficiaries can be a difficult one. When, for example, should you let a child receive principal? When he is 21? Not until he reaches 50 or 60? Perhaps never?

None of these choices is necessarily a perfect solution. A 21-year-old is still usually immature; he could squander away the property within a few years. A person who has to wait until late middle age to receive principal may be too old to use and enjoy it to its fullest extent. The business he wanted to start, the home he wanted to buy, or the education he wanted to give his children—the opportunities to achieve any of these things may have gone by.

Or the person who never receives any of the principal may at some time find himself in serious need. How much security and protection has the trust, created for his benefit, given him if he suffers a prolonged or serious illness or finds himself in unexpected financial difficulties, with the assets of the trust beyond his reach?

One practical solution to the problem is to have the principal paid out in installments; fixed amounts or portions of certain ages or times. For example, your will might provide for payment of one-fourth of the principal to your beneficiary at ages 25, 30, 35, and 40. If he dissipates the first quarter, he may still handle the second or third more wisely.

Another solution is to leave it to the trustee or a member of the family to decide at what time or times, or for what reasons, payments of principal should be made. They could also be given the power to terminate the trust and distribute the remainder to the beneficiary if they consider it to be in his best interest.

Another possible way of handling the problem is to specify the purposes for which principal may be used: for education, buying a home, establishing a business, etc. With an extremely irresponsible beneficiary, your list might be more limited. It could be restricted to serious emergencies or special needs, such as medical care. We remember one trust for such a young man where one of the purposes for which principal could be used was the payment of his medical expenses. He persisted in forwarding his liquor bills (which were substantial ones) to the trustee for payment, on the grounds that the liquor was for medicinal purposes.

Fortunately, many trust beneficiaries are mature, responsible people. Trusts are often created for them for tax or management reasons, sometimes only for convenience. A planner might well give such a beneficiary the right to demand principal—either an unlimited or restricted right.

However, if tax savings is one of its purposes, the beneficiary's right to demand principal should be limited to $5,000 a year, or 5 per cent of the value of the trust principal. Otherwise, he may find all the trust property taxable in his estate when he dies. If he wants or needs it, then he can take up to the specified amount in any year. If he doesn't, the principal is left undisturbed or subject to be paid out in the trustee's discretion. Don't assume that a beneficiary will invade principal just because the trust says that he may. Many people are so conditioned as to the sacredness of principal that they are by nature reluctant to use it, even when necessity demands it.

This reminds us of the turn-of-the-century story of the reunion of a group of graduates of a very fashionable finishing school. The well-groomed, well-dressed ladies were shocked to discover that one of their classmates was obviously a prostitute. Her former friends took her aside to find out why this had happened to her. She explained that she simply needed the money. "But what happened to the trust left you by your father?" they asked. "Oh," she said, "the trust is still there, but the income has dropped considerably and I know Daddy wouldn't like me to dip into principal."

In creating a trust give some thought to using a power of appointment. The trust, remember, creates future interests. No one can predict the future with any degree of certainty. No matter how carefully an estate plan may be worked out today, it may not adequately meet the situation existing 20 or 30 years hence. You can provide the necessary flexibility to handle unforeseen situations and changes in circumstances through powers of appointment.

With such a power you give someone else the opportunity to reassess the family needs at a later date and make any necessary or desirable changes in your plan. He could have the power to do this during his own lifetime or at his death by his will, or both.

You must also decide whether this power is to be a general one so that he may appoint the property to anyone, including himself or his estate, or a special or limited power. A general power naturally gives greater flexibility, but as you recall, it results in tax erosion. The property of the trust is includable in the gross taxable estate of the holder if it is a general power, but not if it is only a special power. If the income beneficiary of a trust has a power which can be exercised during his life, whether general or special, and he exercises it, he makes a taxable gift.

We have seen that a power can be inadvertently exercised and the havoc that can thus be wrought. To avoid such accidents, your will can and should require that in order to exercise the power, the donee must specifically refer to the power you have given him. Furthermore, there should always be a disposition provided for the trust property in case the power isn't exercised. If the disposition is satisfactory, the donee need not exercise the power. If it isn't, he can change it.

Pouring Over into the Living Trust. Have you already set up a living trust or are you planning to do so as part of your program of lifetime transfers? If so, as you recall, it can be the after-death, as well as the lifetime, transfer vehicle. Probate property can be added to it, or in legal parlance, "poured over" into it when you die, by having your will provide for this.

Outright or in Trust. How does one choose between making an outright testamentary gift or leaving it in trust? If it is outright, it is the beneficiary's to use and dispose of freely. A trust limits the beneficiary's rights in the property, but should the dead hand of the testator control the living?

It should be in trust:

• If your beneficiaries are minors—at least until adulthood.

• If your beneficiaries are incompetent, irresponsible, or simply imprudent.

• If you want to save estate taxes on the estates of future generations.

• If you want to keep a particular asset, such as a family business, within the family and out of the hands of outsiders.

• If you want to assure professional management of the property.

The planner who has confidence in his beneficiaries should consider consulting them on the form in which they want their inheritance. You might feel that a mature person should receive the property outright, but he might prefer tax savings to freedom of use.

In the long run it is up to you as the estate planner to make your decisions, weighing the problems—psychological, economic, and personal—and arrive at the best possible solution for your family.

The Final Picture

If you have followed the steps suggested for the trial run, you have a picture of what your distributable estate will look like and how it will be distributed.

Now you can figure out, on the Estimated Income Schedule in the Worksheets, the *estimated available income* for your family after your death. This will show whether your family will have the support you want for them from your estate.

Study the picture carefully. If there are flaws or gaps, you have the opportunity to change it, to correct errors and touch up weak spots. Now is the time to seek professional help—to work with your attorney to make the necessary changes and revisions to guarantee that your after-death objectives will be achieved.

CHAPTER 17

It Pays to Be Charitable

Some time ago, CARE, the international relief organization, celebrated the receipt of its 50 millionth package. On hand for the occasion was the U.S. Ambassador to the United Nations. The lucky donors of the 50 millionth package, Mr. and Mrs. Daniel Gelford of Bayport, Minnesota, had their pictures taken with the Ambassador and were given a trip to Bogota, Colombia, by the Fiber Box Association to present the package in person. The whole affair, with its curious mixture of altruism and commercialism, was typically American. Where else is the impulse to give so strong and the motivation for giving so varied?

Some $61.6 billion are given away to charity each year by Americans both individually and collectively. The donors range from rich to poor and the recipients from great institutions such as CARE to the local library, school, or church. Solicitations are made by mass letter or advertising campaigns, door to door, by nationwide television marathons, and by individuals, both great and small; from the famous movie star to the boy down the street.

People respond to the onslaught of appeals for an amalgam of reasons. For some the motive is a noble one, a desire to help those in need. For others it is a matter of personal satisfaction or the need to repay one's debt to society, or a way of advancing certain principles and beliefs. For others the charitable impulse is stirred more by ambition than by altruism. Philanthropy is a means of attaining status. A person's worth in a community is often measured by the amount he gives away; the larger it is, the larger you believe his fortune must be. What better way of assuring immortality than by giving funds for a wing of a hospital, an endowment to a university, or a collection to a museum?

Adding to all these personal motives—and promoting them as well—is the admixture of tax savings. Our tax laws encourage charitable giving. When you give to charity you pay no gift tax; you receive an income or state tax deduction; in some cases you may even reap a profit from your gift.

The tax aspects of charitable giving make it a significant element in estate planning. Although your philanthropic motives may be of primary importance, it behooves you to plan your program of giving in a way designed to give you maximum tax savings. If philanthropy can pay extra dividends, why not plan them? A sound program of charitable gifts can mean giving more than you might otherwise be able to afford. It can even provide greater security for your family and/or yourself. It can help preserve a family business. It can be a means of carrying out your family objectives.

WHAT IS CHARITY?

Not every gift you make with a philanthropic purpose in mind qualifies for tax deduction under the federal law.

Your gift will qualify under these conditions—if it is made to the United States or one of its states for public purposes; or if it is made to religious, charitable, scientific, literary, or educational organizations, provided their income doesn't inure to the benefit of any individual and provided no substantial part of their activity consists of carrying on propaganda or attempting to influence legislation.

Although the definition covers a multitude of organizations, note that it does not include every nonprofit organization. A donor can sometimes run into trouble in claiming a tax deduction for a "charitable" contribution. A case in point involved the estate of William Nelson Cromwell. The donor, a prominent Wall Street lawyer, left part of his residuary estate to three bar associations. The government denied the estate a charitable deduction for these bequests. The executors, one of whom was John Foster Dulles, sued for a tax refund of over $2 million on the grounds that these associations qualified under the tax laws. The lower court denied the deduction. The organizations, it stated, existed primarily for the benefit of the members of the profession; in addition they engaged in activities to influence legislation. On appeal, however, the higher court found that the organizations were conducted in the interest of the public and granted the charitable deduction.

This story had a happy tax ending, but nevertheless, the moral is clear. Before making a gift, look into the organization you are planning to benefit and find out if it qualifies. Just because it is a nonprofit organization doesn't mean that your donation to it will be tax-deductible.

THE TIMING OF YOUR GIFT

When should you make a charitable donation? While you are alive or at your death? Putting aside personal considerations and viewing it solely from a tax point of view, your decision should be made on the basis of whether you want to save *income* taxes or *estate* taxes. If you give during your lifetime, you will save on the first. If you give at your death, you will save on the second. But sometimes it is possible to arrange matters so that you get both income and estate tax deductions for the same gift.

Generally speaking, lifetime charitable giving is not of significance to the person in the lower income tax brackets. He saves little and so may be better off with a plan which gives him an estate tax deduction. The high bracket planner, on the other hand, may be wiser in making his gifts during his lifetime. His income tax bracket will as a rule be higher than his estate tax bracket; thus his savings will be greater. In addition, the income tax dollars saved increase his spendable income, and so, too, his ultimate estate.

LIFETIME GIVING: THE INCOME TAX APPROACH

All of us make lifetime gifts to charity in some form or other. We make a donation, take our deduction on April 15, and let it go at that. Perhaps we are being careless and are paying out unnecessary tax dollars. A bit of foresight and planning can reduce the actual cost of charitable giving or increase the amount of the gift.

How the Income Tax Deduction Works

Unlike the estate and gift tax laws which carry no restriction on the amount deductible for charitable contributions, the income tax deduction is a limited one. Here's how it works for taxpayers who itemize deductions:

You are allowed a deduction up to 50 per cent of your adjusted gross income, if your gift is to a publicly or governmentally supported organization or if it is to certain types of private foundations which will be later described. Thus a taxpayer whose adjusted gross income is $40,000 may deduct all of a $20,000 gift to these types of organizations.

However, if your gift is to a private foundation, you may only have a deduction up to a maximum of 20 per cent of your adjusted gross income. Certain exceptions are made to this 20 per cent rule. You may have up to a 50 per cent deduction if the gift is made to (1) a private non-operating foundation (usually a family foundation) and if the foundation distributes the contribution to a 50 per cent charity within 2½ months of its reporting year, or (2) to a private operating foundation, or (3) to a community foundation which pools the contributions it receives from many people and administers these contributions as a common fund (all large cities and many small ones have them). An interesting point about the community foundation is that the gift to the common fund is kept in a separate account in the name of the donor and he may designate the charities which are to receive the benefits of his contribution.

Charitable organizations are referred to as 50 per cent or 20 per cent charities depending upon the maximum deductions allowed for gifts made to either type.

If your gift to a 50 per cent charity exceeds 50 per cent of your adjusted gross income, you may carry over the excess for the next 5 years. There is also a 5-year carry-over permitted on gifts to 20 per cent charities. Thus, if you have given amounts exceeding 20 per cent of your adjusted gross income to your family foundation, you can deduct the excess in the current year or in future years.

For corporations, the charitable deduction is different. A corporation gets a deduction of up to only 10 per cent of its taxable income.

In addition, to determining how much to give, the planner

should consider the kind and form of gift. One type of gift may give better tax results than another.

Gifts in Kind

Suppose you want to make a gift of property—whether it be securities, real estate, or insurance. You will get an income tax deduction equal to the fair market value of the property at the time the contribution was made. The fair market value is the price at which the property would have changed hands between a willing buyer and a willing seller. Gifts in kind are particularly valuable when they consist of appreciated property. They will cost the donor less than an equivalent gift of cash and, in some cases, they may even result in a profit to the giver.

Your college asks you for example, to pledge $2,000 to the college's building program. If you pay the pledge in cash, you receive a deduction of $2,000. If you are in the 28 per cent bracket, then your out-of-pocket cost for the donation is $1,440. If you choose instead to satisfy your pledge with securities worth $2,000, which originally cost you $500, the cost of your contribution would be less because you have avoided paying income tax on $1,500. On a sale of this stock, you would ordinarily pay a tax of $420 on the $1,500 appreciation. By donating it to charity, in effect you realize that gain but pay no tax on it, unless you are subject to the alternative minimum tax. The net result is that your $2,000 gift costs you only $1,020.

There are limitations on appreciated property of which you should be aware.

1. You are only allowed a deduction up to 30 per cent of your adjusted gross income if your gift to a 50 per cent charity consists of appreciated property.

2. If the gift of appreciated property is to a 20 per cent charity, the deduction is calculated by subtracting 50 per cent of the unrealized gain from the market value of the donated property.

3. If the gift consists of property which if sold would give rise to ordinary income, the deduction is based on your cost. This is also so for such property as works of art, books, and letters, created or prepared by the donor.

Depreciated Property

Don't make a gift to charity of property which has depreciated in value. You are better off selling the property and donating the proceeds. The charity doesn't suffer because it will receive cash equal to the value of the property it would have otherwise gotten, and you will have a loss deduction in addition to the charitable deduction.

Present Gifts of Future Interests

In order to get a charitable deduction, your gift need not be one which the charity receives immediately. You can make a gift of a remainder interest under any one of three prescribed conditions and still get an immediate deduction for the present value of that interest.

These are the conditions under which a charitable remainder gift will qualify for a deduction:

1. A gift in trust under the terms of which the donor or other beneficiary is to receive a specified annuity (not less than 5 per cent of the value of gift) during the term of the trust and the charity receives the remainder upon the expiration of the trust.

2. A gift in trust with donor or other beneficiary entitled to receive annually a fixed percentage (not less than 5 per cent) of the value of the trust property as determined each year during the existence of the trust, and with the remainder going to a charity at its expiration. In both of these situations the trust must end at the death of the donor or beneficiary or within 20 years of the creation of the trust.

Examples of 1 and 2: In both, a donor creates a trust and funds it with $100,000. In situation 1, she is to receive an annuity of $6,000 during her lifetime, and upon her death the remainder goes to a charity. In situation 2, the donor is to receive annually 6 per cent of the value of the principal of the trust as determined each year during her lifetime, and upon her death the remainder goes to a charity.

3. A gift of a residence or farm to a charity, with the right retained by the donor or his spouse to use it during his or her lifetime or for a specific period of years.

Example: Mr. Country Squire, a 71-year-old property holder, owns a large country estate worth $450,000. He wants to enjoy it during his life, but he plans to leave it at his death to a nearby college. At the same time he'd like to make some lifetime charitable gifts. The tax savings would also mean a lot to him.

His solution is to donate each year to the college an interest in the property worth approximately $30,000, but retain the right to live on it during his lifetime. The gift to the college is a gift of a remainder interest—the right to the donated property at Mr. Squire's death.

He gets a tax deduction of approximately $12,500, which is the remainder value of property worth $30,000 at the end of the life expectancy of a man aged 71 (see the Treasury table in the Appendix). In his 28 per cent bracket, this deduction means an annual tax savings of $3,500.

As Country Squire grows older, he can donate interests worth less than $30,000 each year, since, as his life expectancy decreases, the proportionate value of the remainder interest given to the college increases. As long as the value of the remainder interest he gives away each year is worth $12,500, he will find himself with $3,500 more of spendable income.

Addendum: he might, if he wishes, arrange the gifts so that he retains the right to live on the estate for a certain number of years instead of for his life. Or he might wish to have his wife enjoy it after his death. In this case the college will not get possession of the estate until after his wife dies. Then the remainder interests (the value of the gifts to charity) will be reduced by the joint life expectancies of Mr. Squire and his wife.

Charitable giving can be used to provide secure retirement income for the giver. You arrange to give your favorite charity a sum of money or property. In return for this gift, the charity agrees to pay you or your spouse an annual income for the lifetime of either or both of you for any stated period. These are the ways it may be done:

The Annuity Trust. Under this arrangement a trust specifies an annual amount to be paid to you. This guarantees that you will receive a specific amount which you can depend upon every year.

The Unitrust. Under this trust the annual payment to you must be a fixed percentage of the market value of a trust's assets as determined each year or, alternatively, the lesser of 5 per cent of such value or the trust's income. You can see that there are no guarantees of the specific amount you will receive. Your payments will depend upon the changing values of the trust property or income from year to year.

The Charitable Pool. This way you give the money or property to a public charity to be placed in a pool or common fund. The charity pays your share of the pool's income to you annually. Here again, the annual payment to you is not determined and will probably vary each year.

As you can see, these types of arrangements are particularly valuable to the older person with appreciated property. If he tried to diversify his holdings he would have to pay capital gain taxes and so lose part of his capital through tax erosion. Under these arrangements he exchanges his property for a guaranteed income without any tax on the appreciation of the property. In addition, he gets a charitable deduction of up to 30 per cent of his adjusted gross income. The amount of the charitable gift is determined by calculating his income interest and subtracting that from the value of the property itself.

Many institutions (particularly universities) are offering attractive arrangements of this kind today. They work for the mutual benefit of both parties.

Private Foundations

The philanthropy of the Rockefellers, the Fords, and Andrew Carnegie has made the "foundation" a household word. But the use of foundations is not limited to multimillionaires. It can be a valuable estate-planning tool for people whose estates are not huge, albeit substantial. They are used to obtain the benefits of income tax deductions and also to build up funds to meet specific charitable obligations or purposes.

A private foundation is your own personal charity—a tax-exempt trust or corporation which you create. In order to qualify for this exemption, it must be created and operated for charitable, religious, scientific, literary, or educational purposes. The creator or his family can control the organization as stockholders or trustees, but the activities of the foundation must be directed toward its charitable purposes if its tax-exempt status is to be maintained.

Ms. Community Leader is called upon to donate large sums annually to a number of charities. She finds that sometimes the sum expected from her exceeds her charitable deduction for the year. At times she isn't in a position to meet these obligations. It's easy enough in a good year, difficult in a lean one.

To solve her problem, she sets up her own foundation, either endowing it with a certain amount of property or annually contributing amounts up to 20 per cent of her adjusted gross income, the maximum deduction she will be allowed. She diverts income from herself and realizes further tax savings from her deductions. The foundation's income is received by it tax-free. However, a minimum percentage must be paid out each year for the charitable purposes for which the foundation was created. Otherwise the foundation will be subject to penalty. Mrs. Leader can select the charitable recipients of the fund and determine the amount and time of payments. She gets her charitable deduction, however, when she makes her contribution to the foundation, not when it makes distributions to charities.

Charitable foundations, we shall see, can be particularly useful for estate tax purposes when the major asset is a closely held corporation. For a businessperson, it can be even more than a means of satisfying his charitable obligations and saving taxes. It can help his business.

Phineas Phlump is the president and sole stockholder of Phlump Pump, Inc., a leading manufacturer of bicycle pumps. Phineas makes sizable charitable contributions each year. He wants to get something more out of it than a charitable deduction. He wants to use it to help his business. He creates the Phlump Foundation and makes his contributions to it. The foundation's funds are used to promote cycling through scientific research, scholarships to worthy cyclists, rest homes for retired ones, and bicycle museums. These charitable gifts bearing the Phlump name have two by-products—free advertising and the build-up of good will among the cycling part of the consumer market.

CHARITY AFTER DEATH: HELPING TO CONSERVE THE ESTATE

Unlike the income tax deduction, there is no limitation on the amount of the estate tax deduction. The full amount of any property passing to a qualified charity is tax-free.

Thus the estate tax charitable deduction enables a planner

to satisfy his charitable instincts tax-free at his death, but it can serve other purposes as well. The tax savings realized through use of the deduction can mean greater security for the family.

Using a Charitable Trust

Security for a non-charitable beneficiary can be provided through a charitable trust. You can create a trust to pay the income to someone for life, leaving the remainder to charity.

Ms. Testatrix, a widow, has an estate of $800,000. She wants to leave it in some manner to provide first for the support of her only child, an unmarried woman of 60, and to leave the rest to her favorite charity. If she leaves it all to her daughter, who she knows will eventually leave it to the same charity, there will be estate taxes of about $75,000, after 1986. The net bequest will then be $725,000. At an 8 per cent return, her daughter will receive an income of $58,000.

Instead she leaves her $800,000 estate in trust with an annuity of $64,000 (8%) payable to her daughter for her life and the principal passing to the charity at her death. The charitable deduction for the value of the remainder interest left to charity wipes out the estate tax. The entire $800,000 will be left for the trust. Thus the daughter will receive $6,000 a year more income, and the charity will have $75,000 more principal.

Sometimes it may be better to split the trust in the opposite way: income to charity, remainder to family. This would be so when estate taxes will be great and the family or beneficiary does not have a current need for income.

Let us say Mr. Testator wants to leave his entire $900,000 estate to his only child, a son who has already reached the top income tax bracket. Not only does his son not need the income from his inheritance, but if he received it, 28 per cent of it would go out in income taxes. So Mr. Testator creates a trust in his will under which an annuity will be paid to charity for a stated number of years or until his son reaches a specific age, perhaps 65, and then the principal goes to his son. Mr. Testator's estate taxes will be reduced by the value of the gift of the annuity interest to charity, leaving a larger amount of principal to eventually pass to his son.

The Charitable Foundation
and the Family Business

The person who has created a foundation during his life has a recipient for his charitable bequests. After his death, his family can continue to control its operation. The foundation can be of particular importance in an estate plan where the major asset is the family business, as it was in the case of the Ford family. Henry Ford's estate taxes were so large, a choice had to be made between selling most of the Ford stock to raise the money needed to pay the tax or making a substantial contribution in order to reduce the taxes to an amount which could be paid out of other assets of the estate. Ford common stock was reclassified into voting common and non-voting. The non-voting common went to the Ford Foundation. Control of the corporation remained in the hands of the Ford family, in this case by the retention of the voting stock.

Even a small businessperson may need the help of a foundation in his estate plan. The average small businessperson will find that the larger part of his estate consists of his business. Unless that business can supply the cash that will be needed to pay estate taxes, his other assets may be eaten up. The family's security will then be totally dependent on the business. By giving part of that business to his foundation, he can reduce the estate taxes which will be payable out of his other assets and leave a cushion for the family. The foundation ends up owning part of the business, but the family still controls the enterprise.

However, the Tax Reform Act of 1969 provides a complicated set of percentage limitations on the stock holdings a foundation may have in a business. These rules may require the foundation to either partially or fully divest itself of these stock holdings during periods ranging from 5 to 20 years. Should there be a requirement to divest, it will depend upon the percentage of stock held, the date the foundation obtained it, and whether the stock was acquired by purchase, gift, or bequest.

CHARITABLE GIFTS THROUGH INSURANCE

Gifts of insurance can be made in a number of ways.

1. Give away an insurance policy and get an income tax deduction for its value—approximately the cash value of the policy.

2. Name a charity as irrevocable beneficiary. You receive an income tax deduction for your premium payments.

3. Give more than you would otherwise be able to afford by making your favorite charity the beneficiary of a large insurance policy.

A man aged 45 wants to make a very large gift to a charity he has headed for many years—something impressive and lasting, like a new building. His estate will just be sufficient to take care of his family after his death and now he can't spare more than $7,000 a year out of his capital. $7,000 a year doesn't seem like much but he can use it to build a fund of $500,000 by means of insurance. His net premium for the first year is $8,910, but in his 28 per cent tax bracket, his actual net cost is only $6,415.20. His premium keeps decreasing over the years. Over a period of 10 years, his annual, after-tax premium cost will average out to about $6,700 a year—which buys him a charitable gift worth a half million dollars at his death. In addition, he will not have to pay premiums after the ninth year.

4. Provide a guaranteed income for a member of your family. You name a charity as irrevocable beneficiary of life insurance, and it agrees to pay an annuity or income to your daughter out of the proceeds of insurance. You get an income tax deduction for your annual premiums in the extent they are attributable to the remainder of the proceeds which the charity will keep.

CHARITY: WHICH WAY?

Which is the best way of making your charitable gifts? That, of course, is up to you as the individual planner. Indeed, as we have pointed out, the whole matter of charitable giving, during your life or at death, is one in which many motives, desires, and needs interact; some philanthropic, some personal, and some financial. One type of charitable gift is better than another only insofar as it fits in with and improves both the estate and the personal plan of each individual.

CHAPTER 18

What to Do with Your Business: The Sole Proprietorship, the Family Enterprise, the Part Ownership

Mr. Independent owns his own business. He draws a salary of $60,000. By coincidence, this is just about the same amount as his brother-in-law, Mr. Executive, earns. He is the vice-president of a small manufacturing company.

Equals in income, are they equals in their ability to provide security for themselves and their families?

Independent would tell you that he is better off. After all, if his business continues to prosper, he will have an estate worth at least $750,000, the present value of his company.

Executive, on the other hand, has assets—stocks, bonds, savings, and insurance—that total about $400,000. Not much of an estate in Independent's eyes.

But Independent is only looking at Executive's surface estate. If he were to probe further, he would find that Executive is worth much more than $400,000. He has neglected to consider that the most important part of Executive's estate lies in his employee benefits. Under the corporation's pension and profit-sharing plans, his beneficiaries will receive at least $25,000 a year after he dies. This, together with the income which can be expected from his other assets, will provide his family a yearly income of $50,000 to $60,000. Just about the same as Independent expects his family to receive from his $750,000 estate.

At this point Independent alters his judgment and in his mind raises Executive to an equal position with himself.

But his judgment is still superficial. Again he has neglected to consider an important aspect—the relative stability of the two estate potentials. Executive's fringe benefits on retirement and at death are guaranteed and his investments are diversified. Barring unlikely events, a minimum of $50,000 a year for his family is a sure thing.

In Independent's case, however, the amount of income is predicted on a theoretical assumption—that the business could be sold at its present operating value of $750,000 when he dies, or if continued, would bring in a predictable amount of income for his family.

This is theory only. In fact, no one knows exactly what the business will be worth at his death. Between now and then its value can decrease or increase substantially. Even assuming its value were $750,000 the moment before his death, what would it be worth the moment after? The loss of the key person can have a serious impact on a business, greatly affecting its market value or its value as a going concern.

Even if the business could be continued, a replacement for Independent would have to be found. This could mean that a large part of the profits which Independent had been drawing in salary would be paid out in wages, leaving little income for the family. As an alternative, the business could be put up for sale, but then there would have to be a buyer ready, willing and able to pay its true value. There is often a scarcity of such people. It might come down to a matter of choosing the lesser of two evils.

Where will the money come from to pay the taxes, administration expenses, and debts in Independent's estate? He doesn't have much cash, nor does the business. Will it cause a forced sale or liquidation of his business?

Whichever alternative is selected, continuation or sale, Independent's family could find itself with an annual income of less than $50,000. It could be more, of course, too. The point is that Independent's position as of now is uncertain.

Any Independent, whether he be a sole proprietor, the head of a family enterprise, or a part owner, must have a special estate planning objective—the preservation of his business or its value for his beneficiaries. As a rule, his business is his major asset, perhaps the only asset of real value. Thus his family's security will depend largely or even entirely on whether he is successful in achieving this objective.

Before embarking on an examination of the ways available for meeting this objective, let's see who these independents are and point up the major problems of each.

THE SOLE PROPRIETOR

He is the person who owns all or virtually all of his business. If someone else has an interest in it, it is only nominal. The business may or may not be incorporated and it may be a small shop with a few employees or a large company employing a hundred or more people. No matter what its size the business depends for its success on the skill, acumen, and ability of its owner. The sole proprietor is usually faced with two problems. When he dies, there is no one to take over and so the business will have to be sold. If it is put up for sale it may be difficult for his estate to find a ready market for the business.

THE HEAD OF THE FAMILY ENTERPRISE

He is an owner, too, but members of his immediate family, his spouse or his children, own interests and actively participate in the business. This situation normally calls for continuation of the business for the benefit of the family since he usually has, within the family, the people to take over the management and they are interested in continuing it.

His problem is how to prepare them for their future responsibilities and how to assure them a harmonious working arrangement.

Often, too, there will be beneficiaries who are not in the business. His estate plan must be arranged so that it will not discriminate against the non-participating members of the family, either by some method of having them share in the profits of the business, or by providing their inheritance out of other assets of his estate.

A further problem he must deal with is that of assuring liquidity for the payment of taxes and expenses without impairing the working capital of the business.

THE PART OWNER

He is a partner or a stockholder in a closely held corporation. His partners or fellow stockholders may be relatives, such as brothers or cousins, or strangers, or a combination of both. In all probability the business will continue after his death, but his family may or may not retain its interest in it. If they are going to keep it, then his problem is to assure that they will receive a sufficient income from it. This is particularly important if their interest is a minority one. If their interest is to be sold, he must make arrangements to assure that it will be purchased at a fair price and that cash will be available to carry out the arrangement.

Although the problems of these three independents differ, there are three possible solutions available to each of them: continuation of the business for the benefit of the family; sale at death; sale or gift of all or part of the business interest during life.

Continuation for the Family

A person may be bent on preserving a thriving enterprise for the benefit of his family but before he goes about making arrangements to carry it out he must ask himself this important question: Is my business worthwhile continuing?

This isn't a rhetorical question. What may be a worthwhile enterprise for him may not be worthwhile for his family after his death. The particular industry or the particular business may be subject to periodic slumps. By its nature, the business may depend for its success on his personal leadership. Continuation may mean taking too great a risk with his family's security.

A further consideration is the future of the business. This requires weighing the effects of possible changes in the market, technology, competition, expiration of patents or licenses, and the potential for growth or decline.

Assuming the business is sound and its future looks good, the next important question is whether it will produce the necessary family security in terms of sufficient income. It may do a good job of supporting the family while its head is alive, but that fact in and of itself isn't a guarantee as to future performance.

Take the case of Ms. Entrepreneur, a woman with a corporation worth $300,000. Its annual net profit is very small and every second or third year it has a small loss. However, it pays her a salary of $50,000 a year, so from her point of view, it is a worthwhile enterprise. Now, if at her

death, the family were to sell the business and realize its full
value (ignoring taxes and other expenses), the maximum
income it could expect to receive from investment of the
proceeds at 8 per cent after taxes would be $24,000. On the
face of it, it would seem to be wiser to continue operation of
the business than to dispose of it. But if continuation requires hiring one or two people to replace the owner or
increasing salaries for employees, there might be little profit
left over for the family. Unless it can produce the necessary
profit, the business is not worth continuing.

If the business is sound, however, its future expectations
good, and it can be expected to produce sufficient profit to
support the family, the planner must next turn his attention
to a vital question: who is going to run the business?

Management and the Family Enterprise

The person with a family enterprise probably has his
future management within the business itself. To assure that
it will continue to operate successfully, he must see that the
person or persons he selects to succeed him are properly
trained to take over the responsibilities which will eventually fall to them. It may be of value to pass along some of
this responsibility before his death, not only as part of the
training but also to see how the arrangement will work out.

We know of one businessman who learned a bitter important lesson in that way. His son, whom he envisioned as his
eventual successor, had started by working in the office of
his business, a manufacturing corporation. One day he decided that it was time for his son to learn something about
the production side of the company and so he put him in
charge of a particular project in the factory.

Unfortunately, or perhaps fortunately, his timing was bad.
His son's assumption of responsibility coincided with a business trip the father had to make. When he returned to the
plant a week later, he found it in turmoil. Three of his best
employees had quit. The head of the union local was waiting
to see him. Production was at a complete standstill. His son
had somehow managed to alienate almost everyone in the
plant, regardless of whether they were connected with his
particular job or not. Management was obviously not his
forte. Today he is employed elsewhere and one of his
brothers-in-law is slated for the top job.

When some of the family do not participate in the business another problem is created. On one hand, is it wise to give these "non-participants" interests in a business over which they have no control? Should a widow, for example, have to depend for her security on a business which is run by sons of a prior marriage?

On the other hand, is it fair to those in the business who are contributing their time and energy to the success of the enterprise to let a non-participator have a voice in the operation? Should a father with two daughters and a son give them equal interests, when it is the son who will have all the problems of running the business and the daughters who will have the control?

Arrangements can and should be worked out in such situations, not only in the interest of fairness to the family members but for the sake of the business itself. In the case of a widow whose stepsons run the business, her share of her husband's estate should come from his other assets. If these are not sufficient, additional insurance might be obtained to make up the difference. Another way of providing for her security is through use of a salary continuation agreement between the owner and the corporation, or a pension or profit-sharing arrangement which will be payable to her at his death.

The father with two daughters and a son could make similar arrangements. Or if this were not feasible, he could divide his business equally among them, but permit the corporation or the son to buy out the interests of his sisters. The purchase could be made in installments.

Another method he could use is the reclassification of the corporate stock into preferred and common, the preferred to go to the daughters and the common to the son. This would give the son full voting power, and in addition, any future increase in the value of the business which logically should go to him as the fruits of his labor. It would assure the daughters of an income from the dividends on the preferred. Further, in order to ensure their security, these dividend rights could be made cumulative with the right to convert to common if for any reason dividends on the preferred weren't paid for a specified period of time. Thus the daughters would be able to share in the control of the corporation if the expected income was not forthcoming.

Whichever arrangement the head of a family business

selects, it should be one which will assure adequate protection for the non-participating members and give the participating members some degree of freedom from outside control. At the same time it must provide for efficient and harmonious continuation of the enterprise.

Management and the Part Owner

Continuation of a part owner's interest by his family after his death might seem to present no problems. This is so in many cases. Certain businesses can easily be continued with the former owner's family sharing in its profits. This is true where capital and not services is the major income-producing factor. A partnership or corporation whose assets consisted of real estate would be a case in point.

But when the business is one which depends in large part upon the personal services of its owners, the surviving partners may not be willing to share the profits of their labor with the surviving family. Happy working relationships do not necessarily extend beyond the grave. Consider, for example, this case.

Joe, Jim, and John are equal stockholders in a corporation in which they are all active employees. They receive substantial salaries but rarely declare dividends.

Joe dies. His widow inherits his stock, which is worth about $200,000. But what income does she realize from it? Her husband received a salary; she gets none. No dividends are paid. She wants to sell the stock but there are usually no buyers for a minority interest in a closely held corporation—except, of course, Jim and John. They want to buy her out, but not right now. Why not wait a bit, they reason. Let the widow go hungry for a while and then buy up her shares at bargain basement prices.

The result is a family lockout instead of a family continuation. Jim and John were the villains, but Joe had the basic responsibility; he should have made arrangements to assure that his widow would receive at least a minimum of income from the business. If he wanted her to be able to keep the stock in the corporation, he too could have set up a salary continuation agreement or a pension arrangement which would ensure that she wouldn't go hungry and be squeezed out.

More commonly, troubles of the same sort occur when

there are really no villains at all but only certain unfortunate tendencies of human nature. Three brothers own a business. One dies. The remaining two vow solemnly to take care of his widow—and they mean it. Sometime later the business hits a lean period which lasts for a long time. Little by little the brothers' resolution and devotion wear off until finally they ask themselves, not how long can we take care of her, but rather, how can we get her out of the business?

If you see any such situations possibly arising in your business, then you had better arrange now for a sale. Far better to do this than to risk leaving your family in such a vulnerable position.

Management and the Sole Owner

What happens when the planner wants to continue his business for the benefit of the family but there is no one to take over the management? Obviously, he must create his own successor management.

This is the time when parents should look at their children with a dispassionate eye. Tradition, sentiment, and ego all say that a son should step into his father's shoes. But history tells a different story. Not only are there inefficient sons or wayward sons, there are also artist sons or poet sons; scientist sons or social worker sons—none of whom has either the bent or the desire to take over his father's business.

If your child is one of these, it is better to accept the situation gracefully and make other arrangements for the management of your business.

Creating successor management means bringing in one or more executives and training them for the job. It also means providing them with incentives to ensure their continued, long-term loyalty.

What kind of incentive? Bonuses, profit-sharing, and pension plans which are normally offered by the large corporations are possible. The best form of incentive in this situation, however, is probably some form of ownership interest—a stake in the business. If the business is unincorported this means eventually taking the potential successor in as a partner. It may be better to incorporate so as to obtain more flexibility in working out a suitable arrangement.

With a corporation form of business, key personnel can be given shares of stock as bonuses or in the form of profit sharing. The potential successors might be given an opportunity to purchase shares at a reduced price or over a period of time under advantageous financing arrangements. Another possible way of providing incentive would be by giving them options to purchase stock at a fixed price on the death of the owner.

Yet the incentive plan should not be so great that it jeopardizes the security of the family. The arrangement should be such that an adequate income is assured for the family and/or control remains within its hands. To assure this protection for the family, it may be necessary to change the capital structure of the corporation. For example, the stock might be reclassified into voting common and non-voting common. The family would receive all the voting common and the successor management part or all of the non-voting. The family retains complete control but the key people are given incentive because they share in the company's future growth and earnings by virtue of their stockholdings.

Another method which might be used in reclassification into preferred and common, with the family owning the preferred and successor management the common. Under this arrangement most of the value of the business is put into the preferred and it has preference as to dividends and assets on liquidation. Successor management can afford to buy the common since its value is low. Its incentive will be great since its stock will reap the full benefits of all future increases in the value of the business.

These are not the only ways of re-arranging capital structure to protect the family while providing incentive for outsiders. There are many possibilities, and various features may be added to provide further security. For example, the owner could have a salary continuation agreement. Then the members of the family are not only stockholders of the corporation but also creditors, a more desirable status.

Economic Cushions

If the business is to be continued, whether its management is in the hands of the family or outsiders, the family needs an economic cushion. In a well-planned estate, its security should not rest solely on the fortunes of the business. There should be assets outside the business to provide this reserve. Unfortunately for the average businessperson, most of his estate is his business. How does he create other forms of economic security? He uses the usual methods of estate building: life insurance, outside investments, and funded pension and profit-sharing plans.

The business as well as the family need a cushion—this in the form of extra liquidity. On the death of its head, a sole proprietorship or family enterprise may encounter some rough going for a while. There may be a decrease in business because of the loss of personal contacts or because customers wait to see whether the company will continue or liquidate. Credit may be temporarily withdrawn. Extra cash will help to tide the business over this uncertain period. The corporation can obtain this needed liquidity by insuring the life of its key person or setting up a sinking fund for this purpose.

Liquidity and Taxes

Often a more important reason for providing liquidity is the need to pay estate taxes and administration expenses. It may be possible to pay these out of other estate assets, but unless they are ample (and they rarely are in this type of estate), it is wiser to take the cash out of the business and leave the family as large a reserve as possible. There are two ways of paying the taxes out of the business.

1. *Redemption of Stock.* Ordinarily, cash or other property paid by a corporation to its stockholders out of its earnings and profits is treated as a dividend to the stockholders. One of the exceptions to this rule is a distribution by a corporation in redemption of stock to pay estate taxes. This is popularly known as a "Section 303 redemption." If the value of the decedent's stock exceeds 35 per cent of the value of his adjusted gross taxable estate, the stock can be redeemed without it being considered a dividend, to the extent that the amount received does not exceed the taxes, funeral, and administration expenses. If the redemption price is higher than the tax basis for the stock, some taxable gains will be realized.

In other words, the estate can take money out of the surplus of the corporation with little income tax liability. This is one of the few ways of getting money out of corporate surplus without having it treated as income. Unfortunately, one has to go to the extreme of dying to achieve this tax savings.

In closely held corporations one should be careful in planning a "Section 303 redemption." This is a highly technical matter and cannot be adequately dealt with here. Let it suffice to say expert tax advice is always required in planning a stock redemption to avoid adverse tax results.

2. *Installment Method.* Estate taxes must usually be paid within 9 months after the death of the estate owner. The tax laws, however, permit an executor to pay the portion of the federal tax attributable to the value of a closely held business over a period of 15 years, provided that the value of the business exceeds 35 per cent of the value of the adjusted gross estate. To qualify for this type of payment a business can be a sole proprietorship, a partnership, or a corporation. To meet the over 35 per cent requirement, business entities can be aggregated if, in each, the decedent's capital interest or voting power is at least 20 percent or if there are 15 or fewer partners or stockholders.

During the first 5 years the estate need only pay interest on the deferred taxes. The tax with the interest can then be paid in up to 10 annual installments. In addition, the tax on the first $1,000,000 of such business property has a special low interest rate of 4 per cent.

The installment method allows an estate to pay the estate tax over a period of time and perhaps do it out of earnings of the business without impairing its capital. Remember, though, that it only applies to the part of the tax which is attributable to the value of the business interest. The balance of the tax must still be paid within 9 months. There is another problem to consider in using this method of payment. Since an executor is personally liable for estate taxes, by paying in installments he is extending the period of his liability. If the business should fail or estate assets decline in value, he might have to pay the balance of the taxes out of his own pocket. However, the tax law allows the discharge of executors from such personal liability if certain requirements are met.

Continuation and Your Will

The last, but by no means the least, thing that must be done to carry out a plan of continuing your business is the granting of authorization in your will. In the absence of a specific authorization to do so in the will, the executors may be required to sell or liquidate, or risk personal liability for failing to do so. The executors and trustees should therefore be given the broadest powers to carry out the plan of continuation.

SALE AT DEATH

If the business is to be sold and its full value realized by the family there must be a market for the business. There may be willing buyers for it today but this is no assurance that the same will hold true at the time of the owner's death. Moreover, the death of the owner or key person tends to reduce the price offer. Buyers are always in a better bargaining position if the estate or family is forced to sell.

Then, too, there is an interim period between the death and sale during which profits may drop, making the business a less attractive investment. If a ready buyer cannot be found, the estate may be forced to liquidate the business and realize substantially less on the sale of the assets than the true value of the enterprise as a going business.

The conclusion is obvious. If you plan to have your business interest sold at your death, it is better to make the arrangements for that sale while you are alive than to leave it to chance.

The best market may be found within the business itself—your partners, fellow stockholders, key personnel, the corporation's pension plan, or possibly a family foundation.

1. *Partnership Agreement.* A partnership agreement should make provision for having the surviving partners buy the estate's interest. The scale can be worked out to permit installment payments over a number of years or it can be financed by each partner owning insurance on the lives of the others.

2. *Buy-Sell Agreement.* If the business is incorporated, you can have an agreement requiring the other stockholders or the corporation to buy or redeem your stock after you die. Some agreements obligate only the estate to sell or the stockholders to buy, while others make it mandatory on both sides. In most cases the planner should be sure that under his agreement the purchase and sale are mandatory

unless he has valid reasons for wanting his estate to have flexibility.

Such agreements can be financed by the stockholders insuring each other if they are the potential purchasers, or by the corporation insuring its stockholders if the agreement calls for redemption. The price to be paid is set forth in the agreement. It may be a fixed amount, which should be adjusted periodically to reflect increases or decreases in value, or can be based upon a formula involving net worth and good will.

3. *Key Personnel.* The person who has no partners or fellow stockholders to buy out his interest must create his own market. He can do this perhaps through his key personnel. Financing the sale may be difficult but installment and other methods can be worked out.

4. *Family Foundation.* If the owner has set up a family foundation it can be used as a market for the business. The owner provides the funds for the purchase through his annual contributions or by having the foundation insure his life. If he pays the premiums for the insurance he has an additional benefit. The premiums are charitable contributions and he receives an income tax deduction for them.

5. *Employee Stock Ownership Plans.* These are also possible purchasers. These plans already own large shares of the businesses which created them. If the employees' trust is not in a position to finance such a purchase, it can carry insurance on the owner's life to provide the necessary funds.

LIFETIME TRANSFERS

Like any other asset, a business may be sold or given away, in whole or in part, during the owner's lifetime in order to carry out his estate plan. The decision to make a business transfer a lifetime one might be motivated by any one of a number of reasons: inability to arrange for a profitable after-death sale; desire to benefit or provide incentive for family members or successor management; need to diversify investments; need for liquidity; and of course the classic motive for lifetime transfer—removing the subsequent growth on a substantial asset from the taxable estate.

Lifetime sale has its economic disadvantages as well as its advantages. On the one hand, a living owner can probably get a better price than the executor of his estate. On the other hand, the gain realized on the sale is subject to taxes and so reduces the planner's capital during his lifetime.

If the decision is to sell, however, this present era is a particularly good time for it. We are in a period when many companies are attempting to grow by acquisition or merger and are seeking diversification. Now may be the time to take advantage of the opportunity to be "acquired."

There are a number of methods of lifetime transfer. Which of them you select will depend to a large extent on your objectives.

Sale for a Lump Sum

This is the simplest method. The problem may be that a potential buyer doesn't have the available funds. An employee stock ownership plan or your family foundation may be able to pay a lump sum.

Installment Sale

Under this arrangement the seller usually, but not always, gets a down payment. The balance is paid to him over a period of years. This is a common practice where the sale is made to a member of the family or key personnel. The buyer, by being allowed to spread out his payments over a period of time, is able to finance it, at least in part, out of the earnings of the business.

Sale Plus Contract

For the owner who really doesn't want to retire this can be a good solution. The sale is tied in with an employment contract retaining the owner as manager or consultant at a specified salary. When there is such an employment arrangement, the sales price of the business might be contingent on future earnings. For example, the sales arrangement might involve a lump sum or installment payments combined with a percentage of the profits for the next 5 or 10 years.

Exchange of Stock

Large companies interested in acquiring businesses generally offer their own stock in exchange. The stock received by the seller is usually listed and therefore readily marketable.

This arrangement is highly recommended for owners who will realize large gains on an outright sale. On the exchange of stock there is no tax payable. The tax is payable only when you sell the new stock. One way to reduce the tax impact is to sell the new stock gradually over a period of years.

Private Annuity

This arrangement (the sale of your business in exchange for an agreement by the buyer to pay you an annuity) has its tax advantages, as we know. It is especially well suited to the sale of a business since annuity payments, like installment payments, can be financed out of the profits of the business.

Private annuities carry some risk, however. The buyer could default in his obligation to make payments. That's why these are customarily limited to arrangements between members of the family.

Gifts

In Chapter 11 we saw how the gift of an asset has the potential to reduce both income and estate taxes. When the gift is of a business interest, it has some added advantages. It can provide incentive for successor management. It can create potential buyers—a part owner may be induced to buy the rest of the business.

It can solve a difficult but common problem—the reluctance of children to remain in a family business where they have no control or authority. This way they can be given a measure of both and so increase their own self-respect. At the same time the gift will serve to accomplish another purpose—the training of family members to take over on the death of the owner.

A person who wishes to keep down the size of his taxable estate might do well to give away the future expectations of the business, particularly if he sees great future growth in his business and does not want to give it away in the form of estate taxes.

He reclassifies the corporate stock into voting preferred and non-voting common. Ninety per cent of the entire value of the business goes into the voting shares; 10 per cent goes into the non-voting. He keeps the voting shares which give him control of the company. At the same time he makes a gift of the non-voting stock (which has little present value) to his children. When and if the business experiences growth, the increase in the value will redound to them.

Thus the value of the owner's interest remains fixed; he receives dividend income from his preferred shares and he keeps control of the company during his life. The result is that his estate will not be subject to increased taxation because of the growth of the company. And since the initial value of the common stock is low, it can be transferred to the children with little or no gift taxation. Thus, a potentially valuable asset, which might otherwise represent a large asset in the owner's estate, is transferred to the ultimate beneficiaries at little or no cost.

Going Public

As many owners of small corporations have discovered, it can be worthwhile to go public. The usual method is for the owner to sell only part of his interest while retaining enough to keep control. In this way he is able to convert some of his closely held interests into cash and can diversify his investments. At the same time he has created a market which can be used for future sale of his remaining stock, either during his life or at his death.

HOW TO VALUE YOUR BUSINESS

The determination of the worth of a business is vital to many aspects of estate planning. If your business is the major part of your estate you can scarcely begin your plan of transfer without coming to grips with this problem.

You must know the value of your business in order to calculate your estate taxes. The failure to make these estimates can frustrate the formulation of a satisfactory estate plan.

The valuation of a business is also important in another aspect of estate planning—lifetime transfers and gift taxes.

The planner who is making gifts to his children or other members of his family must place a value on any business interests he gives in order to determine whether it comes within his annual exclusion and unified credit and, if not, the amount of gift taxes will be payable.

Valuation has income tax ramifications as well. If an employee is given stock or an interest in the business, it is considered compensation and therefore income to him. The value of what has been given to him must be established. If a businessperson makes a charitable gift of, for example, shares of stock to his foundation, its value must be determined in order to calculate his income tax deduction.

How to Determine Value

For tax purposes the fair market value of a business interest is the net amount which a willing buyer would pay to a willing seller. When dealing with publicly traded securities, we have a ready reference—market quotations. With stock of a closely held corporation or an interest in an unincorporated business, determining valuation can be a difficult matter.

For estate tax purposes, if a business or business interest is sold within a reasonable time after death, the sales price will usually establish the value—provided it is an arm's length transaction. The price paid, for example, on a sale by an estate to the children of a deceased owner would be subject to very close scrutiny. If it was obviously not reasonable, it might not carry any weight as evidence of true value.

A partnership agreement or stockholders' agreement or an option to purchase, which fixes the sales price beforehand, determines the value for estate tax purposes. The price set in the agreement or option will be taken as the value (even though it is less than actual value) provided the estate is obligated to sell. For example, Corporation X is owned by two stockholders. They enter into an agreement which provides (1) that if either wishes to dispose of his stock, he must first offer it to the other at a price of $1,000 per share; and (2) at the death of either, the survivor has the right to purchase the shares at the same price. One of them dies. Although a share might be actually worth $1,500 the estate's obligation to sell the stock makes its value for tax purposes the price set in the agreement.

Other Methods

In the absence of actual sales or buy-sell agreements, other methods to determine value must be used. Unfortunately, there is no pat formula or set of rules for valuing a business. The Internal Revenue Service does offer certain "factors" stating that these are not "all-inclusive" but that they are "fundamental and require careful analysis in each case."

• "The nature of the business and the history of the enterprise from its inception." This means looking at its past record to determine potential stability.

• "The economic outlook in general and the condition and outlook of the specific industry in particular."

• "The book value of the stock and the financial condition of the business." In spite of the fact that the book value is almost always considered in dealing with valuations, a planner shouldn't rely on it. Since book value rarely reflects actual value, it isn't often accepted by the Internal Revenue Service.

• "The earning capacity of the company." Potential future income is a major factor in the value of most businesses and past earnings are used as an indication of future performance. Due weight is given to any trend toward increasing or decreasing net income.

• "The dividend-paying capacity." This means more than just dividends which are actually paid in the past. It means what could have been paid after retention of a reasonable amount of profits in the company. In a family corporation this factor is given less weight. Here profits can be taken out in the form of salaries and a dividend-paying policy may be determined by the needs and tax brackets of the family.

• "Whether or not the enterprise has good will or other intangible value." There is no general definition of good will and no set formula for its valuation. The Internal Revenue Service generally values good will by capitalizing the excess of net earnings over and above a fair return on the net tangible assets. In actual figures how would this work out? A company has a net worth of $500,000, and makes a profit of $50,000. Using 6 per cent as the norm, a reasonable return would have been $30,000. But since they have earned $20,000 more than this, the amount is attributed to good will.

• "Sales of the stock and the size of the block of stock to

be valued." First of all, to be a test of value, sales must be arm's length transactions. Forced sales or distress sales or small isolated sales will not be relied upon to determine actual value. If the stock represents a controlling interest, its value may be greater than its per share value. On the other hand, if it is a minority interest it might be less.

• "The market price of stocks of corporations engaged in the same or a similar line of business having their stocks actively traded in a free and open market." The companies must truly be comparable in order to make a valid comparison. This includes comparable capital structures as well as market and business trends.

Although there are these various factors to be given consideration, certain ones carry more weight than others. Earnings will be a more important factor for a company which sells products or services. However, for an investment or holding company, such as a real estate corporation, the value of its underlying assets is of greatest importance.

A great deal of emphasis is put on capitalization of earnings and, at times, capitalization of dividends. One of the most difficult aspects, however, is the determination of the capitalization rate to be used. There is no formula even within the same industry. In addition, it varies from time to time depending on economic conditions.

To repeat: in the absence of a buy-sell agreement or actual sale, there is no way to be sure of what the ultimate valuation of a business will be for tax purposes. Certainly, the businessperson himself can't determine it. He needs the help of his accountant and attorney. He might be well advised to get expert appraisals.

If possible, you should try to establish the value now—during your life—rather than leave it for your executor to argue it out with the tax authorities. This can be done by making taxable gifts and filing gift tax returns, or by making charitable donations and claiming income tax deductions. It might involve litigation, but because valuation is so difficult and each side is bound to have conflicting appraisals, the usual result is a compromise. While the valuation of one purpose is not necessarily binding on the government, it is some evidence and carries weight for the future.

KEEP IT WORKABLE

Your business transfer plan should not be treated differently from the rest of your estate plan. Like it, it must be periodically reviewed. Changes of circumstances, whether personal or economic, can turn a good arangement into an unworkable one. Be sure it doesn't happen to yours.

CHAPTER 19

Choosing Your Estate Managers

While a person is alive, he is the one who provides for his family, ensures their security, and makes plans for their future. He wishes he could do the same thing after he is dead. He wants a form of immortality.

If that wish is not attainable, something close to it is. In the people whom he selects to manage his estate, to take care of the needs of his family, he begets an immortality of a sort. Competent representatives can be found to act in his name and in his image to do the same as he would.

The word that defines these people is "fiduciary." It refers to the executor, the trustee, the guardian of a minor's person and property. Technically and actually, the fiduciary is a person who has assumed the responsibility or duty of acting for the benefit of another person with whom he stands in a relationship of confidence and trust.

Confidence and trust it indeed is—or should be. Choosing a fiduciary is not a mere formality; no legal fiction is involved here. Few people realize the responsibilities they are assigning when they select their fiduciaries, and so leave the choice until the last minute. Then the tendency is to choose someone who is a friend or relation without any thought as to whether he, she or they possess the necessary abilities, let alone the willingness to do the job.

Let us take just one of the fiduciary roles—guardianship. Guardianship of the person of a minor implies one set of qualities—the ability (and the desire) to give children love and affection, to raise them according to the values and principles held by their parents. Guardianship of property implies another set—the ability to handle their financial affairs, to invest and use their money wisely, to conserve their capital. Skill in financial affairs is the requirement here.

Sometimes these two sets of abilities are combined in one person, but more often they are not. Yet how many people, in making a will, consider this? A couple make a devoted aunt the guardian of their children's property *and* person. They think they have done the right thing.

But suppose the aunt knows nothing about financial matters? Wouldn't it have been wiser to separate the guardianship functions, appointing her the guardian of the persons of the children, and another, guardian of their property? This would relieve her of an unwanted burden as well as ensuring the financial security of the children.

The function of a fiduciary, then, is often a double one: it may involve both personal and impersonal responsibilities; it demands both sense and sensibility. That is why it is often necessary to have multiple fiduciaries, and why their selection is a serious matter which calls for careful consideration and the balancing of many requirements. It is just as important to the small estate as it is to the large one—if the amount of money involved is not substantial, that does not mean that the need for sound management is lessened; it may indeed be that much greater.

The Executor

The source of the executor's function is twofold: the law and the will. Under the law, someone must collect the assets of the estate, protect the property against loss or harm; assert any claims against third parties which the deceased or the estate may have; value and inventory the property; liquidate assets; pay all debts and expenses; prepare and file estate and income tax returns. These duties end when the beneficiaries are accounted to and the property is distributed.

The person who does these things is the executor. If you die without a will or if the people you designated as your executors refuse to take the job, or resign or die, or cease to act for any reason, the law steps in, and the court appoints someone to do the job of the executor. He is called an administrator.

As testator you have the right to impose additional responsibilities and duties on your executor. You can leave it up to him, for example, to select certain beneficiaries, to choose charities, or perhaps to distribute personal effects among relatives. He might also be given powers of investment—broader or more limited than the law accords him.

The executor (or administrator) has a time-consuming and important function. He will need the services of a lawyer and possibly also of an investment counselor. But even so, it is he who is responsible for the decisions made, the steps taken. If he acts recklessly or imprudently, or oversteps his authority, then he will be held responsible and is personally liable for any consequent losses.

The Trustee

The trustee receives, and is responsible for, the administration, investment, and distribution of trust property. He collects the income, pays the trust expenses, distributes the income and/or the principal in accordance with the directions of the trust instrument or will.

The executor's job is over in a few years at the most but the trustee will probably have to act over a long period of time. An estate might require trustees for as long as 75 years. The financial security of not one but several generations may be involved. The trustee's investment duties may require repeated investments with periodic reviews of holdings and appraisals. Over the years he will have to make accountings to the beneficiaries, and he will have to file income tax returns for the trust every year.

Beyond this the trustee usually has to work personally with the beneficiaries. He may be required continuously to exercise his own discretion as to the distribution of the trust monies; deciding between one beneficiary and another, settling rival claims. He may have the duty to sprinkle income among a group of beneficiaries to keep himself informed of their needs and resources. And especially, the trustee must be able to assess, re-appraise, and deal with all the changes and cycles that inevitably occur in the economic world over a period of time.

All this means that a trustee must be a person of experience and mature judgment—or an organization which is capable of handling these many duties. Don't forget that the trustee—as well as other fiduciaries—need not be an individual. It can also be a corporation.

Like the executor, the trustee is responsible for the administration of the trust property and thus can be subject to personal liability for any losses due to his reckless or imprudent exercise of authority.

The Guardian

As we know, guardianships are of two types: personal and property. The duty of the guardian of the person is, of course, to assume the responsibilities of personal care which the dead parents had. The personal guardian may be—and usually is—a member of the family. But it could also be a trusted friend.

The guardian of the property, as the name implies, handles only property. He makes investments, collects income, pays expenses, and uses or applies the income or the principal for the benefit of his ward. His duties last until his minor is of age. Then he submits his account and turns the property over to his former charge.

The law limits the authority of a property guardian, however. He is bound to seek and follow the directions of the court. He is limited to his ability to exercise discretion. Because of this it is far better to leave property to a minor in trust under the care of a trustee who is provided with all the powers for carrying out the objectives of the estate owner.

But this doesn't mean that the guardian of the property should be completely eliminated. Even if you leave everything in trust you should designate one, so that there will be someone to take care of property which the child now owns or may later acquire from other sources.

Choosing Your Fiduciaries: How Many?

As a testator you have a choice in your selection of fiduciaries. You can have one person perform all the functions, acting simultaneously and continuously as executor, trustee, and guardian. Conversely you may appoint several people for each of the jobs. Or you may choose a corporate fiduciary, a bank or trust company. Which is best depends on the size and character of your estate, the needs of your beneficiaries, and your own feelings as to who will be able to carry out your objectives most effectively.

Co-fiduciaries: A Special Problem

When two or more people are given the responsibility for one function, whether it be as guardians, trustees, or executors, they are co-fiduciaries.

There are often excellent reasons for appointing co-fiduciaries. You may want to use the special talent or experience of one person, but feel that he isn't qualified to take on the entire job. For instance, a person might want a business friend to take on the job of managing his estate investments, but at the same time want someone else who is closer to his family to take on the responsibilities of evaluating their needs. His solution is to have his friend act as co-trustee with his spouse or another relative. Sometimes co-fiduciaries are appointed for reasons of family harmony. A planner, for instance, might want one of his brothers to be his executor, but doesn't want to offend his second brother. So he names them jointly.

The life of a co-fiduciary does not always run smoothly, however, and a planner should be aware of this. If he's going to appoint co-fiduciaries, he should try as far as is humanly possible to make sure that they are people who will be able to work together. Disagreement or dissension is serious; it can result in court proceedings, with a consequent waste of time and money.

Some planners have tried to solve this problem beforehand by appointing odd numbers of people as co-fiduciaries, and specifying in their will that the majority rules. But committees are burdensome things: too often they complicate rather than simplify estate administration.

Successor Fiduciaries

If you appoint an individual or individuals, you must be sure also to appoint successor or substitute fiduciaries as well. The person you select might die, become incapacitated, resign, or simply refuse to serve. If you haven't nominated a substitute in your will or trust instrument, the appointment of one is left up to the court. You can also take care of this contingency by giving a fiduciary or one of your beneficiaries the authority to name a successor. If you have a corporate fiduciary, however, there is usually no reason to name a successor. A bank or trust company is immortal and can be expected to last for the duration of its assigned responsibility.

CHOOSING YOUR FIDUCIARIES: WHO?

This is, of course, the key question, for upon your selection of the proper people or groups depends in large measure the future of your estate.

There are only a few restrictions on your choice. Some states do not allow non-residents to be appointed. Others allow them to qualify only if they are blood relatives. In some states corporations cannot serve unless they are qualified to do business in that state. And, of course, the court will not permit the appointment of someone obviously not qualified to serve, such as a minor, an incompetent, or a felon.

The main problem in fiduciary selection is whether to select individuals or corporations, or possibly a combination of both. Let's see some of the ramifications involved in each case.

The Individual Fiduciary

First, some general qualifications. Whoever you select should be a responsible, mature person. Beyond this, he should have some experience in business and financial matters. That doesn't mean that he has to be a specialist, just that he has the information and judgment to know how and know where he can find specialized advice when he needs it, plus the ability to evaluate this advice when he receives it.

He should be someone whose opinion and judgment, whether in business or personal affairs, you value and respect. In addition, he should know your family, and know your goals and aims for them. It's just as important that your family, too, have confidence and respect for him. In a sense your fiduciary is taking over as head of the family. This is a big job, and unless there is mutual confidence all around, there is likely to be trouble.

We remember one case of a frustrated executor who was

trying to work out an investment portfolio which, in conjunction with the widow's own investments, would be well-balanced and produce the most after-tax income for her. The widow, who happened to be his sister-in-law, refused to give him any information concerning her personal affairs. We tried to help by explaining to her that his purpose was not to pry into her business but to help her. Her answer: she understood why he wanted the information and appreciated his efforts in her behalf. It wasn't that she didn't trust him; it was his wife. Who knew what information he might pass on to her?

This was the result of bad planning on the part of the estate owner. Perhaps the brother-in-law should not have been selected to do the job. There is, after all, no point in selecting someone who—for whatever reason—will not be able to elicit full cooperation from your beneficiaries.

Leaving the personal question aside, there are also some practical considerations. The individual selected should not be too old and he should be in good health. As planner you should make sure, too, that he has the time and the willingness to carry out his duties.

Family Members as Fiduciaries

Most people turn to their own family for fiduciaries. This is usually both proper and just. Naturally you want those closest to you to carry on after you. But when you come to decide which member of your family to select, reasons and not sentiment should rule.

One's husband or wife is usually the first choice as executor, but what happens when it comes to choosing an alternate if there is no spouse surviving? Too often the planner wants to do "the right thing" and lets wisdom and judgment go to the winds. Thus he names all four of his children as excutors or in some way gives responsibility to the whole family. This rarely works out. There's bound to be trouble. Better to make a decision and a selection now based on your own assessment of the individual qualifications of your family's members.

It goes without saying that the individual selected, no matter what his specialty, should be a person of integrity. Instances of malfeasance are rare, but they can happen. Fiduciaries can be bonded, of course, but this is expensive—and, more important, it is, or should be, unnecessary. If you are so unsure of a person that you think he should be bonded, then choose someone else. Or if you cannot find anyone whose integrity you know you can rely on, then you would certainly be better off with a corporate fiduciary.

The Corporate Fiduciary

The usefulness of the corporate fiduciary is becoming more and more recognized. We believe that in many types of estates a corporation is preferable to an individual. When the estate is sizable or complicated, an institutional fiduciary is usually a wise choice. Handling an estate of this type is quite a burden for an individual—often too much so. In addition, it takes experience and know-how which few individuals can be expected to have. How can one person be investment counselor, tax expert, accountant, and administrator at the same time?

The bank or trust company contains all these elements. It offers a packaged service which is often cheaper and more efficient in the long run. Take for instance the corporate trust officer. Not only is he a person with background and training in his specialty; he also has at hand, when he needs them, the experience and background and training of the entire bank staff.

A corporation provides full-time management; it is financially responsible; it is experienced.

And it has continuity. This is a great plus. We have mentioned the fact that a trust can last through several generations. No one person can handle such a trust. But a bank or trust company will be able to.

Corporate fiduciaries do tend to be more conservative in their investments than most individual investors. This is a factor you should take into consideration. Depending on your aims and desires, it may or may not be a point in their favor. Remember, however, that you can direct your fiduciaries to follow any particular program of investment you think advisable. In other words, the inherent conservative tendency of the corporate fiduciary is not really a stumbling block to a more imaginative and aggressive investment program, if that is what you want.

Corporations are more impersonal in their administration. Again, this is advantageous or disadvantageous depending upon the circumstances. A bank or trust company can't give an intimate, personal touch to its administration, but sometimes its very impersonality prevents pressures and strains that might otherwise occur if a family member is made a fiduciary. It usually can deal more effectively with the "problem" beneficiary. It is more difficult to harass or pressure a corporate fiduciary. It is impossible to call a bank at midnight and complain that you can't live on the income of a trust.

Compromises are always possible too. The person who wants both the impersonal, experienced management of a corporation and the personal touch of an individual can appoint both of them, either formally as co-fiduciaries or under a more informal (but clearly spelled out) arrangement. The bank is made the executor or trustee, and an individual is given certain powers over the distribution of income and principal, but not over investment or administration. A variety of collaboration arrangements are possible.

If your decision is to use a corporate fiduciary, be sure to consult with them beforehand. They can help you to set up your estate transfer program in the most efficient way possible; they can review your will and your trust arrangements with your lawyer to make sure that both are properly organized for good administration.

You should be aware that corporations, just like individuals, may decline an appointment. This is most likely to happen if the estate or trust is not set up to be easily administered, or if the estate is a small one and commissions aren't adequate to compensate them for the work involved. A trust company, for instance, would probably decline to serve as a trustee of a $100,000 to $200,000 trust fund unless it will receive the minimum commission it specifies.

Fiduciary Powers

Beyond those provided by law, what sort of powers should a planner give his fiduciary?

Investment

Unless you specifically empower him with additional authority, a fiduciary's investment freedom is limited by law.

In some states he can invest only in property which is specified by law, known as "legals" or "legal lists." In other states his scope of investments is limited by what is called a "standard of prudence," i.e., measured by how prudent people of intelligence and discretion would act in managing their own affairs.

Under your will or in the trust instrument, however, you can do pretty much as you please: either making investment power a broad one, or limiting it to specific kinds of investments. On the whole we favor giving wide powers for a number of reasons. First of all, if you have carefully chosen your fiduciaries, you should have sufficient confidence in them to rely on their judgment.

Further, a live investor obviously is a better judge of the changing economic needs of the estate than a dead one. As the past decades have proved, few can guess with real accuracy the swing of an economic cycle; what was a sound investment 25 years ago may no longer be. Many an estate has diminished because the testator has not foreseen this possibility and has not armed his executor or trustee with the power to switch, change, re-invest, etc., according to his own discretion. The principle that the dead hand of the testator should not rule the living is especially applicable to investment powers.

Just as you may make the investment power flexible, so also with the people you confer it on. The power can be limited to one of the co-fiduciaries or it can even be given to a beneficiary or a third person.

Property Retention

It is usually wise to give a fiduciary the power *to retain* property in the estate. This power is important when the estate has a variety of investments, some of which do not fall within the usual permissible investment categories. Unless the fiduciary has the right to retain them, they must be sold, sometimes to the detriment of the estate.

In 1950 an estate was probated in New York State which consisted almost entirely of high-grade corporate stocks worth about $400,000. The portfolio was well-founded, the dividend return was high, and each individual stock represented a good investment. The will, however, did not give the executor or the trust any authority to keep the property and was silent on investments. Until 1951, in the absence of specific authorization, a New York fiduciary could not invest in common or preferred stock. Therefore the executor had to liquidate all these securities and invest in "legals" which provided a smaller income return.

Business Disposal

A businessperson should always specifically empower his fiduciaries to continue his business or to enter into new partnership arrangements. Otherwise sale or liquidation is required with the possibility of losses being incurred.

Real Estate

Broad powers are particularly important here since the authority granted by law can be especially limited with respect to real estate dealings in many states. A fiduciary might be able to sell a million dollars worth of securities but would not be allowed to dispose of a $10,000 piece of real estate without judicial approval. By all means, give your fiduciary the power to deal with real estate, including the right to mortgage and lease, as well as to sell.

Borrowing and Lending

Unless he is given the authority, the fiduciary may not be able to borrow or lend. If the estate needs cash to pay taxes but the executor is unable or doesn't want to liquidate assets, this restriction can be onerous. Sometimes beneficiaries may need cash funds at a time when distribution cannot be made. All this makes the borrowing and lending power an important one.

Tax Savings

Give your fiduciary the right to exercise options, file joint returns with your spouse, and consent to prior gifts. This will allow him to take advantage of many possible tax savings.

COMMISSIONS: FIDUCIARY COMPENSATION

All fiduciaries are entitled to compensation for their services. It is fixed by statue or determined by the court.

State laws on commissions vary greatly. In some states, depending on the size of the estate or trust, each fiduciary gets a full commission. In other states there is one commission which is divided among the fiduciaries, usually according to the service rendered. If a fiduciary performs special services, such as managing a business or real estate, he may be entitled to a "management commission" which is in addition to his regular fee.

Suppose the estate uses an attorney who is also a fiduciary. He has a double function, but in most states he cannot receive both commissions and attorney fees. In these states you will probably be saving money if you make an attorney a fiduciary. Even if you live in a state where an attorney is entitled to commissions as well as attorney's fees it may still be best to use him. His experience and knowledge and the confidence which you and your beneficiaries have in him make the cost worthwhile. Remember, too, that your executor and often your trustee will need legal services, so the alternate cost will be no greater. Moreover, many attorneys who act as executors or trustees waive their commissions and take only legal fees.

If you wish, you can enter into an agreement to fix your fiduciaries' commissions, either by agreement during your life or by the terms of your will. Members of the family, for example, will serve as fiduciaries without compensation. When there is a prior agreement on commissions, this takes precedence over the statute or court-fixed commissions.

FINALLY

The people who administer your estate are just as important as its assets. Be sure that you select them with at least the same care as you use in selecting your investments.

CHAPTER 20

A Last Word on Estate Planning: Don't Do It All Yourself

With a book like this to use as a reference and with guides and charts to aid him, could an intelligent person do his own estate planning? Are estate creation and transfer a matter of technique, like house building, which the knowledgeable amateur can master?

The idea is alluring but dangerous. For this is precisely what estate planning is *not*. It does not demand the mastery of a single area of knowledge but of many. It is by nature made up of many parts, and requires the use of many skills, which, while interrelated, are yet quite different. It deals with such subjects as the laws of trusts, taxation, corporations, wills, personal and real property, and many others. It involves a knowledge of economics and financial dealings, and the ways people make their livings, and then their fortunes. It must take into account not only material things, but also the delicate and involved problems of personal and family relationships. It is, in a sense, as broad and complicated as life itself. It has a philosophy of its own evolved over the years and is based on the experience of countless numbers of people.

What must you know to plan an estate? Much more than is in this book. What is contained here are only general principles and broad statements. To cite all the exceptions to these would take volumes. As a matter of fact, there is a great body of legal literature on each aspect of any one of these chapters. It is beyond the capacity of any one individual to absorb all this knowledge. And even if he could, there is always the difference between knowledge and action. Assuming the possibility of acquiring the former, putting it into practice is another matter. This takes experience, something that no do-it-yourselfer can readily come by.

Let us cite three do-it-yourself estate plans and their unfortunate outcome.

The first one concerns wills and how they are drawn. A man had one prepared by his lawyer which gave the bulk of his property to his wife. A few years later his wife died, and eventually the man remarried. He realized that he needed another will, but saw no need to consult a lawyer. He used the old will as a guide and drew a new one, substituting the name of his second wife for his first. He executed the will in his own handwriting, and therefore did not bother to have witnesses; these were only necessary, he thought, when the will was typed or written by someone else.

If he had lived in any one of a number of states other than where he did, New York, he would have been on safe ground. What he did not know was that the principle that a handwritten will does not need witnesses does not hold true in New York. Only if he had made the will while in service as a soldier or sailor would it have been valid.

The result: when he died, the will came to probate and was declared invalid. The laws of intestacy prevailed and his property was not distributed the way he wanted.

The second do-it-yourself plan concerns insurance. A widower had made the proceeds of a $200,000 term life insurance policy payable to his estate. This was to make sure that there would be sufficient cash available to meet expenses at the time of his death. He knew there would be estate taxes of about $70,000 due on this when he died but thought this was inevitable. The fact is that it wasn't; had he transferred the policy to his children, they would have received the $200,000 free of estate or income taxes. The proceeds could then have been paid to the estate to meet its liquidity needs. He could have, alternatively, transferred the policy to a trust which could have purchased property from the estate with the proceeds, with the same results.

The third concerns that most-important-of-all estate tax savings tools, the marital deduction. This last do-it-yourselfer thought he had qualified the proceeds of a life insurance policy for it. He had made sure that his wife had the power to withdraw the principal. This was one of the key requirements for qualifying an insurance policy for the marital deduction before the Economic Recovery Tax Act of 1981.

But this particular insurance policy had certain technical requirements for withdrawals; they could only be made on certain dates, a limited number of times a year, and in specified minimum amounts. This is not an unusual provision in many policies. The Internal Revenue Service, however, claimed that because the widow did not have the right to withdraw the proceeds according to the language of the statute "in all events," a marital deduction could not be taken. The court upheld its contention. As a result a substantial additional tax had to be unnecessarily paid.

The annals of estate planning abound with similar stories. The point is clear. No matter what the size of your estate, you will need advisors and helpers to assist you in its planning. If the estate is small, perhaps there need be only two, the lawyer and the insurance broker. If it is larger, then a team of experts is required.

The Attorney

He is the captain of your team. As such it is his function to analyze the existing situation, to make recommendations for improvements and changes, to carry out a program of gifts and sales, and to perform such services as the reorganization of corporations, the drawing up of stockholder and partnership agreements. He plans and draws wills, sets up trusts, and gives tax advice.

Beyond this the lawyer brings to his job a special type of expertise without which the entire estate plan would flounder—language. By this we do not mean grace of style or expression, but the use of language to convey precise meaning. Like any discipline, the law has developed its own language over the years because of the need to express a particular meaning, or shade of meaning which is not accurately communicated by the use of ordinary words. Take the simple word "residence," for instance. A person may have several residences, but only one of them can be what is commonly known as his legal one. Which one? A great deal may depend upon how this word is construed. Many thousands of dollars in taxes or perhaps the way an estate may be distributed could be involved. The lawyer solves this semantic dilemma by using the word *domicile*, which in its meaning at law signifies the place of residence which a person intends as his official and legal one.

This technical usage of language comes into play with the execution of the numerous documents which are required for estate transfer. Once a person dies and the transfer process goes into motion, these papers are all that remains to express what his intentions were. To make these as precise, as clear, as truly reflective of the estate planner's intentions as possible is the attorney's all-important function, one that only he can perform.

The attorney should also be of aid in helping you to go through a dry run of your estate plan. By all means, ask him to prepare a hypothetical administration of your estate to show mathematically just what the taxes, costs, and the eventual distribution will be. He is the person who will help you figure out exactly how the plan will operate once put into action.

Just as the estate planner cannot do his job of planning by himself, neither can the attorney perform his function in isolation. He must coordinate many elements and so will need to call continuously on the aid and advice of other specialists on the team.

The Accountant

As the one who annually audits a person's financial affairs and prepares income tax reports on the basis of his analysis, he is perhaps closer to the changing financial condition of your estate than anyone else. When a business is involved, he has intimate knowledge of its operations. When property is involved, he is continuously aware of its changing value. All of this knowledge comes about because of his concern with your continuing financial health and the proper preparations of your income tax returns. He is the team member who functions as the keeper of your records, alerting the others to new circumstances and fresh requirements.

The Life Insurance Underwriter

His role has changed and deepened as modern estate planning has become more complex, and equally, as life insurance has come to play a more important part in it.

The old-fashioned way of buying life insurance—from a

friend or relative who needs the commission—won't do for
the serious estate planner. He needs to seek out a professional life insurance person with a background and experience in estate analysis, one who can operate on equal terms
of expertness with the other members of the team. He is
your authority on insurance. He knows the different forms
of life insurance to be used, presents the way it can be paid
for, and the methods by which the proceeds can be most
effectively employed. He coordinates the life insurance estate with the general estate. Twenty-five years ago such an
individual was hard to find. Today there are many such
professionals. It is up to you as the planner to make sure
that you find one, and not to fall back on the favor-to-a-
friend approach.

The insurance person is out to sell insurance. Strangely
enough, this makes him of special use to the estate planner.
He must analyze estates to find how and where life insurance needs can be met. As a solicitor (which the lawyer
cannot be) the insurance broker is, in fact, the person who
most often initiates the idea of an estate planning effort. His
part is that of a gadfly to see that this effort is not only
begun but carried out to a conclusion so that the life insurance program he presents is truly integrated into your overall plan.

Be sure that your insurance underwriter gives you an
audit of all your life insurance policies, showing the types,
the amounts, the premium payments and their dates, the
cash values, the ownerships, the beneficiary arrangements,
the modes of settlement and options. This audit should then
be given to the attorney. Without it he cannot fit the life
insurance plan into the overall estate picture.

The Bank or Trust Officer

Your attorney will call on him frequently because of his
special background; he has experience in the actual operation of estates. He knows how property can be conserved,
how a business can be run when the owner has died. He is
an authority on investment and the marketability of securities and property.

He is also the person who, in all likelihood, will be the
one who takes over most of the job of handling the estate
after you have died. Therefore it's important to get his

advice on exactly what powers he will need to do his job well, and on the various administrative problems that may arise. He should work with the attorney in drawing up the plan or the documents which will form the basis for the administration.

We have spoken before of the special function of the trustee—of the demands, both personal and financial, that will be made on him. If you want him to be able to act in your place, you must take him into your confidence now, while you are alive and making all these plans. He needs to know—not generally, but specifically—your aims and objectives for each member of your family. If there are special problems, let him know about them. Forewarned is forearmed.

The Investment Advisor

His function is obvious. He reviews the present holdings of the estate and plans the future investments. His particular contribution is the balancing off of the long-term and short-term needs of an individual during his life. His advice on diversification of securities holdings will be of special value.

We call this group an "estate-planning team," and we use the word "team" in its real sense—a group which meets regularly, acts in concert, consults with each of its members.

Unfortunately, this rarely happens. Most estate plans are not reviewed frequently enough, are not prepared collectively. This is a mistake—and a costly one. When sizable estates are involved, it is absolutely necessary to preserve this team principle. It is up to you as the estate planner to see that this is carried out. You must take the initiative in seeing that your team is a working one.

Nor can you leave anything up to the team. If that were true, there would be no need for books such as this one, no reason why a person should inform himself of the basic ideas and concepts of estate planning. In actuality, the more the planner knows about the subject, the better the plan will be. If he cannot and should not act as an expert, he must nevertheless be a knowing amateur.

Any lawyer can tell you that a knowledgeable client is a pearl of great price. It is difficult, almost impossible, to advise a person on how to plan his finances, his savings, his investments, his insurance, and all the multitude of things that make up his estate unless the client himself has a good general grasp of the principles involving creation and transfer of this estate.

In the long run the expert is a technician, and only that. He is not a seer, not a prophet. He cannot plan your estate for you if he has no idea of what your objectives are—if he does not know how and why and where you want to distribute your property.

There are decisions you must make. But how can you make them unless you are aware of the number and extent of possibilities and choices open to you? Or, in other words, unless you are knowledgeable.

APPENDIX

U.S. INCOME TAX TABLES

For 1988 and thereafter

Tax Rates	Single Individuals	Joint Returns	Heads of Household
15%	0–$17,850	0–$29,750	0–$23,900
28%	over 17,850	over 29,750	over 23,900
33%*	43,150–89,560	71,900–149,250	61,650–123,790

*Includes an additional 5 percent tax on the amounts shown. Above these amounts, the 28 percent tax rate applies.

For 1987

Tax Rates	Single Individuals	Joint Returns	Heads of Household
11%	0–$1,800	0–$3,000	0–$2,500
15%	1,800–16,800	3,000–28,000	2,500–23,000
28%	16,800–27,000	28,000–45,000	23,000–38,000
35%	27,000–54,000	45,000–90,000	38,000–80,000
38.5%	Above 54,000	Above 90,000	Above 80,000

See page 353 for information on personal exemptions and standard deductions.

UNIFIED ESTATE AND GIFT TAX RATES

Rate Schedule

If the amount with respect to which the tentative tax to be computed is:	The tentative tax is:
Not over $10,000	18 percent of such amount.
Over $10,000 but not over $20,000	$1,800, plus 20 percent of the excess of such amount over $10,000.
Over $20,000 but not over $40,000	$3,800, plus 22 percent of the excess of such amount over $20,000.
Over $40,000 but not over $60,000	$8,200, plus 24 percent of the excess of such amount over $40,000.
Over $60,000 but not over $80,000	$13,000, plus 26 percent of the excess of such amount over $60,000.
Over $80,000 but not over $100,000	$18,200, plus 28 percent of the excess of such amount over $80,000.
Over $100,000 but not over $150,000	$23,800, plus 30 percent of the excess of such amount over $100,000.
Over $150,000 but not over $250,000	$38,800, plus 32 percent of the excess of such amount over $150,000.
Over $250,000 but not over $500,000	$70,800, plus 34 percent of the excess of such amount over $250,000.
Over $500,000 but not over $750,000	$155,800, plus 37 percent of the excess of such amount over $500,000.
Over $750,000 but not over $1,000,000	$248,300, plus 39 percent of the excess of such amount over $750,000.
Over $1,000,000 but not over $1,250,000	$345,800, plus 41 percent of the excess of such amount over $1,000,000.
Over $1,250,000 but not over $1,500,000	$448,300, plus 43 percent of the exccess of such amount over $1,250,000.
Over $1,500,000 but not over $2,000,000	$555,800, plus 45 percent of the excess of such amount over $1,500,000.
Over $2,000,000 but not over $2,500,000	$780,800, plus 49 percent of the excess of such amount over $1,500,000.
Over $2,500,000 but not over $3,000,000	$1,025,800, plus 53 percent of the excess of such amount over $2,500,000.
Over $3,000,000 but not over $3,500,000	$1,290,800, plus 55 percent of the excess of such amount over $3,000,000.

For the year 1988 and thereafter, the maximum tax rate on amounts in excess of $2,500,000 will be 50%.

THE UNIFIED TAX CREDIT

For Transfers Made and Decedents Dying in	Unified Credit	Exemption Equivalent
1987 & thereafter	192,800	600,000

An estate tax return is required only if the decedent's cumulative gifts and the value of the decedent's estate exceed the amount of $600,000.

NOTE: There is a federal tax credit allowed for the estate or inheritance tax you will have to pay to the state in which you live. States like Florida and Nevada have a tax which exactly equals the federal estate tax credit, while others will equal or exceed it. Thus, in these states the combined U.S. and state taxes will be the amount of the U.S. tax, whereas in other states the combined U.S. and state taxes may be larger than the amount shown on this table.

The Tax Reform Act of 1976 eliminated the $60,000 federal estate tax exemption and replaced the exemption with a unified tax credit, which is set forth in the above table. The amount of the credit is determined by the year of death and further reduces the federal tax.

Examples

1. Mr. A is a resident of Florida. He wants to determine what his prospective estate taxes will be. He estimates that his taxable estate will be $1,000,000. Referring to the U.S. Estate Tax Table, he finds that his tentative U.S. tax will be $345,800. The federal credit for state taxes on a $1,000,000 taxable estate is $33,200. Inasmuch as Florida's estate tax is equal to the amount of the credit, Mr. A's estate will pay Florida $33,200. The federal tax (after applying the state tax credit) comes to $312,600 and this total is further reduced by the unified credit (see the Unified Tax Credit table above). Thus, projecting taxes on a post-1986 estate, Mr. A's federal tax of $312,600 would be reduced by the 1987 unified credit of $192,800, resulting in a net federal tax of $119,800. The combined U.S. and Florida taxes come to $153,000.

2. Ms. B lives in New Jersey. Her U.S. estate tax will be the same as Mr. A's. Her estate will also receive a $33,200 credit for state tax to be paid. However, New Jersey's estate tax on a taxable estate of $1,000,000 is about $46,500. This amount exceeds the U.S. tax credit by $13,300. Thus the combined U.S. and New Jersey taxes will be $166,300.

LIFE EXPECTANCY TABLES

EXPECTATION OF LIFE IN YEARS

Age	Total	White		Black	
		Male	Female	Male	Female
20	56.0	53.0	59.9	47.2	55.4
21	55.1	52.1	58.9	46.2	54.4
22	54.1	51.2	58.0	45.3	53.4
23	53.2	50.3	57.0	44.5	52.5
24	52.3	49.4	56.0	43.6	51.5
25	51.3	48.4	55.0	42.7	50.6
26	50.4	47.5	54.1	41.8	49.6
27	49.5	46.6	53.1	40.9	48.7
28	48.5	45.7	52.1	40.1	47.7
29	47.6	44.7	51.2	39.2	46.8
30	46.6	43.8	50.2	38.3	45.8
31	45.7	42.9	49.2	37.5	44.9
32	44.7	41.9	48.2	36.6	44.0
33	43.8	41.0	47.3	35.8	43.0
34	42.9	40.1	46.3	34.9	42.1
35	41.9	39.1	45.3	34.1	41.2
36	41.0	38.2	44.4	33.2	40.3
37	40.0	37.3	43.4	32.4	39.3
38	39.1	36.3	42.5	31.6	38.4
39	38.2	35.4	41.5	30.7	37.5
40	37.2	34.5	40.6	29.9	36.6
41	36.3	33.6	39.6	29.1	35.7
42	35.4	32.7	38.7	28.3	34.8
43	34.5	31.8	37.7	27.5	34.0
44	33.6	30.9	36.8	26.7	33.1
45	32.7	30.0	35.9	25.9	32.2
46	31.8	29.1	34.9	25.1	31.4
47	30.9	28.2	34.0	24.4	30.5
48	30.1	27.3	33.1	23.6	29.7
49	29.2	26.5	32.2	22.9	28.9
50	28.3	25.6	31.3	22.2	28.0
51	27.5	24.8	30.4	21.5	27.2
52	26.7	24.0	29.6	20.8	26.5
53	25.8	23.2	28.7	20.2	25.7
54	25.0	22.4	27.8	19.5	24.9
55	24.2	21.6	27.0	18.9	24.1
56	23.4	20.8	26.1	18.2	23.4
57	22.6	20.1	25.3	17.6	22.7
58	21.9	19.3	24.4	17.0	21.9
59	21.1	18.6	23.6	16.5	21.2
60	20.4	17.9	22.8	15.9	20.5
61	19.6	17.2	22.0	15.3	19.8
62	18.9	16.5	21.2	14.8	19.2
63	18.2	15.8	20.4	14.3	18.5
64	17.5	15.2	19.6	13.8	17.9
65	16.8	14.5	18.9	13.3	17.2
70	13.7	11.6	15.3	10.9	14.1
75	10.8	9.1	12.0	8.8	11.3
80	8.3	7.0	9.0	6.7	8.6

Source: National Center for Health Statistics, *Vital Statistics of the United States, 1982*

VALUATIONS OF ANNUITIES, LIFE ESTATES, AND REMAINDERS

TREASURY TABLE A

The following is the single life, unisex, 10 per cent Treasury Table for valuation of an annuity, life interest or remainder interest, effective December 1, 1983.

(1) Age	(2) Annuity	(3) Life estate	(4) Remainder	(1) Age	(2) Annuity	(3) Life estate	(4) Remainder
0–19*				51	8.3874	.83874	.16126
20	9.7365	.97365	.02635	52	8.2969	.82969	.17031
21	9.7245	.97245	.02755	53	8.2028	.82028	.17972
22	9.7120	.97120	.02880	54	8.1054	.81054	.18946
23	9.6986	.96986	.03014	55	8.0046	.80046	.19954
24	9.6841	.96841	.03159	56	7.9006	.79006	.20994
25	9.6678	.96678	.03322	57	7.7931	.77931	.22069
26	9.6495	.96495	.03505	58	7.6822	.76822	.23178
27	9.6290	.96290	.03710	59	7.5675	.75675	.24325
28	9.6062	.96062	.03938	60	7.4491	.74491	.25509
29	9.5813	.95813	.04187	61	7.3267	.73267	.26733
30	9.5543	.95543	.04457	62	7.2002	.72002	.27998
31	9.5254	.95254	.04746	63	7.0696	.70696	.29304
32	9.4942	.94942	.05058	64	6.9352	.69352	.30648
33	9.4608	.94608	.05392	65	6.7970	.67970	.32030
34	9.4250	.94250	.05750	66	6.6551	.66551	.33449
35	9.3868	.93868	.06132	67	6.5098	.65098	.343902
36	9.3460	.93460	.06540	68	6.3610	.63610	.383690
37	9.3028	.93028	.06974	69	6.2088	.62086	.37914
38	9.2567	.92567	.07433	70	6.0542	.60522	.39478
39	9.2083	.92083	.07917	71	5.8914	.58914	.41086
40	9.1571	.91571	.08429	72	5.7261	.57261	.42739
41	9.1030	.91030	.08970	73	5.5571	.55571	.44429
42	9.0457	.90457	.09543	74	5.3862	.53862	.46138
43	8.9855	.89855	.10145	75	5.2149	.52149	.47851
44	8.9221	.89221	.10779	76	5.0441	.50441	.49559
45	8.8558	.88558	.11442	77	4.8742	.48742	.52258
46	8.7863	.87863	.12137	78	4.7049	.47049	.52951
47	8.7137	.87137	.12863	79	4.5357	.45357	.54643
48	8.6374	.86374	.13626	80	4.3659	.43659	.56341
49	8.5578	.85578	.14422	Over 80*			
50	8.4743	.84743	.15257				

*Not shown.

VALUATIONS OF ANNUITIES, INCOME INTERESTS, AND REMAINDERS
TREASURY TABLE B

The following is the 10 percent Treasury Table showing the present worth of an annuity or income interest for a specified period of years and of a remainder interest postponed for that specified period, effective December 1, 1983.

(1) No. of years	(2) Annuity	(3) Term certain	(4) Remainder	(1) No. of years	(2) Annuity	(3) Term certain	(4) Remainder
1	.9091	.090909	.909091	31	9.4790	.947901	.052099
2	1.7355	.173554	.826446	32	9.5264	.952638	.047362
3	2.4869	.248885	.751315	33	9.5694	.956943	.043057
4	3.1699	.316987	.693013	34	9.6086	.960857	.039143
5	3.7908	.379079	.620921	35	9.6442	.964416	.035584
6	4.3553	.435526	.584474	36	9.6765	.967651	.032349
7	4.8684	.486842	.513158	37	9.7059	.970592	.029408
8	5.3349	.533493	.466507	38	9.7327	.973265	.026735
9	5.7590	.575902	.424098	39	9.7570	.975696	.024304
10	6.1446	.614457	.385543	40	9.7791	.977905	.022095
11	6.4951	.649506	.350494	41	9.7991	.979914	.020086
12	6.8137	.681369	.318631	42	9.8174	.981740	.018260
13	7.1034	.710336	.289664	43	9.8340	.983400	.016600
14	7.3667	.736669	.263331	44	9.8491	.984909	.015091
15	7.6061	.760608	.239392	45	9.8628	.986281	.013719
16	7.8237	.782371	.217629	46	9.8753	.987528	.012471
17	8.0218	.802155	.197845	47	9.8866	.988662	.011338
18	8.2014	.820141	.179859	48	9.8969	.989693	.010307
19	8.3649	.836492	.163508	49	9.9063	.990630	.009370
20	8.5136	.851356	.148644	50	9.9140	.991481	.008519
21	8.6487	.864869	.135131	51	9.9226	.992258	.007744
22	8.7715	.877154	.122846	52	9.9296	.992960	.007040
23	8.8832	.888322	.111678	53	9.9360	.993600	.006400
24	8.9847	.898474	.101526	54	9.9418	.994182	.005818
25	9.0770	.907704	.092296	55	9.9471	.994711	.005289
26	9.1609	.916095	.083905	56	9.9519	.995191	.004809
27	9.2372	.923722	.076278	57	9.9563	.995629	.004371
28	9.3066	.930657	.069343	58	9.9603	.996026	.003974
29	9.3696	.936961	.063039	59	9.9639	.996387	.003613
30	9.4269	.942691	.057309	60	9.9672	.996716	.003284

Compound Interest Table

The magic of compound interest on regular savings in the creation and building of an estate is indicated by the following table. It shows the amount to which $1.00, invested at the beginning of each year, will accumulate, in the number of years and at the interest rates indicated.

YRS	7.00% ANNUAL RATE	8.00% ANNUAL RATE	9.00% ANNUAL RATE	10.00% ANNUAL RATE
1	$1.000	1.000	1.000	1.000
2	2.070	2.080	2.090	2.100
3	3.214	3.246	3.278	3.310
4	4.439	4.506	4.573	4.641
5	5.750	5.866	5.984	6.105
6	7.153	7.335	7.523	7.715
7	8.654	8.922	9.200	9.487
8	10.259	10.636	11.028	11.435
9	11.977	12.487	13.021	13.579
10	13.816	14.486	15.192	15.937
11	15.783	16.645	17.560	18.531
12	17.888	18.977	20.140	21.384
13	20.140	21.495	22.953	24.522
14	22.550	24.214	26.019	27.974
15	25.129	27.152	29.360	31.772
16	27.888	30.324	33.003	35.949
17	30.840	33.750	36.973	40.544
18	33.999	37.450	41.301	45.599
19	37.378	41.446	46.018	51.159
20	40.995	45.761	51.160	57.274
21	44.865	50.422	56.764	64.002
22	49.005	55.456	62.873	71.402
23	53.436	60.893	69.531	79.543
24	58.176	66.764	76.789	88.497
25	63.249	73.105	84.700	98.347
26	68.676	79.954	93.323	109.181
27	74.483	87.350	102.723	121.099
28	80.697	95.338	112.968	134.209
29	87.346	103.965	124.135	148.630
30	94.460	113.283	136.307	164.494
31	102.073	123.345	149.575	181.943
32	110.218	134.213	164.036	201.137
33	118.933	145.950	179.800	222.251
34	128.258	158.626	196.982	245.476
35	138.236	172.316	215.710	271.024
36	148.913	187.102	236.124	299.126
37	160.337	203.070	258.375	330.039
38	172.561	220.315	282.629	364.043
39	185.640	238.941	309.066	401.447
40	199.635	259.056	337.882	442.592

Example:

If you invest $1,000 a year at 9 per cent, compounded annually, your total investment will be worth $51,160 in 20 years; $136,307 in 30 years; $337,882 in 40 years.

Estate Planning Worksheets

MY ADVISORS ARE

	Name	Address
Attorney:		
Accountant:		
Life Insurance:		
General Insurance:		
Stockbroker:		
Investments:		
Bank Officer:		
Other:		

MY RECORDS AND DOCUMENTS ARE KEPT AT

	Name	Address
Wills and Trusts:		
Securities:		
Insurance Policies:		
Receivables:		
Mortgages and Deeds:		
Business Interests:		
Safety Deposit Box:		
Other:		
1.		
2.		
3.		

PROPERTY RECORD

Properly filled out and kept up to date, this section will provide you with a continuous record of your family's property. Be sure to differentiate between that held separately by the husband or the wife, or jointly by both. A simple code beside each listing, such as (h) for husband, (w) for wife, and (j) for jointly held will make the ownership clear.

CASH

On hand..		Amount
On deposit		
Bank	Interest Rate	
1.		
2.		
3.		
4.		

SECURITIES

Number of Shares	Company	Cost	Value	Income

302

BONDS

Company	Cost	Value	Income	Due Date

RECEIVABLES

Debtor	Address	Amount	Income	Due Date

MUTUAL FUNDS, SYNDICATES, REALTY TRUSTS, ETC.

Name	Cost	Value	Income

REAL ESTATE

	Property 1	Property 2	Property 3
Type Location Title Cost Value Mortgage Upkeep Income			

MORTGAGES RECEIVABLE

Mortgagor	Address	Amount	Income	Due Date

PATENTS AND ROYALTIES

Description	Value	Income

PERSONAL PROPERTY

Description	Cost	Value

BUSINESS INTERESTS

	Business 1	Business 2	Business 3
Name of Business			
Form of Doing Business			
Fiscal Year Ends			
Parties to Business and Participating Shares			
Book Value			
Estimated Estate Tax Value			
Is there an agreement to sell at disability? at retirement? at death?			
If so, has cash been provided?			
Are the partners insured? In what amounts?			
If interest is not to be sold at death: 1. Who will receive it? 2. Who will take over management? 3. What incentives should be arranged?			

EMPLOYMENT BENEFITS

	Company	Amounts Vested, Contributed, or Deferred	Estimated Income or Lump-sum Payments	Death Benefit
Pension Plan Profit-sharing Plan Thrift Plan Deferred Compensation Salary Continuation Health, Accident, etc. Self-employed Retirement Fund Other				

GOVERNMENT BENEFITS

	Description	Social Security or Registration No.	Retirement Benefit	Death Benefit
Social Security Veteran's Pension Veteran's Death Benefits Disability Benefits Other				

HEALTH, ACCIDENT, MEDICAL-SURGICAL-HOSPITALIZATION INSURANCE

Company or Source	Description	Benefits	Policy Number	Issued	Expires

FIRE, LIABILITY, OTHER INSURANCE

Company	Description	Amount	Policy Number	Issued	Expires

LIFE INSURANCE

Company	Face Amount	Type*	Policy Number	Date of Issue	Cash Value	Owned by	Beneficiary
On Husband's Life							
On Wife's Life							

*Such as, 5-year term, ordinary life, endowment, etc.

OTHER PROPERTIES OR INCOME SOURCES

Description	Cost	Value	Income

NOTES OR ACCOUNTS PAYABLE*

Amount	Creditor	When Due	Interest Payable	Remarks

*Include in this schedule all amounts owed on notes and accounts payable, mortgages, income taxes, etc.

TRUSTS

Grantor	Revocable or Irrevocable	Principal	Income	Termination Date	Life Beneficiaries	Remainder Beneficiaries

ANTICIPATED INHERITANCES

Source	Age	Estimated Principal	Estimated Income	If Inheritance Will Be in Trust		
				Termination Date	Life Beneficiaries	Remainder Beneficiaries
Father						
Mother						
Others						
1.						
2.						
3.						

ESTATE ANALYSIS SCHEDULES

These schedules will help you to analyze your estate and show you to what extent it can provide security for your family. They will supply you with (1) a summary of your family's property inventory, (2) how much cash will be needed at your death to pay your estate's taxes and expenses, (3) the source of the cash and what property will have to be sold to raise it, (4) what property and other sources of income will be left to your family, and (5) how much annual income your family can expect to have in the event of your disability, retirement, or death.

INSTRUCTIONS

Schedule A—INVENTORY VALUATION

The first step is to make an inventory of your family's property. This inventory can be taken from the property record entries on pages 302–10.

Enter the present market value of each asset in the appropriate columns. If the husband owns the property, enter it in col. 1. If the wife owns it, enter it in col. 4. If it is jointly owned enter one-half of the value of the property in each of cols, 2 and 3. Enter the total value of each type of asset in col. 5. Total all columns at the bottom.

Schedule B—COMPUTATION OF ESTATE COSTS AND TAXES

1. Add together the values of each asset in Schedule A, cols. 1 and 2, and enter them in col. 1 of Schedule B. Total the entries at the bottom of col. 1 to arrive at your "Gross Estate Valuation."
2. Transfer that figure to the top of the schedule in col. 3, opposite the words "Gross Estate Valuation."
3. For your deductions, enter in col. 2 the amounts you estimate as estate expenses such as mortgages, loans, funeral expenses, income or other taxes due, and 7½ percent of all property which will pass under your will for administration costs. Total your deductions and enter them in col 3. Subtract them from the "Gross Estate Valuation" above. Enter the net figure as your "Adjusted Gross Estate" in col. 4.

4. If you plan to use a marital deduction, total up the value of the property which will qualify for the deduction (see page 214 and enter the amount opposite the words "Marital Deduction" in col. 3. You should also make an alternate calculation without a marital deduction for your estate plan in the event your spouse dies before you. The amount to be entered would be "0."

5. Next, enter the value of charitable contributions opposite the appropriate heading in col. 3.

6. Total the last two items in col. 3, enter the total in col. 4, and subtract it from "Adjusted Gross Estate." Enter the net figure as your "Net Taxable Estate" in col. 4.

7. By using the U.S. Estate Tax Table in the appendix, you can calculate the federal estate taxes which will be payable. There will, in most cases, be a state inheritance or an estate tax to pay as well.

Schedule C—ESTATE CASH REQUIREMENTS

This schedule will show how much cash your executor will need to pay off the estate costs. It also shows how much your estate will shrink as it passes to your beneficiaries.

1. Fill in the first three items from the figures you developed in Schedule B.

2. Enter the total amount of cash bequests in your will.

3. An addition of these items will show the "Total Cash Needed."

Schedule D—LIQUIDATION AND AFTER-DEATH INCOME SCHEDULE

Col. 1—Enter each type of property and after-death income source.

Col. 2—Enter the value of each item which will have to be liquidated to supply the cash needed to pay off the estate cash requirements. The total at the bottom of this column should be equal to the "Total Cash Needed" in Schedule C.

Col. 3—Deduct col. 2 from col. 1.

Col. 4—Enter spouse's property and jointly held property from Schedule A.

Col. 5—Add cols. 3 and 4.

Col. 6—Estimate income from items in col. 5. If in doubt, use an overall return of 4% on income-producing property.

Schedule E—ESTIMATED INCOME SCHEDULE

Col. 1—Enter items from Schedule A, col. 5.

Col. 2—Enter estimated present income from items in col. 1 as well as income from present employment.

Col. 3—Enter the estimated income you will receive from all sources in case you are disabled *now* and the length of time you will receive each item of income.

Col. 4—Enter the estimated income you will receive from all sources when you retire and the length of time you will receive each item of income.

Col. 5—Enter the items of income listed in Schedule D, col. 6 and the length of time your family will receive them after your death.

The totals at the bottom of Schedule E will show the all-important estimates of what income your family will have if you become disabled, or retire, or die.

Schedule A
INVENTORY VALUATION

Inventory	(1) Husband's	(2) Jointly Owned Husband	(3) Jointly Owned Wife	(4) Wife's	(5) Total
Type of Property					
Personally Owned?					
Cash					
Securities					
Stocks					
Bonds					
Receivables:					
Notes and Mortgages					
Real Estate:					
Income Producing					
Non-income Producing					
Business Interests					
Mutual Funds					
Investment Syndicates and Trusts					
Trusts, Patents, and Royalties					
Oil, Cattle, Timber, etc.					
Residence					
Personal property					
Other Property					
Employment Benefits?					
Pension Plan					
Profit-sharing Plan					

Thrift Plan
Deferred Compensation
Salary Continuation
Stock Options
Self-employed Retirement Plan
Other Sources

Government Benefits

Social Security
Veterans Benefits

Life Insurance and Annuities

Personal Life Insurance
Group Life Insurance
Pension Life Insurance
Annuities; Personal or
  Qualified Plans

Other Sources

Present Employment

TOTAL

Schedule B

COMPUTATION OF ESTATE COSTS AND TAXES

(Assuming husband predeceases wife)

Inventory	(1)	Computation of Estate Costs and	(2)	(3)	(4)
Type of Property	Estate Tax Valuation*	*Taxes*			

Gross Estate Valuations
  Deduct:

Personally Owned:
Cash
Securities:
  Stocks
  Bonds
Receivables:
  Notes and Mortgages
Real Estate:
  Income Producing
  Non-income Producing
Business Interests
Mutual Funds
Investment Syndicates and Trusts
Trusts, Patents, and Royalties
Oil, Cattle, Timber, etc.
Residence
Personal Property
Other Property

Employment Benefits:
Pension Plan
Profit-sharing Plan

Computation column items:

Debts and Expenses
  Debts
  Funeral and Last Illness
  Income or Other Taxes Due
  Administration Costs

Deduct Total
Adjusted Gross Estate

Deduct:
  Marital Deduction
  Charitable Contributions
  Deduct: Total

NET TAXABLE ESTATE
U.S. ESTATE TAX (tentative)
Less: UNIFIED CREDIT
U.S. ESTATE TAX

(state death tax credits not dealt with)

Thrift Plan
Deferred Compensation
Salary Continuation
Stock Options
Self-employed Retirement Plan
Other Sources

Life Insurance and Annuities:

Personal Life Insurance
Group Life Insurance
Pension Life Insurance
Annuities: Personal or
    Qualified Plans

Other Sources

TOTAL GROSS ESTATE

*To help you figure the estate tax valuations for Schedule B you should carefully read Chapter 15. This is especially so for certain items of your inventory

- *Business Interests.* see pages 269 to 272.
- *Trust Interests.* see Chapter 13.
- *Life Insurance.* see page 40.

Schedule C

ESTATE CASH REQUIREMENTS SCHEDULE

Total Debts and Expenses, as above

Charitable Contributions, as above

Estate Taxes, as above

Cash Bequests, as per Will

TOTAL CASH NEEDED

½Schedule D

LIQUIDATION AND INCOME SCHEDULE

(After death of husband)

Inventory *Type of Property and Income Source:*	(1) Valuation	(2) Property Sold to Meet Estate Costs	(3) Balance Available to Family	(4) Other Family Property	(5) Total Property Available to Family	(6) Estimated Income to Family
Personally Owned:						
Cash						
Securities:						
Stocks						
Bonds						
Receivables:						
Notes and Mortgages						
Real Estate:						
Income Producing						
Non-Income Producing						
Business Interests						
Mutual Funds						
Investment Syndicates and Trusts						
Trusts, Patents, and Royalties						
Oil, Cattle, Timber, etc.						
Residence						
Personal Property						
Other Property						
Employment Benefits						
Pension Plan						

318

Profit-sharing Plan						
Thrift Plan						
Deferred Compensation						
Salary Continuation						
Stock Options						
Self-employed Retirement Plan						
Other Sources						
Government Benefits:						
Social Security						
Veterans Benefits						
Life Insurance and Annuities:						
Personal Life Insurance						
Group Life Insurance						
Pension Life Insurance						
Annuities: Personal or Qualified Plans						
Other Sources:						
TOTAL						

½Schedule E

ESTIMATED INCOME SCHEDULE

Inventory	(1) Total	(2) Present	(3) Disability		(4) Retirement		(5) Death	
Type of Property and Income Source:	Value	Income	Income	Period	Income	Period	Income	Period
Personally Owned:								
Cash								
Securities:								
Stocks								
Bonds								
Receivables:								
Notes and Mortgages								
Real Estate:								
Income Producing								
Non-Income Producing								
Business Interests								
Mutual Funds								
Investment Syndicates and Trusts								
Trusts, Patents, and Royalties								
Oil, Cattle, Timber, etc.								
Residence								
Personal Property								
Other Property								
Employment Benefits								
Pension Plan								
Profit-sharing Plan								

320

Thrift Plan
Deferred Compensation
Salary Continuation
Stock Options
Self-employed Retirement Plan
Other Sources

Life Insurance and Annuities:
Personal Life Insurance
Group Life Insurance
Pension Life Insurance
Annuities: Personal or
Qualified Plans

Other Sources:

TOTAL

Estate Financial Planning Survey

For the estate planner, investment acumen lies not as much in the ability to select a certain "right" security as in the ability to create a long-term, well-balanced investment program that will produce the capital needed to carry out estate planning objectives. How you as an investor-planner accomplish this and how well you accomplish it is a highly individual matter. There are a number of factors to consider that will help you gain a clearer idea of what you must accomplish and why. Below is a list of such factors. Your responses to them will begin to give you an idea of what your individual investment objectives should be.

1. How many years do you have to reach your intermediate or long-range financial goals?
2. How many college-bound children do you have? How many years from now do you need to have funds for their education?
3. At what age do you hope to retire? How much time do you have before you need to draw income from investments?
4. How much income do you expect you will need at the time of your retirement?
5. Will you need capital to start a business after early retirement? How much do you think you will need?
6. What is the degree of risk you are willing to take in growth-oriented investments (emotionally and financially)? How much risk are you willing to take to achieve capital appreciation that will be required to reach your financial goals?
7. What is the amount of capital you have available to initiate your plan? How much and when can you put in additional capital?
8. How experienced are you as an investor? How much advice or management do you require?
9. What tax advantages are available to you?

Using this list of questions and your responses as a starting point, make a list of your goals for building your estate. Having your goals clearly in mind is the first and most critical key to setting up a balanced investment program.

A PROGRESSION OF INVESTMENT STRATEGIES FOR ESTATE PLANNING

Earlier you were asked to consider a series of factors that help to establish your investment goals for planning your estate. Not everyone presents the same profile, and the variations of needs and aspirations are vast. Here are some guidelines that should be of use to you in focusing on both short and long term investment strategy:

1. Most people's first major outlay of capital is basic—buying a house.
2. Purchase life insurance for yourself and your spouse both as an investment and to provide for early loss of the other's income and support for the family in the event of early death.
3. Save capital sufficient to meet the minimum entry requirements for your desired investments.
4. Select an investment in which the risk factor meets your comfort level (see section below on "Degrees of Safety") and that is geared strictly for increasing your capital. (See also the section below entitled "Making Investment Decisions.")
5. Establish and implement a plan to build capital for college education for your children. Such investments could include:
   - *Zero Coupon Bonds.* These bonds let you know the exact amount you will have at maturity and are useful for building toward the predicted sums you will need. They have long-term maturity that can coincide with the projected time children will be entering college.
   - *Annuity Single Premium Whole Life Insurance.* This is insurance with an investment component that allows the accumulation of capital. At a certain point, you can take out a given amount of money as a loan at little or no interest and leave the rest to maintain the investment.
   - *Bonds with a Fixed Return.* These bonds allow you to work on the basis of projected earnings needed. In this way you can determine the amount to invest at a certain time, or over a period of time.
6. Once the children finish school, you can concentrate

on retirement funds and begin to build capital beyond your pension plan with growth-oriented investments that allow you optimum appreciation of your capital (commensurate with your risk/comfort level). Often one's peak earning years occur at about this time of life. For instance, a corporate climber who works his way up to a substantial income reaches peak income during the last 20 percent of his working life. During this time, you should be able to accumulate large sums of money, especially if you plan ahead and avoid the temptation to raise your standard of living beyond your ability to continue saving and investing. Most people really focus on building funds for their retirement out of these peak earnings when they are between the ages of 50 and 60.

7. Any time that your capital has appreciated to a sufficient level, you can begin to diversify your portfolio with a variety of investments with which you feel comfortable. The goal at this point is to generally build your estate for family use and for your retirement. The priorities you place on growth versus income, however, may shift in emphasis as you approach and then begin your retirement.

ESTABLISHING A BALANCED PORTFOLIO

Estate planning can be confusing given the variety of investments available, fluctuations in the economy, and changes in your own needs as time goes on. The classic investment portfolio can, however, be laid out in simple categories that will assist you in structuring the one that suits and adjusts to your evolving needs.

A model portfolio is diversified so that no one type of investment or no one sector of the economy is the sole focus. The basic investment categories are: cash, growth, fixed income return. Because you are trying to build the value of your portfolio, the emphasis should be on capital appreciation. The actual percentages of funds in any of the three categories may change from time to time depending upon the state of the economy, the market dynamics, and the period of your life.

For example, the larger amount should probably be in the

growth category (ownership of shares in such things as stocks, mutual funds, etc). The amount you have in cash, such as a money market account, fixed income investments, bonds, CD's, annuities, etc., will vary depending upon the economy and whether you need income more than appreciation. It may also depend upon the liquidity needed to shift to investments that have greater potentials in changing economic conditions. If the economy is volatile and you are in doubt about what will happen, cash placed in a money market fund, certificates of deposit, treasury bills, or savings accounts (low yield but safe and liquid) is probably your best bet until economic and market factors become clearer. During a time of growth in the economy you may want to place larger amounts in growth investments, such as stocks and mutual funds.

A Simple Rule of Thumb

To simplify the matter, the proportions of cash, growth, and fixed income investments should vary over your lifetime, and should be monitored by you and your investment counselor. Your changing goals for greater appreciation or greater income will tip the balance one way or another, but a rule of thumb after you have built your solid base of capital and perhaps the security of a home might be something like the following:

GROWING ECONOMY				HIGH INTEREST RATES		
CASH	GROWTH	FIXED INCOME		CASH	GROWTH	FIXED INCOME
10%	70%	20%		20%	50%	30%

RETIREMENT YEARS		
CASH	GROWTH	FIXED INCOME
20%	30%	60%

These are not by any means hard and fast percentages, but are meant to illustrate a point about shifting times and advancing years.

Structuring Your Investments

Having established the long-term goals for building your estate, you then need to have a strategy for operating in the world of investing. To begin with, your strategy will depend upon your financial status—that is, how much capital you have available for investment, whether you have purchased a home, and if you have established liquid funds for emergencies for at least 6 months.

Below are five levels of estate building at varying points in life and financial worth. Finding where you fit will help you to determine some strategies to follow.

Level 1: Zero capital. Ready to save. Need to establish a regular program of saving to build capital for initial investments.

Level 2: May have purchased a home. May have set aside liquid funds for emergencies. Put together a small additional nest egg of, say, $3,000 or $4,000, and are ready to make an initial investment.

Level 3: Have surplus capital ($10,000+). Have several conservative investments that are performing well on a steady basis. Ready for higher capital appreciation and growth (therefore ready for a higher level of risk).

Level 4: Ready to shift to more conservative investments that provide fixed income while maintaining those that provide appreciation and growth.

Level 5. Receiving income from your investments. Beginning to live off investments with fixed returns.

Once you know your needs and have considered your priorities among the three segments of your portfolio (cash, growth, fixed income), you are ready to select investments on the basis of how well they meet your current financial status and goals.

Making Investment Decisions

Keeping an objective perspective is crucial for successful investing. Your level of understanding of the bottom line of investment can really make the difference between low performance or loss of your money, and achieving high performance and gain. In this experienced advisors can help you. You must know that in building your estate the only way to truly increase your wealth is to obtain a significant *real* return on your money. The real return is the rate at which you increase the value of your invested capital after taking into consideration the factors of inflation, taxes, and investment and management costs. Low risk, conservative investments are important for psychological and financial reasons, when safety is the key element in your planning. If you decide to stay with such investments for safety reasons, you should be aware that you have made an informed choice, knowing that you paid a price for that safety— namely, low return and perhaps a real loss on your investment. As an example, if you are receiving 5½ percent interest on your savings account, your net after a 28 percent tax would be just short of 4 percent. Should the inflation rate be more than 4 percent you have obviously lost the difference in real value. On the other hand, if your investment earns a return or profit that is in excess of the inflation rate you have increased the real value of your assets accordingly.

Common stocks and mutual funds have on average provided a greater margin of profit than most other investments. Stocks and mutual funds investing in stocks are obviously the media of investment which are most likely to increase the value of your estate. It is uncertain, however, that the general rise in market values will continue at the same rate as in the past. It is possible that changed economic and market conditions will cause values to plummet as much as one-third or more, as occurred in 1952 and 1973, with the consequent loss of your hard-earned money. If you have the stamina to stay with your investments, experience has shown that the market will attain its former value or possibly increase in value. However, in the short term and in a fluctuating market, the critical factor is to remain objective. Becoming emotionally wedded to an investment is the pitfall. If a security shows consistently poor performance, you must be willing to dispose of it. Timing, objectivity and facts are the essential elements. This is where the objective analysis of the merits of your investment program by a professional advisor or manager can be of crucial value to you. He has no interest other than the success of your investment strategies. Your success will further his own potential for success.

Degrees of Safety

To determine which categories of investment are suitable for building low-risk investments consult the following lists.

Low Risk/Low Return Investments

- A home (if desired)
- Life insurance
- Annuities
- Bank certificates of deposit
- Treasury bills, bonds and notes
- 401 (k) plans
- U.S. savings bonds
- Municipal bonds (grade A or better)

Once you have built a foundation of secure, low risk/low return investments, you can begin to consider ways of achieving greater capital appreciation. Investments that allow you to achieve this can still involve only minimum to moderate risk. They include the following types of investments:

Moderate Risk/Moderate Return Investments

- Blue chip stocks
- Preferred stocks
- Mutual funds (well-established/well diversified)
- Corporate bonds
- Real estate trusts
- Real estate partnerships

After you have begun to achieve your moderate capital appreciation goals and have built a comfortable margin of fairly reliable growth, you can then assess the amount of discretionary income you have for some of the more speculative types of investments that offer high rewards. These speculatives are not for everyone. Your tolerance for risk is a factor to consider before venturing into such aggressive investments, and the funds used for them must be dispensible, since there is always the possibility of losing them. These, then, are the high-risk/high-return investments. They are capital gains-oriented, but tend to be volatile and may reflect sudden swings in the market.

High-Risk/High-Return Investments

- Specialized mutual funds (concentrate on one industry group only—e.g., a fund with stocks only in companies involved in high technology manufacturing).
- Commodities (metals, currencies, agricultural products, oil)
- Futures contracts
- Options
- Warrants

Diversification

As stated earlier, it is important to keep your investments diversified so that no one economic factor has a disproportionate effect on your estate. You must seek to achieve diversification not only in the relationship of each investment to the other, but also in the relation to the rest of your assets and your sources of income.

Degrees of Liquidity

Another factor to consider in building a portfolio is the degree of liquidity available in your various investments. Being able to liquidate easily allows you to handle emergencies, take advantage of sudden investment opportunities, and at the time of death allows for greater ease in handling estate taxes, expenses, and debts. The list below shows samples of degrees of liquidity from greatest to least.

- Cash/checking account
- Passbook savings account
- Money market account
- Treasury bills, 90 days, 6 months, 1 year.
- Treasury notes (1–5 years)
- Treasury bonds (5+ years)
- Stocks (always liquid, but at the risk of being in a loss position at the time you wish to sell)
- Mutual funds
- Real estate (considered to be the least liquid investment)

Inflation Hedge

As previously mentioned you need to consider how well a particular investment will preserve your capital against inflation. It is just as important to protect the purchasing power of your capital as it is to protect yourself against the possible loss of capital. In any inflationary period, it won't do to just maintain the number of your dollars. If that is all you do, you will suffer an economic loss. Here again, the whole question of diversification enters the picture. A portfolio that is invested entirely in a savings account or other low interest investments is no protection against inflation. Only a portfolio based on a variety of investments—some with fixed returns and some with potential for capital appreciation—will do that.

Growth

What is growth potential? It is the inherent ability of the investment not just to protect against inflation, but to actually appreciate the capital beyond a normal inflationary increase. Generally speaking, these investments are found in the industries that have great growth potential. Growth areas in the economy shift over the years. In the early part of the century it was the railroad and the steel industry. In recent years it has been automobiles and chemicals, then electronics, then high technologies and overseas manufacturing.

Income

What is the expected income return on the investment? It is expected future income production as well as to current income. Is the income guaranteed? Will the income return be available in bad times as well as in good times? Is it fixed? Will the rate of return move up and down with general money rates so as to reflect the state of the economy and the probable changing costs of living?

Marketability

What is the marketability of the investment? Is this a security that you can readily sell? Or will buyers perhaps be hard to find? There are many securities that are not readily marketable, but still make worthwhile investments. Obviously, however, your investment portfolio should not be weighted with these. Liquidity is extremely important to many aspects of estate planning.

Tax-Deferred Investments

Portions of your portfolio should allow for long-range planning. Here you need not be concerned with issues of immediate liquidity or fluctuating markets. These are the investments you enter into for the sake of planning for retirement and for college education expenses for your children. They allow you to defer payment of taxes on both the principal you invest and on the earnings made from the investment itself. These include annuities (including Single Premium Whole Life), 401 (k) plans, IRAs, and Keogh plans.

Tax-Advantaged Investments

With the sweeping changes in the 1986 Act, there are few investments that allow for substantial tax advantages. These are:

1. *Tax-free municipal bonds.* Earnings are not subject to tax at the federal level or in the issuing town and state.
2. *Single premium whole life insurance.* Taxes are deferred on earnings until withdrawn. Interim borrowings of the cash value may be available with little or no net interest cost.
3. *Deferred annuities.* Similar to single premium whole life in that taxes are deferred on earnings until withdrawn. Partial withdrawals may be made up to the amount of your investment.
4. *Individual Retirement Accounts (IRAs).* Taxes on earned income that is contributed plus earnings are tax-deferred until withdrawn at retirement. However, this tax advantage is available only to individuals not covered by a company plan or whose income is less than $25,000 a year (or $40,000 a year if filing jointly).
5. *Master Limited Partnerships.* Return on principal is only 50-60 per cent taxable.
6. *Real Property.* Interest on principal and second residence mortgages and taxes may be deducted. Interest, taxes, and depreciation may be deducted on commercial properties.
7. *Oil, cattle, timber and certain other natural resources.* Depletion allowances are deductible.

INVESTMENT CHECKLIST

This checklist provides an overview of the gamut of investments generally available. They are grouped according to the investment characteristics that make them appropriate for varying programs and objectives: cash, growth and fixed income return.

Cash

There are many reasons for keeping funds in cash or cash equivalents. They are a saving medium; they are available for unforeseen family needs; they are a reservoir of which uninvested amounts are kept for later investment; they are generally free of risk and as such a source of psychological and financial security.

Investment	Source	What It Is	Use	Risk	Advantages	Disadvantages	Minimum Entry
Money Market Deposit Account.	Banks, savings & loans, brokerage firms.	Funds invested in short-term instruments: CD's, U.S. T-bills government securities, short-term municipal bonds.	Preservation of capital, liquidity and highest possible interest income given these objectives.	Low.	Rates not subject to federal regulation. Banks set their own. Insured by federal agency up to $100,000. No withdrawal penalties.	Monthly fees, limited check writing, minimum balances required.	$1,000–$2,500
Savings Account.	Banks, savings & loans, credit unions.	Passbook account wherein money deposited earns interest.	Earns interest income.	Low.	Insured by federal agency up to $100,000. Yield is guaranteed. Can use balance as collateral.	Interest rates are low. In some cases minimum balances required.	$5–$100

Investment	Source	What It Is	Use	Risk	Advantages	Disadvantages	Minimum Entry
Super Now Account.	Banks, savings & loans, credit unions.	Bank/checking account that is interest bearing.	Earns low interest.	Low.	No ceiling on interest rates banks can pay if minimum rate is maintained. Insured by federal agency up to $100,000. Liquidity. Check-writing privileges.	Minimum balance required to receive interest. If balance falls below minimum, penalties are imposed.	$2,500

Growth

The purpose of placing funds into equity-type investments is to achieve greater growth potential for your capital. Such investments carry various degrees of risk that generally correspond to their potential for reward. They can be short- or long-term investments, depending upon the amount of time you hold the investment to maximize your return. As of 1986 the new tax laws no longer offer any advantage to long-term versus short-term capital gains. As a result, you are now free to move into and out of equity positions at the times most advantageous for you to obtain the greatest profit.

Investment	Source	What It Is	Use	Risk	Advantage	Disadvantage	Minimum Entry
Annuity.	Life insurance companies, employer's 401(k) programs	Investments made by insurance companies that guarantee a fixed return with no risk of capital for a fixed duration.	Retirement income; building of retirement funds within a 401(k) plan. Tax deferral.	Low.	Very secure. Guaranteed minimum interest rate allows for higher fluctuating rate. Usually can borrow the cash value at low interest rates.	Low returns.	Varies
Common Stock.	Brokerage firms; in a few cases employees can purchase their company's stock directly from their company.	A security that represents a stated amount of ownership in a company.	Dividend income and/or appreciation in value.	Medium to high.	Carries the potential for a high rate of return.	Carries risk of market fluctuations on a daily basis. Not insured by federal government.	$1,000

Investment	Source	What It Is	Use	Risk	Advantage	Disadvantage	Minimum Entry
Convertible.	Brokerage firms.	Preferred stock or a bond, or a debenture that may be exchanged by holder for common stock—generally of the same company.	Income and/or appreciation.	Medium.	Carries safety of preferred stocks and bonds along with potential for capital appreciation of common stock.	Yields are lower than similar quality noncovertibles. They sell at premiums to conversion value of the common stock purchased.	$5,000
401 (k) plans.	Various Employers.	Tax-deferred investment plans. You regularly contribute portions of pre-tax salary dollars to a variety of investment options.	Appreciation, tax deferral.	Low.	High yield growth of savings on tax-deferred income. Provides growth of retirement funds. Diversified, professionally managed.	Not liquid until retirement. 10% penalty on early withdrawals. Annual deferrals limited to $7,000.	No minimum
Individual Retirement Account (IRA).	Banks, mutual fund companies, brokerage firms, credit unions, insurance companies.	Tax-advantaged retirement accounts for individuals not covered by company plans or whose income is under $25,000, or under $40,000 if filing jointly.	Retirement income.	Varies.	If you qualify, contribution of up to $2,000 a year is fully tax deductible. Growth of account is tax-free until withdrawn.	Subject to penalty of 10% if withdrawn before age of 59½.	$250

Investment	Source	What It Is	Use	Risk	Advantage	Disadvantage	Minimum Entry
Master Limited Partnershps.	Investment brokerage firms.	Group ownership of specific diversified properties (Real estate, oil, gas). Can buy and sell like stock, or hold until properties are sold.	Appreciation, tax advantage.	Low.	Liquidity—can buy & sell as desired. Reasonable yield. 50-60% tax-exempt. Potential for appreciation.	Subject to fluctuation in real estate market—you could be tempted to sell out at low point before property reaches projected appreciated value.	$800-$1,500
Mutual Fund.	Brokerage firms, mutual fund companies, insurance companies.	An investment trust. Your money is pooled with that of other investors. Professional managers invest this pool of funds in specified assets in the U.S. or overseas.	Income and/or appreciation.	Varies.	Mangement by professionals. Risk reduced by diversification. Wide selection of specialized funds within a family of funds. Can switch from one to another within a family. Low minimums.	Not insured by federal government. Yield influenced by fluctuation in stock market and interest rates.	$1,000
Real Estate Investment Trusts (REITS).	Brokerage firms.	A trust or corporation that invests in or finances real estate (shopping centers, office buildings, apartments, etc.). Sold as securities.	Appreciation, income.	Medium.	Allows for participation in real estate with little money.	Dependent upon inflation—value fluctuates with real estate and stock market.	$2,000.

Investment	Source	What It Is	Use	Risk	Advantage	Disadvantage	Minimum Entry
Real Estate as Your Residence.	Real estate brokers, individual owners, banks.	A house, condominium, or apartment in a cooperative.	Appreciation, tax advantage.	Average.	While providing residence, allows for tax write-off or loan interest, appreciation potential, and collateral for other loans.	Value can depreciate; not liquid; ongoing maintenance costs.	Varies
Real Estate Limited Partnerships/ Public Partnerships.	Investment brokerage firms.	A group ownership of diversified properties (office buildings, apartment complexes, shopping centers). Can buy units of the package offered during a specified period.	Appreciation, tax advantage.	Low to high.	Can invest in real estate for little capital. Diversified properties—not dependent upon any one property. Professional management.	Must hold units bought until partnership sells the properties. Not liquid. Dependent upon inflation. Subject to fluctuation in real estate market.	$3,000–$5,000
Real Estate Limited Partnerships/ Private Partnerships.	Investment and brokerage firms.	Group ownership of a specific property of any size and kind. Can buy units of the package offered during a specific period.	Appreciation, tax advantage.	Low to high.	Chance to invest in major property with fewer partners (higher percentage of ownership). Professionally managed.	Not diversified. Subject to specific fluctuation in real estate market. Not liquid. Dependent upon regional inflation.	$3,000–$5,000

Investment	Source	What It Is	Use	Risk	Advantage	Disadvantage	Minimum Entry
Single Premium Whole Life.	Insurance companies, brokerage firms	Policy with a one-time, lump sum premium with guaranteed tax-free death benefits, and tax-deferred earnings.	Appreciation retirement, tax deferral.	Low.	Tax-free or tax-deferred earnings at competitive interest rates. Guaranteed principal. Tax-free death benefits. Can borrow against earnings on policy in large amounts tax-free.	Tax-deferred earnings subject to tax if policy is cashed in.	$5,000

Fixed Income Return

The purpose of fixed income investments is to provide for reliable sources of predictable income from your capital. Such investments generally allow for the reinvestment of earnings when growth is still a goal. Once you want or need to live off your investments, however, fixed income-providing investments should occupy a higher proportion of your portfolio.

Investment	Source	What It Is	Use	Risk	Advantage	Disadvantage	Minimum Entry
Certificates of Deposit.	Banks, savings & loans, credit unions, brokerage firms.	A set sum of money left in a bank for a set period earns agreed-upon interest rate. Deposit plus interest paid at end of period.	Interest Income.	Low.	Insured by federal government for up to $100,000; interest rates competitive	Penalties for early withdrawal.	$500

Investment	Source	What It Is	Use	Risk	Advantage	Disadvantage	Minimum Entry
Commercial Paper.	Brokerage firms, corporations, bank holding companies.	Short-term unsecured notes offered by large corporations.	Interest income.	Varies.	Yields are competitive. Backed by the credit of the borrowing company.	More risk than a CD. No secondary market. Not covered by collateral of the issuing company.	$25,000
Corporate Bond.	Brokerage firms.	Debt obligation of corporation for your loan of the bond price.	Income.	Medium.	Assured return over long period of time with high quality available through bond ratings.	Could be called in before maturity and paid off only to that date.	$5,000
Keogh Plan.	Banks, brokerage firms, credit unions, mutual fund companies, insurance companies.	Retirement plan for self-employed.	Tax deferral retirement income.	Varies.	May contribute 25% or $30,000 (whichever is less) each year tax-deductable. Funds grow tax-free until withdrawn.	Subject to 10% penalty and taxes if withdrawn before age 59½. If a defined benefit plan, cannot receive full benefits until age 65.	$250
Mortgage-Backed Securities.	Securities dealers, brokerage firms, issuing institutions.	Shares of ownership in pools of mortgages that are backed by federal, state or local governments (Ginnie Maes, Fannie Maes, etc.)	Interest income, retirement income.	Low.	High yields. Liquidity, backed by government agencies. Pays regular prorated monthly income.	Subject to fluctuations in interest rates. As mortgages are paid off, payments diminish and eventually cease.	$1,000 (in a mutual fund) or $25,000

Investment	Source	What It Is	Use	Risk	Advantage	Disadvantage	Minimum Entry
Municipal Bonds.	Banks, brokerage firms.	Debt obligation of town, city, or state (or their agencies) for your loan of the bond amount.	Tax-free income.	Low if bonds are rated A or better.	Interest paid is tax-free at the federal level and in issuing state and city.	Lower return than on taxable bonds. If you have to liquidate, may be subject to prices below market value.	$5,000
Preferred Stock.	Brokerage firms.	Stock that pays fixed dividend. Has priority over common stock if company is liquidated.	Income.	Varies.	Provides a fixed rate of return and is more secure than common stock.	Dividend never increases. Value is subject to stock market fluctuations.	$2,000
Treasury Bills.	Banks, federal reserve banks, brokerage firms, U.S. Treasury.	U.S. Treasury securities with short-term maturity (13, 26, and 52 weeks).	Interest income.	None.	Interest paid is exempt from state and local taxes. Backed by the U.S. government. May be traded like corporate securities.	Not redeemable until maturity date. Value if selling them is subject to the market value.	$10,000
Treasury Bonds.	Banks, federal reserve banks, brokerage firms, U.S. Treasury.	U.S. Treasury securities with long-term maturity of 10 years or more.	Interest income.	None.	Interest paid is exempt from state and local taxes. Backed by the U.S. government. Maybe traded like corporate securities.	Not redeemable until maturity. Trading value is subject to market fluctuations. Interest rates may be lower than other fixed-return investments.	$1,000

Investment	Source	What It Is	Use	Risk	Advantage	Disadvantage	Minimum Entry
Treasury Notes.	Banks, federal reserve banks, brokerage firms. U.S. Treasury.	U.S. Treasury securities with medium term maturity (not less than 1 year, not more than 10).	Interest income.	None.	Interest paid is exempt from state and local taxes. Backed by the U.S. government. May be traded like corporate securities.	Same as T-bills	$1,000 (4 plus years) $5,000 (less than 4 years)
U.S. Savings Bonds.	Banks, savings and loans, federal reserve banks, U.S. Treasury.	Debt obligation of U.S. Treasury for amount of bond. Designed for small investors.	Interest income.	None.	Exempt from state and local taxes. May defer until federal tax. Principal and interest guaranteed. If held 5 years they return about 85% of average T-bill while paying minimum 7.5% guaranteed.	Usually lower interest rate than available with other fixed income investments.	$25
Zero Coupon Bonds.	Banks, brokerage firms.	Discounted from face value with zero annual interest paid out. Capital appreciation is realized at maturity.	Appreciation.	Medium.	Low expense initially. Balloon payment to you at maturity. Good for long-term planning since you know the exact amount you will receive.	Lower yield than regular bonds. Have to pay annual taxes (as if you had received interest.)	$1,000

341

CHECKLIST
FAMILY OBJECTIVES AND NEEDS
ESTATE PLANNING QUESTIONS

Estate planning begins with an appraisal of yourself and your family. What, exactly, do you want to accomplish during your life? What are your chances of realizing these aims? Will these aims meet the needs of your family? What are those needs now and in the future, while you are alive, after you are dead, when you retire, if you become disabled: for yourself, your spouse, your children, your parents, your grandchildren?

Here, for your guidance, a checklist which can help you. It has none of the answers—those you must evolve yourself. It should start you thinking, provide the framework on which you can build your estate plan—the determination of your objectives.

All the questions in this checklist are dealt with in the main book. Use the book as a guide and aid. It contains much of the information you will need to formulate your own personal estate-planning objectives.

FAMILY INCOME AND REQUIREMENTS

A. During My Working Life
   1. How much income do I have, and from what sources?
      a. Employment or business.
      b. Investments.
      c. Other sources.
      d. What will my income probably be in 5, 10, 15, or 20 years?
   2. How much are my living costs?
      a. Household expenses.
      b. Rent or home-ownership expenses.
      c. Business incidentals, i.e., commuting, lunches, entertainment, etc.
      d. Taxes.
      e. Miscellaneous—interest, medical, auto, etc.
      f. What will my family's outlay probably be in 5, 10, 15, 20 years?
B. In the Event I Become Disabled, Retire, or Die
   1. *If I become disabled now*
      a. How much income will I need?

    b. How much income will I have? From employment or from business?

    c. How much income will I have from investments or other sources?

    d. How much income will I have from my disability insurance, social security, veteran benefits?

    e. How much more disability insurance do I need to make up a probable income deficit? How can I pay for it?

    f. What would the differences be if I became disabled, 5, 10, 15, 20 years from now?

2. *If I retire*

    a. Will I have to retire?

    b. How much income will I need if I retire?

    c. How much income will I have? From employment or from business?

    d. How much income will I have from my investments or other sources?

    e. How much income will I have from annuities and social security?

    f. What am I equipped to do after my retirement? What training should I have?

    g. What business can I start now to prepare for my retirement years?

    h. Shall I live in the same place or shall I move to one of the retirement states? What advantages are there, if any, in these states from income, health, and tax-shelter points of view?

3. *If I die now*

    a. What will my estate consist of and how much will it be worth?

    b. What will the estate costs amount to?

        (1) Debts and obligations.

        (2) Administration expenses.

        (3) Estate and inheritance taxes.

    c. What specific assets of my estate will have to be paid out or sold to meet these estate costs?

    d. How much will be left for the support of my family?

    e. How much income will my family need and for how long?

        (1) For my spouse.

        (2) For my children.

(3) For children's education.

(4) For parents.

f. How much income will be available and in what form and for how long?

g. Will some part of principal have to be paid out to support my family and, if so, how long will it last?

h. How much income will be available to my family 5, 10, 15, 20 years after my death?

i. What would the differences be if I died, 5, 10, 15, 20 years from now?

ESTATE CREATION OBJECTIVES

A. Residence

1. Where should I live on the basis of my income, my family's needs, and occupational convenience?

2. Should I rent or own?

3. Would a move increase my standard of living, and what would be the consequent costs?

4. Would the additional costs, if any, interfere with my long-term estate creation objectives?

B. Savings

How much am I setting aside to create an estate?

a. Cushion savings account. How much should I have to meet a 3-6 months' loss of income?

b. Investment savings account.

c. Life insurance investment.

d. Other investments.

e. Do I have a systematic, enforced savings program?

f. How much can I save in 5, 10, 15, 20 years?

(1) How much would it be worth at 4%, compounded?

C. Personal Insurance

1. How much insurance do I need to make up my family's income deficit?

2. How much can I invest each year in insurance? Am I using tax-sheltered methods of financing the premiums?

3. Are the policies owned and payable in a way so as to minimize taxes and maximize use of the proceeds?

4. Who are the beneficiaries: the estate, spouse, children, parents, charity; a trust in behalf of spouse, children, parents, charity; the trustees under my will?

5. Are the death payments to be made in a lump sum or

according to what option? In what installments and during what period?

6. Has my insurance been integrated with my will and the rest of my estate?

7. When did I see my insurance underwriter last? Has he given me a complete written audit and analysis of my insurance portfolio?

D. Employment

What opportunities do I have for creating or increasing my estate through my employment or business?

1. *The Employed Executive*

   a. Pension, profit sharing, stock options, thrift plans.

   b. Group life, disability, medical and surgical and split-dollar insurance.

   c. Deferred compensation, salary continuation, bonuses, and deferred bonuses.

   d. How can I bargain for position, salary, capital gains returns, or any fringe benefits not now available to me?

2. *The Professional*

   a. Fringe benefits from unincorporated associations, professional corporations, corporation owning professional building, etc.

   b. Self-employed retirement act, tax-exempt organization annuities, forfeitable plans.

   c. Can I take part of the deal instead of a fee?

   d. If I have partners, have arrangements, been made to cover the sale of a partner's interest at the disability, retirement, or death of a partner?

3. *The Business Owner*

   a. Am I using the best forms of doing business—individual ownership, partnership, or corporate forms—in order to obtain maximum tax advantages?

   b. Can I obtain corporate fringe benefits as a stockholder-executive (see employed executive)?

   c. Should I use Subchapter-S treatment?

   d. Should I sell the business or an interest in it, reorganize stock, merge, etc., to obtain capital gains advantages?

   e. Have I arranged proper disposition of my business or shares in case of sale of an interest, or the disability, retirement, or death of a partner?

E. Investments
   1. Have I looked at my investment portfolio critically?
   2. How much cash value do I have in my insurance policies?
   3. Have I established a proper ratio as between my fixed return and equity investments?
   4. Should I have tax-free bonds?
   5. Am I getting the most mileage from capital gains treatment?
   6. Am I looking at my investment program on the basis of long-term objectives?
   7. Have I looked into the feasibility of an outside or a second business?
   8. Have I examined the possibilities for real estate investment: undeveloped land, income-producing property, syndicates, investment trusts, corporations, etc.?

ESTATE TRANSFER AND CONSERVATION OBJECTIVES

A. My Family
   Have I assessed the character, abilities, and needs of my family and each of its members?
   1. *My Spouse*
      a. Is she my primary beneficiary?
      b. What is her life expectancy? How long will she need support?
      c. Has she the ability to manage and invest property?
      d. How can I prepare her during my life for the management and investment of property?
      e. If property were left to her outright, could she maintain it intact for her own use by resisting the demands upon her of children and relatives?
      f. Should property be left to her outright or in trust?
   2. *My Children*
      a. What is the educational status of each child?
      b. Have I supplied sufficient funds to assure that each child can complete his education?
      c. Does one child require special consideration because of disability or handicap or, on the other hand, because of special educational requirements?
      d. Should boys be treated differently from girls?

    e. If they are adults, have they had experience in the management and investment of property?

    f. Are they stable and reliable?

    g. Should property be left to them outright or in trust? If in trust, should distribution of principal from the trust be made to them when they reach certain ages, or should it be kept in trust for life?

B. Conservation

  1. *Taxation*

    a. Am I using available tax-shelter opportunities to reduce the combined total family income tax during my life and after my death?

      (1) Would lifetime gifts of income-producing property to members of my family or to trusts in their behalf spread income and take advantage of lower tax brackets?

      (2) Am I using multiple trusts, living and testamentary, to receive the proceeds of my estate, such as insurance policies, qualified retirement plans, deferred compensation, etc., so as to reduce my family's combined income tax after my death?

    b. Am I using available tax-shelter opportunities to reduce estate and inheritance taxes?

      (1) Do I know how much the estate taxes and administration costs on my estate will be? Have I had my attorney do a hypothetical administration (dry run) of my estate to determine these costs?

      (2) Are the transfer patterns of the estates of both my wife and myself integrated so as to incur minimum transfer taxes and administration expenses in both?

      (3) Should I make lifetime transfers of property in order to reduce the size of my taxable estate?

      (4) Am I using the maximum marital deduction? Should I?

      (5) Will there be double taxation on some part of my property, both in my estate and in my spouse's estate?

      (6) Should I save estate taxes on my spouse's estate if she survives me, by setting up a "wasting" marital deduction trust in my will?

(7) Should I use the charitable deduction to reduce estate taxes?

2. *Liquidity*

   a. Have I calculated the amount of cash which will be needed to pay estate taxes, expenses, and debts?

   b. Will there be sufficient liquid assets to pay for these items?

   c. If not, what steps shall I take to provide the necessary cash?

      (1) Shall I rearrange my investments to make them more liquid?

      (2) Do I need more insurance?

      (3) Can I get money out of the surplus of my business through a tax-free redemption of stock?

   d. Will my estate have to be paid within 15 months or within 10 years of my death?

3. *Management*

   a. When was the last time I discussed my estate and my objectives with an attorney, accountant, life insurance advisor, trust or bank officer, and investment counselor?

   b. Have we carried out the plans we made?

   c. Have I ever had a conference of all my advisors to work out an integrated, overall estate plan?

   d. Should my investments be managed by a trust or an investment management organization?

   e. Have I arranged for efficient management of my estate after my death?

      (1) Have I appointed executors and trustees who have both a personal interest in my family's welfare and the experience to do an efficient job of investment and management?

      (2) Have I considered the use of a corporate fiduciary?

      (3) Should members of my family be named as executors and trustees? If so, who?

      (4) Should the investment duties and the discretion to distribute income and principal be placed in the hands of different fiduciaries?

      (5) Has the guardian I have named for my minor children skill and experience in financial matters?

    (6) Have I arranged for substitute or successor fiduciaries?

    (7) Have I given my executors and trustees broad powers to handle any changing requirements of my estate and my family? If I have a business, do they have the power to continue it?

C. Charitable Contributions

  1. Do I have charitable objectives?

  2. Should I make charitable contributions during my life or at my death? Or both?

  3. Would a charitable foundation help me achieve charitable, family, and business objectives?

  4. Would life insurance further my charitable objectives?

  5. How can I obtain maximum income and estate tax benefits in my charitable program? Can I have the advantage of both?

D. Business Interests

  1. Shall my business interests be continued or sold at my death or retirement?

  2. If they are to be continued, who will continue their management? What training does successor management need? What incentives must be offered? Will there be sufficient cash and working capital available to the business? Will the family's income be assured?

  3. If they are to be sold, who will buy them? Is there a buy-sell or stock-redemption arrangement? Are the funds available to finance such an arrangement? Are there key people in the business who can purchase an interest? Should the transfer be made now through an outright sale or by a public issue of stock?

E. My Will

(All the following questions apply equally to spouse's will.)

• When was my will executed?

• When was it last reviewed by me? By my attorney?

• Have any changes occurred in my business or family situation which would require changes in the will provisions?

• Have I made an inventory of property which will pass under my will?

• Have I made an inventory of property which will pass at my death outside of my will?

- Have I integrated the transference of both of these types of property with my will so that my objectives will be achieved?
- Does my will use available opportunities to reduce my estate taxes and administrative expenses?
- Does my will use available opportunities to reduce income taxes for my beneficiaries after my death?
- Does my will take advantage of the maximum marital deduction?
- If my spouse has property of her own, should I use the maximum marital deduction?
- Does my will provide for distribution of my property, either outright or in trust, in such a way as to meet the specific needs of each of my beneficiaries?
- Does my will have a *common disaster clause?*
- Have I provided a guardian for minor children?
- Have I exercised any powers of appointment which I may have? Do I want to?
- Have I provided that adopted children or descendants shall inherit in the same way as natural-born ones?
- Have I provided that estate and inheritance taxes shall be paid out of the residuary estate and shall not be apportioned among any beneficiaries? Do I want to?

OUTLINE OF MY WILL

My will was executed on   (date)

My will was prepared by   (attorney)

It provides the following distribution of my property:
A. Specific Bequests
  1. Personal property to:
       Name   Property Description

  2. Money Bequests to:
       Name   amount

  3. Charitable Bequests to:
       Name   amount

  4. Business Interests or Other Property to:
       Name   Property Description

B. Residence and Real Estate Devised to:
       Name   Property Description

C. Distribution of the Rest
  1. To My Spouse

   a. If outright, how much and what property?

   b. If in trust, how much and what property?

   (1) If one trust, what are the provisions dealing
       with the distribution of income and principal
       during her life and after her death?

   (2) If there is a second trust for her, describe its
       income and principle distributions during her
       life and after her death.

2. To My Children
   a. If outright, how much and what property goes to each?

   b. If in trust, how much and what property is set up in trust for each?

   (1) Describe its income and principal distributions during each beneficiary's life and after his death.

3. To Others
   a. Describe how much and what property each will get, and the way it will be distributed (outright or in trust).

I have appointed the following fiduciaries:

Executors

Successor Executors

Trustees

Successor Trustees

Guardians of Minor Children

Successor Guardians

SUMMARY OF THE TAX REFORM ACT OF 1986

This summary is a general and nontechnical explanation of those provisions of the act that have the most widespread application and effect on estate planning. Since it does not deal in detail with these provisions or cover many of the minor changes made, and moreover, since the effective dates vary from one provision to the next, it is recommended that the reader consult his lawyer or tax adviser on matters that may be relevant to his personal situation.

How It Affects Your Income Tax Return Computation

For tax year 1987 only, there are four income tax brackets;

Tax Rates	Single Individuals	Joint Returns	Heads of Household
11%	0–$1,800	0–$3,000	0–$2,500
15%	1,800–16,800	3,000–28,000	2,500–23,000
28%	16,800–27,000	28,000–45,000	23,000–38,000
35%	27,000–54,000	45,000–90,000	38,000–80,000
38.5%	Above 54,000	Above 90,000	Above 80,000

For tax years beginning in 1988, there are two income tax brackets—15 per cent and 28 per cent. Single taxpayers with income up to $17,850, and taxpayers filing joint returns with income up to $29,750, are taxed at 15 per cent. Income in excess of these levels is taxed at 28 per cent. The act phases out the benefit of the 15 per cent rate by imposing an additional 5 per cent tax on income levels between $71,900 and $149,250 for joint returns and $43,150 and $89,560 for single taxpayers.

The personal exemption will be increased to $1,950 in 1988, and $2,000 in 1989. Beginning in 1990 the $2,000 exemption will be indexed for inflation. In 1988 the personal exemption will be phased out for taxable incomes above $149,250 for joint returns and $89,560 for single individuals. Beginning in 1989 the phaseout will be indexed for inflation. The additional exemption for the blind or the elderly has been repealed.

The standard deduction for 1988 is $5,000 for individuals

who file joint returns and $3,000 for single taxpayers. For an unmarried individual who is either age 65 or blind, the standard deduction is increased by $750. The increase is $600 for each married person who is age 65 or blind.

How It Affects Your Deductions for Personal Expenditures

The charitable deduction for those who do not itemize is repealed.

The floor for the medical expense deduction is increased from 5 to 7.5 per cent of the individual's adjusted gross income.

The deduction for personal interest including interest on car loans, credit cards, and life insurance policy loans has been repealed. However, under the phase-out rules 65 per cent of the interest is deductible in 1987, 40 per cent in 1988, 20 per cent in 1989 and 10 per cent in 1990.

Qualified residence interest is deductible for interest paid or accrued on indebtedness secured by a first or second home. If the principal amount of home loans exceeds the purchase price of the house plus the cost of improvements, interest attributable to that excess will not be deductible unless the debt was incurred for education or medical expenses effective for loans made after August 16, 1986.

How It Affects Your Capital Gains

The 60 per cent capital gains deduction has been repealed, thereby taxing long-term capital gains at the same rates as ordinary income. Capital losses are allowed in full against capital gains.

How It Affects the Alternative Minimum Tax

The alternative minimum tax is an additional tax on what is known as "tax preference items." The act raises the rate from 20 to 21 per cent. Due to the repeal of the 60 per cent long-term capital gain deduction it is no longer a preference item. Preference items have been expanded to include the unrealized appreciation portion of capital gain property to charity.

How It Affects Your Individual Retirement Account

Individuals who are not active participants in qualified retirement plans may still take a full $2,000 deduction and an additional $250 for a nonworking spouse. Active participants in qualified plans with incomes exceeding certain levels will lose the availability of a deduction for all or a part of the IRA contribution.

For married couples filing a joint return when at least one is covered by a pension plan, the deduction is phased out at adjusted gross income levels between $40,000 and $50,000. For single individuals covered by a pension plan the deduction is phased out for adjusted gross income between $25,000 and $35,000. Taxpayers will be entitled to make nondeductible contributions to IRAs up to the point when the total of deductible and nondeductible equals the maximum limits of $2,000 and $250 for a nonworking spouse.

How It Affects Family Tax Planning

All unearned income of a child under age 14 in excess of $1,000 is taxed to the child at the top marginal rate of the parents. Earned income of the child continues to be taxed at the child's rate.

Income of a trust that by its terms reverts the assets to the grantor before the death of the beneficiary will be taxed to the grantor. This eliminates the tax advantages of the Clifford trust.

The generation-skipping transfer tax has been expanded to include direct transfers to beneficiaries more than one generation below that of the transferor (direct skips). A specific exemption of $1 million per transferor replaces the current credits and exclusions on the generation-skipping tax. A special $2 million dollar per grandchild exemption applies to direct skips made before January 1, 1990.

How It Affects Corporate Taxes

For 1988, the maximum tax rate for corporations is reduced from 45 per cent to 34 per cent and graduated as follows:

Taxable Income	Tax Rate
$0 to $50,000	15 per cent
50,000 to 75,000	25 per cent
over 100,000	34 per cent

An additional 5 per cent tax up to $11,750 is imposed on taxable income over $100,000 and up to $335,000.

Index